The
Shared Space

The
Shared Space

*the two circuits
of the urban economy in
underdeveloped countries*

MILTON SANTOS

adapted for publication in English by

CHRIS GERRY

Methuen
LONDON AND NEW YORK

First published as *L'Espace Partagé*
© Editions M.–Th. Génin 1975

English translation © 1979 by Methuen & Co Ltd
First published in Great Britain 1979 by Methuen & Co Ltd
11 New Fetter Lane, London EC4P 4EE
Published in the USA by Methuen, Inc
733 Third Avenue, New York, NY 10017

Typeset by Inforum Ltd, Portsmouth
Printed in Great Britain by
Richard Clay (The Chaucer Press) Ltd,
Bungay

British Library cataloguing in publication data

Santos, Milton
The shared space.
   1. Underdeveloped areas – Economic conditions
   2. Underdeveloped areas – Urbanization
   I. Title
   330.9′172′4   HC59.779–42878

   ISBN 0–416–79660–5
   ISBN 0–416–79670–2 Pbk

Contents

Preface

This book was written with the express intention of elaborating and analysing more comprehensively a number of problems already touched on in my study *Les Villes du Tiers Monde* (Génin/ Librairies Techniques, 1971). In this way, I hope to contribute to the establishment of a theoretical framework which can be used for the analysis of the spatial implications of urbanization, a field in which there remains much to be said, especially with respect to the Third World. But these specific problems cannot be solved unless we have at our disposal a more profound understanding of the global process of development and underdevelopment. The spatial aspects of this process are of particular importance when we consider the role played by territorial expansion, control and competition in the historical development of contemporary nation-states.

I have also attempted to lay stress on the spatial impact of technological change in the Third World; this has not been achieved simply by taking a narrow technical view, but rather through the recognition that economic and political forces are of paramount importance. I would have been more satisfied if I had been able to devote more time to the discussion of the importance of the spatial dimension on planning, but on reflection this seemed to be an area so rich that it deserved the full attention of a separate study. The objective of any book which purports to lay before its readers a newly elaborated set of ideas or concepts should be to provoke comment and discussion and to encourage

subsequent empirical studies which may confirm or disprove its
principal hypotheses. It is only in this way that the theoretical
framework may be tested and, if necessary, reformulated.

The lengthy process of data collection and theoretical formulation which culminates in the publication of this book was
considerably facilitated by the fact that I am part of the Third
World myself, and that I have had the opportunity to travel
extensively in Latin America and Africa, meeting and talking to
people from all sections of society – on the one hand, the theorist
who confronts the problems of the Third World in a relatively
abstract manner, and on the other hand, those who are faced with
the day-to-day task of overcoming the concrete problems of survival. Nevertheless, the necessary work was not accomplished
unaided. I was able to expose myself to a number of different
schools of thought during my various attachments to European,
Latin American and North American universities, a contact
which I found most stimulating and profitable.

The reader will perhaps be struck by the wide range of sources
used in the present study: the collection of these data was made
possible with the invaluable assistance of the libraries at the Sor-
bonne in Paris, at Harvard and M.I.T. in the United States, and
finally at the University of Toronto in Canada, where I was
fortunate enough to be helped by Professor Jacob Spelt. I am also
indebted to a number of friends and colleagues around the
world: when my ideas were in their earliest stages of development, they had the patience to discuss a wide range of subjects
with me. The letters which passed between Terry McGee and
myself, relating to our common interest in the economic activities
of the urban poor in the Third World, were a constant stimulus to
my work. At the University of Toulouse the numerous and frequent discussions I had (and continue to have) with my friend
Bernard Kayser and his fellow geographers and sociologists were
of decisive importance for me. The same must be said of my
collaboration with Guy Lasserre in Bordeaux. The comments and
criticisms of my students and colleagues at *l'Institut d'Étude du
Développement Économique et Social (IEDES)* frequently caused me
to willingly reformulate a number of my initial ideas. My friend
D.F. Maza Zavala of the Faculty of Economics at the Central
University of Venezuela, whom I consider to be one of the Third
World's finest economists, must take the credit for encouraging
me to seek the answers to a number of questions for which
Western economists appeared to have little time or interest. I

would also like to extend my thanks to Paul Claval and Harold Brookfield, general editors of the French and English series of which the present study forms a part, for the interest they have shown in my work.

My son Milton was always keen to keep me informed of the problems being encountered by our home country of Brazil; he used his understanding of and commitment to the problems of the Third World to assist me in data collection during his vacations, which he customarily spent in whichever country I happened to be working at the time. Finally, I owe a great debt of gratitude to my wife, Marie-Helene, whose perceptive comments and invaluable help in defining and refining many of my ideas contributed significantly to the completion of this study.

Milton Santos *University of Paris, 1970*
University of Toronto, 1973

PART I

1

Towards a new paradigm

It is only in recent years that the urbanization process in under-developed countries has been treated in a theoretical manner. The 1950s saw pioneering work in this field and produced the type of speculative analysis capable of generating a wide spectrum of descriptive terminology. Redfield and Singer (1954) advanced the concepts of orthogenetic and heterogenetic cities; Davis and Hertz Golden (1954) returned to and reinterpreted the concept of primacy and Jefferson (1939) introduced the idea of overurbanization. In 1960, Sjoberg added the notion of the pre-industrial city, and Hoselitz (1960a) characterized Third World cities as either 'generative' or 'parasitic'.

These different approaches, and particularly the dichotomy proposed by Hoselitz, were sufficiently well received for them to be adopted as paradigms upon which the subsequent important work on Third World urbanization was to be based. They remained to the fore throughout the 1960s, though they were interpreted in a number of different ways. For example, Emrys Jones (1966: 38–54) used the term 'pre-industrial city', whilst Friedmann and Lackington (1966) replaced 'overurbanization' with 'hyperurbanization'. Though initially critical of such super-latives, Sovani (1964) later inclined towards the use of some qualification when advancing the idea of 'primary' and 'mature' urbanization (1966). Bose (1965) defined Calcutta as a premature metropolis.

Those who initially undertook the search for a general theory of Third World urbanization may be exonerated for retaining what might be called a 'qualificative' approach; they were working at the inception of our initially slow progress towards an understanding of the nature of underdeveloped countries. With hindsight, and considering how much more is now known on the subject, it is clear that this school of thought had not been able to grasp the fundamental reality of Third World urbanization. Instead, it restricted itself to the superficial approach which was productive only of a wide range of qualifying terminology, much of which had been transferred from the environment with which these writers were already familiar, namely the urban phenomena of Western countries.

Twenty years of experience has placed the futility of this approach beyond dispute; the time is more than ripe for a reorientation towards a substantive analysis more conducive to an understanding of the reality and internal dynamic of urbanization in underdeveloped countries, and away from speculative and comparative studies.

National planning with immature theories

The 1950s also saw the introduction of systematic planning in underdeveloped countries, whilst the first studies of spatial planning appeared during the 1960s. Using Perroux's (1955) now classic work on growth poles as a base, Boudeville (1961, 1966), Rodwin (1961), Alonso (1968), and Friedmann (1963, 1966) attempted to introduce a spatial dimension into the analysis of urbanization. Similarly, Christaller's (1933) seminar on central place theory regained popularity, and numerous studies were devoted to these two themes. Lasuen (1971) considered that growth poles and central places were manifestations of the same theoretical problem. However, national planning was rapidly subordinated to political expediency, notably in the sphere of international relations.

Analyses of Third World urbanization have also been handicapped by political preoccupations. In many studies, urban realities have been identified as elements of instability.[1] Studies of urban housing, employment, marginality, migration, and overcrowding are dominated by a greater preoccupation with the symptoms than with the causes of urban poverty. Moreover these latter are becoming increasingly serious on an international scale.

The whole question of foreign aid can be viewed from the same standpoint; again we see the results of basing analysis on an hypothesis yet to be validated. Despite the critical attention which foreign aid has attracted (Hayter 1971; Mende 1972) it is still advanced as a miracle cure. The expected critique of that assertion is rarely forthcoming for the simple reason that it no longer appears necessary or even desirable to treat the subject to a scientific analysis (Myint 1965a:491). Exactly the same can be said of the most urgent problems of urbanization, the study of which has been restricted by a narrow and almost exclusively political perspective. Thus virtually all analysis is invalidated from the start when the researcher feels himself obliged to provide, often in a limited period of time, the results expected of him.

As a result, research is distorted and weakened, whilst the results are inevitably a compromise. Also, the researcher is torn between the desire to understand reality objectively and the temptation to prophesy and offer solutions. But the difference between the perspective required of the theorist and that required of the technical adviser is fundamental: the adviser has to consider the particular variables of a given situation, which means considering the objectives of the bureaucrats and administrators, as Moore (1965:13) so perceptively pointed out. The results of such analyses can only be disappointing. Moreover, they give rise to a pressing demand for studies of an even more detached and systematic nature (Wurster 1964:10).

Mathematical methods have been applied to the story of urbanization in underdeveloped countries in the hope of providing a more rigorous and well-focused analysis. But we know the results. Theoretically, the use of multivariate techniques facilitates an understanding of the functioning of urban systems. However, when the methodological framework and spatial theories are patterned on Western realities, mathematical rigour serves to perpetuate not only inappropriate theories but also errors in their interpretation. Moreover, not all economic problems are amenable to mathematical treatment; those that are may not necessarily be the most important. Although in certain cases, as for example in the studies of Abiodun (1967, 1968), the possibility of description of non-dynamic conditions has been refined, the use of quantitative models unsupported by an understanding of local realities has not contributed to the advancement of theoretical models.

Underdevelopment: the historical context

To understand the processes of underdevelopment we must use a more explicitly historical methodology. The fundamental mistake that many researchers have made is to rely on comparisons between the developed and the less developed world. In this way concepts formulated on the basis of data from developed countries have been indiscriminately applied to Third World countries. As the availability of data on underdeveloped countries increases so it becomes possible to base an historical analysis on Third World reality rather than on the assumption that all social evolution is simultaneously comparable and complementary. Researchers who use raw data collected in underdeveloped countries and who are free from the need to make comparisons with developed countries reach very different conclusions from those researchers who depend upon spurious cross-sectional comparisons.

Reissman thus draws parallels between developing and developed countries: 'the urban process in the developing countries is presently repeating many of the characteristics observed in the Western world.' Supposedly this can be explained 'by the similarity of development in the two periods and in the two types of societies' (Wellisz 1971:39; Smailes 1971:5). Bauer (1957:36) goes still further by risking a parallel between contemporary India and medieval Europe.

Such views are based on the postulate that the Third World is 'developing', i.e. in a state of transition towards the contemporary situation in developed countries. In reality, this idea of 'similar path models' is inadequate (McGee 1971a). The ostensible *world in development* is actually an *underdeveloped world* with inherent characteristics and mechanisms which are clearly in need of explanation.

An historical approach to the study of the underdeveloped countries shows that they did not evolve in the same way as the developed countries. This difference shows up well in the social, economic and spatial organization of Third World society, whose process of urbanization can be seen as just one element in a spectrum of complementary processes. The contemporary situation in underdeveloped countries is in no way comparable to that of the 'advanced' countries prior to their industrialization. Bettelheim (1962: Chapter III) points out that the economies of the advanced countries 'were neither dependent, distorted, nor

in disequilibrium, but rather integrated and autocentred'.
Despite strong warnings from Polly Hill (1966) and Paul
Wheatley (1969) against the dangers of ethnocentricity, the
influence of Western theories is sufficiently strong to ensure that
their supercession will be a slow process. We wonder, as does
Gakenheimer (1971:55–66), whether 'it would not be better to
categorically refuse imported methods and start from scratch, i.e.
with the formulation of the initial'.

The spatial characteristics of underdevelopment

Two fundamental deficiencies impel us to propose an analysis
based upon the organization of space. Little of the work on
underdeveloped countries has involved a rigorous analysis of
spatial dynamics. Additionally, most of the available studies were
undertaken in the 1950s and early 1960s when insufficient was
known about the wide-ranging effects of high technology on
spatial organization. Never has there existed a greater need for
an assessment of the comparative spatial organization of both
developed and Third World countries.

The essential components of spatial reality are universal and
form an historical continuum, varying nevertheless in their quantitative and qualitative balance, interaction and recomposition on
the basis of location; thus we see the emergence of spatial differentiation. Though the constitution and reconstitution of space
in underdeveloped countries is conditioned by external interests
often operating on a world-wide scale, their impact on spatial
factors is localized and subject to considerable inertia (Santos and
Kayser 1971). However, the differential impact of modernizations, whether these have internal or external origins, is
highly selective, making itself felt at different times and locations
to different extents. At every phase of modernization, new zones
of formerly 'neutral' space are drawn into the orbit of
'operational' space; with the advent of continuous imbalance and
adjustment, instability in spatial organization becomes the
dominant trend.

In the underdeveloped countries there are enormous income
disparities. At the regional level, they are manifested in the
hierarchical employment-structure; at the local level, they can be
felt in the co-existence of two economic systems, each operating
on a different level. Income disparities are much smaller in

developed countries and have little influence upon the accessibility of a wide range of commodities. An individual's capacities to both produce and consume largely depends on his location; consequently, in underdeveloped countries, such potentialities are subject to much greater variability than in the developed world.

The whole spatial dynamic is thus influenced by enormous geographic and individual disparities. Such spatial selectivity at an economic as well as a social level appears to hold the key to the elaboration of a spatial theory. Spatial selectivity can be interpreted in two ways, according to whether production or consumption is considered. Production, especially that requiring a high level of technology, tends to be concentrated at specific points. Consumption responds to forces of dispersion; since, however, spatial factors strongly influence the ability to consume in both qualitative and quantitative terms, such social differentiation operates as a brake on the forces of dispersion.

At the national level, new economic demands are superimposed over existing 'traditional' ones. The economic system is thus forced to accommodate both new and inherited social realities, and faces the need for dynamic modernization. This applies equally to the productive and distributive systems. Two economic circuits are created, responsible not only for the economic process, but also the process of spatial organization.

Two circuits

The city, therefore, can no longer be studied as a single homogeneous entity, but should be thought of as two subsystems, namely the 'upper' or 'modern circuit' and the 'lower circuit'.

The first objective is to define adequately each circuit of the urban economy, their reciprocal relations, and their relations with society and their surrounding space. Urban life is conditioned by the characteristics of each circuit, yet each circuit maintains a discrete relationship with urban space.

The upper circuit is the direct result of technological progress and its most representative elements are the monopolies. Most of its relations take place outside the city and surrounding area and operate in a national or international framework. The lower circuit consists of small-scale activities and is almost exclusively for the poor. Unlike the upper circuit, the lower circuit is well entrenched in the city and enjoys privileged relations with its environment.

Though each circuit constitutes a subsystem of the city, only the modern circuit has been systematically examined. For too long, both economists and geographers have identified the modern component of the urban economy with the whole city. Friedmann (1961:89; 1964:346) declared that the 'folk' sector existed within the city without being a part of it. Most research thus examines only one sector of the city rather than all of it, thereby precluding the emergence of an authentic theory of urbanization.

The recognition of the existence of two circuits necessitates a reappraisal of concepts such as urban exports, central places and growth poles, which have until now furnished the theoretical base of regional planning. The lower circuit must now be recognized as an element indispensable to the understanding of urban reality. Measures must be found to increase the lower circuit's productivity and sustain its growth while at the same time retaining its privileged role as a supplier of employment.

This new approach entails close control of the dialectic between the two circuits; to do this, many more detailed statistical and market studies and a systematic analysis of the lower circuit are required. Such an approach would constitute a new urbanization paradigm. Kuhn (1962) phrased it well when he stated that science does not develop through an accumulation of experience based on outdated concepts of reality, but rather through the elaboration of new approaches based on contemporary reality.

The lower circuit

Many authors have turned their skills towards the study of the lower circuit in underdeveloped countries, but usually *en passant*, as part of some wider perspective. To such classic texts as those of Boeke (1953)[2] and Geertz (1963) can be added the work of McGee to whom we owe a debt of gratitude for his transcendence of the conventional approach and his theoretical innovations. For too long students of the Third World have neglected to accord sufficient attention to the pressing questions of urban markets and the role of the city as a commercial centre, for example. However, the findings of McNulty (1969:176), Saylor (1967:98), Bohannan and Dalton (1962), Mintz (1956, 1964), Skinner (1964) and Brookfield (1969), among others, have suggested that the importance of these phenomena is universal. But these efforts have not encouraged a second wave of equally perceptive studies: apologists claim that a lack of data has prevented any further advance, whilst others cannot even muster such an excuse. Geographers and economists have been particularly slow in bending their energies to the analytical task.

But a mere analysis of markets as such will not suffice; commercial phenomena must be seen at least as a subsystem of commerce in general, or better still, as a component of the general system of spatial relations in which the city plays a central, or at least a significant, role. But components other than commerce are also significant in this context: the lower circuit includes traditional productive (e.g. artisanal), transport and service activities.

Little is known in concrete terms about the lower circuit of the urban or domestic economy (Saylor 1967:5; Kay 1970:152) and even less about petty commerce. The existing data concerning the number of moneylenders and market traders (Bauer and Yamey 1968:4), occupations so important to the functioning of both the urban and regional economy, is extremely vague. What appropriate information is available of the numbers of self-employed in a small-scale production (Beguin 1970:228–9)?

This is a multifaceted problem; ignored by official statistics, the lower circuit is the object of numerous misconceptions which constitute both the cause and the consequence of data deficiencies. But the situation can be easily explained: the collection of statistics in underdeveloped economies is often undertaken in an inappropriate manner (i.e. on the basis of Western models) and the intervention of international agencies seems to only aggravate the problem. The seemingly rational application of common statistical measures denies the individual and historical specificity of different countries, yet is supported by the dominant ideology of development theory. In the context of international comparisons, information is gathered in the main from the modern sector of the economy, whilst the rest of the economy is ignored; even Marxist writers such as Kus'min (1969) are guilty of this myopic preoccupation.

Field studies must therefore fill in these enormous gaps in our knowledge, as McGee has done with respect to the hawkers in Hong Kong, and as the present author has attempted to do in Venezuela, Brazil and Algeria with respect to the two circuits of the economy. Polly Hill has shown that for researchers to underestimate this need on the pretext that data is lacking, is nothing short of academic cowardice; the use of meaningless but readily available official statistics still seems to be more attractive than having no data at all.

Some advances have been made: research into the provision of industrial goods has given rise to information on both the maldistribution of income and consumption. Data collected for government housing projects, etc. add a little to our knowledge of the standard of living 'enjoyed' by the mass of the population. These must be carefully interpreted, however, within a methodology reflecting the reality of the underdeveloped country.

In our own study, we shall attempt to provide a systematic analysis conducive to the formulation of some general principles applicable to Third World urbanization. This will necessarily be applicable to the majority of underdeveloped countries (namely, those whose economies could be described as 'liberal'). For contemporary development theory to be reformulated, pride of place must be accorded to the *spatial* dimension (Pinto and Sunkel 1966:86). In a sense, we are responding to Wheatley's challenge (1969:26) that a general theory of urbanization, radically different from the received wisdom of Western academics, is no longer just a distant dream of the future. The realization of this theoretical reformulation and re-orientation will be our major preoccupation here; however, for its success, it will require an urgency and *collective* motivation among those who are sincerely concerned over progress in the Third World.

2

The two circuits of the urban economy: evolution and characteristics

To understand fully not only the contemporary characteristics of the two circuits in a particular underdeveloped country but also the changing pattern of its spatial organization, the history of that country must be taken into account. Only by doing this can we avoid what Wilbert Moore has called 'temporal myopia' (1965:15) – that is, erroneously interpreting phenomena as if they had the same historical origins. A periodization of history is vital if such commonly and often imprecisely used terms as 'traditional' and 'colonial' are to be placed in a valid spatial and historical context.[1]

A particularly fruitful approach to evaluating the historical processes that have operated on a given country is to think in terms of *modernizations*. The semantics of the term 'modernization' are still subject to heated discussion, particularly among sociologists. However, if we accept Moore's definition that modernization involves 'entering the modern world economically, politically and socially' (1965:6), then we can recognize that several 'modernizations' (see Santos 1972a) have occurred in the world to date. Such an approach also reduces the ambiguity of such terms as 'growth' and 'development'; these are often but not necessarily concomitant. For example, industrialization need not result in growth *and* development but instead may lead to a 'pseudodevelopment' if economic activities are not integrated at the national level and a worsening distribution of income is in evidence.

A modernization, then, is the diffusion of an innovation from a 'polar' region to peripheral subordinate regions, and/or from an anterior historical period to a subsequent one. On a global scale, 'polar' regions are developed countries, peripheral regions are underdeveloped countries. The evolution of any given Third World country therefore depends on when it first felt the impact of external forces of modernization and, secondly, on the sequence of successive modernizations. The first impact of modernization brings a country or region into a global economic system; the order in which subsequent modernizations are experienced determines the contemporary economic, social, political and spatial characteristics of a country or region.

However, such an historical periodization is inevitably subjective and will depend upon the objectives of the researcher (Braudel 1958:488). Therefore, for the present study the major influences exerted by the West can be summarized more generally: a first stage from the end of the sixteenth century until the Industrial Revolution: the second, from the mid-eighteenth to the mid-twentieth century (with the effects being particularly marked after 1870), and the contemporary, post-Second World War period. Three major revolutions characterize these periods: first the transport revolution; second, the Industrial Revolution to 1870 and its consolidation; finally the post-Second World War technological revolution (Santos (ed.) 1972; Alonso and Meyer 1972).

Whenever the complex of economic, social, political, cultural and moral subsystems causes old variables to re-emerge or creates new ones, the influence of the world system over its dependent space takes on different forms. Thus the dominant forces of the mercantilist period will differ from those of the subsequent phases of manufacturing, early industrialization and large-scale industry, and of the contemporary technological period. Equally, their effects on peripheral countries are different. History has given us therefore a *commercial*, and *industrial* and finally a *technological* modernization closely corresponding to the historical periodization of underdevelopment.

During the first phase of modernization, an international division of labour, strengthened by the metropolitan legislative superstructure, began to evolve. The colonizers systematically and increasingly appropriated the wealth of other nations; an impoverished countryside co-existed with urban areas characterized by a limited market for consumer goods and a demand for labour commensurate with their almost exclusively commercial and administrative functions.

In the second, post-Industrial Revolution phase, urban areas capitalized on their already privileged position through the development of modern land and maritime transport, thereby facilitating large-scale metropolitan capital accumulation. At the same time, a growing demand for foodstuffs and raw materials in the metropolis reinforced the orientation already taken by the international division of labour.

The third phase of modernization was characterized by not only a revolution in consumption but also the growing importance of warfare in directly and indirectly encouraging the industrialization of many underdeveloped countries. Equally, economies of scale became available through the resurgence of technical change. Currently, the rapid rates of population growth and urbanization are adding a new dimension – that of industrial production – to the internationalization of the division of labour. However, the impact of modernizations on contemporary Third World countries has been differential and selective, both in spatial and historical terms. In order to stress this fact, a classification of underdeveloped countries is required, based upon the extent of the impact of the various waves of modernization.

Historical periods and systems

Many sociologists implicitly associate modernization with development, giving the impression that both terms apply only to recent historical change. Others (e.g. Lerner 1967:21) define modern societies as those 'capable of self-sustaining growth over the long run'. Eisenstadt (1966:1) suggests the seventeenth century as the beginning of the modernization process, defined as the penetration of the rest of the world by the key elements of Western social, economic and political systems. But the roots of modernization in fact lie further back; the influence of the 'modern' world was first felt by the 'non-civilized' world at the end of the fifteenth centry with the emergence of the Spanish and Portuguese mercantile revolution. Previously, no pole of civilization, including the relatively more advanced societies such as the Arab World or China had been able to impose itself on the entire world.

Having established the roots of the modernization process, an historical periodization can be attempted; five periods can be isolated, with the first stretching from the end of the fifteenth to the end of the sixteenth century, the second lasting until about

1720, the third until almost the end of the nineteenth century (approximately 1870), the fourth from 1870 to about 1950, and the fifth being the present period.

Technological modernization and the evolution of the two circuits

Itself a product of the pervasive influence of technology (Roweiss 1970), contemporary modernization is controlled by large-scale industry, which basically consists of multinational firms and their supporting systems (such as the means of mass communication).

The rapid rate of change clearly differentiates the present period from preceding ones. The implications of the present-day period for underdeveloped countries are manifold and profound. For the first time in the history of underdeveloped countries, two variables emanating from the centre of the world economic system have become generally diffused throughout the periphery. The two variables in question are information and consumption, the former serving the latter (Table 2·1); together they transform economy, society, and spatial organization. They generate the forces of concentration and dispersion, which determine spatial organization. Information permeates all levels of society and creates demands that mirror those of the developed countries. This process is facilitated by the more recent advances in communication.

The effect of introducing new goods into the range of products available for consumption in the poor countries is well known. According to Nurske (1953:61–62), 'the presence or the mere knowledge of new goods and modes of consumption tends to raise the general propensity to consume', acting as an 'obstacle to capital formation and development'. This hypothesis is known as the international demonstration effect (Hirschman 1964:179).[2] One result of the demonstration effect is to reduce demand for local products. This diversifies demand without a parallel increase in income (Dasgupta 1964:182; Merhav 1969:28). As a result, more individuals are drawn into 'modern consumption' though the latter will be intermittent and/or marginal among the poorest sections of society.

Technological modernization in the Third World creates only a limited number of jobs when the capital-intensity of the industries is given. Furthermore, much of the resulting indirect employment is generated in central countries or for expatriates wor-

Table 2.1 Increase of number of radios in selected underdeveloped countries

Countries	Population (1000's)	1948	1953	Annual increase '48-'53 (%)	1963	Annual increase '53-'63	1964	1965	1966 (%)	1967	Annual increase '64-'67	No. radios per 100 inhabitants 1967
Algeria	12,540 (1966)	157	259	10.5	1500	19.2		470	550	700	20.7	5.6
Ghana	8,139 (1960)	8	24	24.6	504	35.6	555	505	555			6.8
Morocco	14,140 (1961)	86		23.2	615	9.7	650	700	748	800	7.1	5.7
Mexico	45,671 (1960)	700	2300	27.2	6506	10.8	7281	8593	9897	10932	14.5	23.9
Argentina	23,255 (1960)	2200	2582	3.3	5800	8.4	6200	6600	7000	8000	8.9	34.4
India	511,125 (1961)	282	838	24.3	3737	16.1	4315	5401	6485	7579	20.7	1.5
Hong Kong	3,834 (1961)	30	87	23.7	139	8.1	529	529	585	623	5.6	16.2
Pakistan	107,258 (1961)	62	98	9.6	459	16.7	549	972	1014		35.9	0.9

Source: United Nations, Statistical Yearbooks, 1966 and 1968.

king locally. Industry is becoming increasingly incapable of meeting an increasing local need for increased employment. Agriculture is also witnessing a decline in manpower due to modernization even in the more backward areas; this is one of the factors behind the phenomena of rural exodus and tertiary urbanization. In the cities of underdeveloped countries, the labour market is deteriorating and a high percentage of persons have neither stable employment nor income.

The choice of production techniques available in the leading sectors of underdeveloped countries is generally restricted to relatively capital-intensive ones (Eckaus 1955:545). However, the decrease in employment in both agriculture and industry through technological modernization has resulted in the creation of a large number of small-scale activities.

The presence of a mass of people with very low wages or depending upon occasional work for a living, alongside a minority with higher incomes,[3] creates in urban society a distinction between those who have permanent access to the available goods and services and those who have similar needs but who are unable to satisfy them. This creates both quantitative and qualitative differences in consumption.[4] These differences simultaneously cause, are manifested in and reproduce the two circuits of the urban economy, each of which produces, distributes and consumes its own goods and services. One of the circuits is the direct result of modernization and includes activities created by technological progress. The other is an indirect result of modernization, since it involves those individuals who benefit only partially or not at all from recent technical progress and its repercussions.

The two circuits: composition

The two-circuit formulation is useful in understanding the functioning of the city as a living organism;[5] it also facilitates the explanation of the city's external relations both with its immediate hinterland and with other urban centres.

One must distinguish countries with a long history of urbanization from those which have undergone this phenomenon only recently. In the former case modernization creates new structures which impose themselves upon existing urban structures and thus modify them. In the latter case, technological modernization creates two integrated forms of urban economic organization. Nevertheless in all cases, the two circuits are present.

Geertz (1963:34) spoke of a 'firm–centred economy' and a 'bazaar economy'. In order to consider the variety of situations in the Third World, we prefer to call these two circuits of the urban economy the 'upper circuit' and the 'lower circuit' (Santos 1971, 1972), thereby highlighting the dependence of the lower upon the upper circuit.

In simple terms, the upper circuit consists of banking, export trade and industry, modern urban industry, trade and services, and wholesaling and trucking. The lower circuit is essentially made up of non-capital-intensive forms of manufacturing, non-modern services generally provided at the 'retail' level and non-modern and small-scale trade (see Fig. 1).

In the upper circuit, one may differentiate integrated, non-integrated and 'mixed' activities. Modern urban industry, trade, and modern services are integrated elements since they are at the same time activities peculiar to both the city and upper circuit. Export orientated industry and trade are non-integrated activities, for, while they may be situated in the city in order to benefit from locational advantages, outputs are consumed outside the city and most activities are controlled by external interests. Banking is also included in this category, since it acts as a link between the modern activities of the city and larger cities both within the country and abroad. Wholesaling and trucking are 'mixed' activities, for they are linked to both upper and lower circuits of the urban regional economy. The wholesaler is at the top of a descending chain of intermediaries reaching down to the itinerant hawker and street vendor. Through these middlemen and through credit, the wholesaler provides a large number of products to the lower levels of trade and manufacturing as well as to an extensive range of consumers. The total volume of his business transacted within the lower circuit determines his status with the bank and thus the extent of his activities in the upper circuit. An integrating factor within the upper circuit, wholesaling is also the apex of the lower circuit.

Similarly, trucking plays two distinct roles; one vehicle may however serve successively in these two roles. By transporting goods the trucker provides a two-way link between the activities of the two circuits whether within the city, between two cities, or between the city and rural areas. On the other hand, the trucker himself may become a trader, in which case he participates direc-

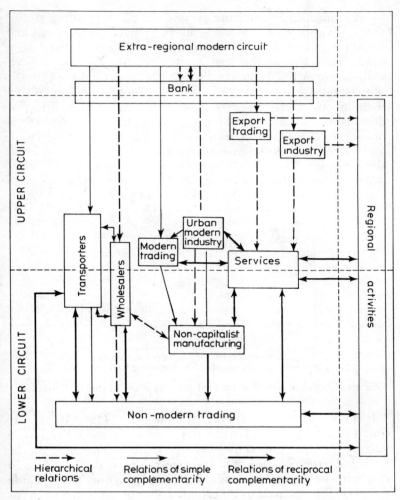

Figure 1

tly in an activity that may belong to either economic circuit.

The existence of mixed forms of activity in no way affects the definition of each circuit. However, a mere enumeration of each circuit's components is not an adequate definition. Each circuit is defined by: (i) the totality of activities undertaken in a given context; (ii) the section of the population linked to each circuit by consumption and employment. Nevertheless members of one social stratum may consume outside the corresponding circuit, although this consumption will be partial and occasional. Middle-class consumption patterns may be as much related to the upper classes as to the less-favoured classes. Moreover, individuals more directly attached to the lower circuit do not constitute a labour force exclusive to that circuit for they occasionally sell their labour to the upper circuit. Some activities having predominant characteristics of one circuit may also have characteristics of the other. This occurs more frequently in the upper circuit and for certain types of manufacturing where the co-existence of firms using different technologies and organizational modes is still possible. One could even speak of the existence of a 'marginal' upper circuit alongside the upper circuit proper.

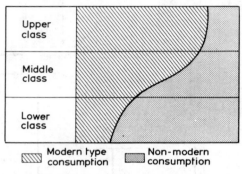

Upper
class

Middle
class

Lower
class

Modern type consumption   Non-modern consumption

Figure 2 Income distribution and participation in the two circuits

It is important to remember that not every Third World city contains each element of the model sketched above; indeed some may have only a limited number of activities, depending on the historical circumstances of urban growth. It could almost be said that no two cities were exactly alike, though this does not preclude the need for research to determine common characteristics for both Third World urban circuits irrespective of the city's location.

The two circuits: characteristics

The fundamental differences between the activities of the upper and lower circuits are of a technological and organizational nature.

The upper circuit uses an imitative imported, high-level and capital-intensive technology; in the lower circuit, though technology is labour-intensive and often either indigenous or locally adapted, it often has considerable innovative potential.

Activities in the upper circuit can rely on bank credit. Indeed large firms often establish and administer banks in order to first control and then absorb other activities; many of these manipulations are carried out on paper – Caplovitz's 'bureaucratic credit' (1963:2). The activities of the lower circuit are simultaneously based upon credit and cash. Here, however, credit is, to a large extent, of the direct and personal type essential to those who are themselves unable to accumulate money. Because borrowers are obliged to repay the debt by instalments, the search for cash becomes periodically frantic. Even wholesalers and other middlemen need cash to honour their commitments to the bank.

The upper circuit deals with a large volume of merchandise, whilst both the production and distribution aspects of the lower circuit work with small quantities (Brookfield 1969). Nevertheless, in the upper circuit quantities may also be limited, as is the case of the specialist shops where high prices are charged on the basis of fashionable quality merchandise demanded by a specified type of clientele.

This difference is based upon the capital available to each circuit and its characteristic type of organization. In the upper circuit, the volume of capital is of a magnitude commensurate with the level of technology used. Lower circuit activities are labour-intensive and may do without a bureaucracy.

In the upper circuit, wages are the dominant form of labour relation. Over time, progressively fewer people are employed in relation to the volume and value of production, whilst there is also a steady reduction in the labour force required in industry (though opportunities for government and other service employment will increase).

Employment opportunities in the directly productive sector and its adjuncts are mostly generated in the more developed cities or regions, both within the country and abroad.

Employment in the lower circuit is seldom permanent and its remuneration is often at or below the subsistence level. Employment often takes the form of a personal agreement between the hirer and hired, though family and self-employment are of greater importance. The average number of persons employed per enterprise is low; however, the number of production units being large, the total number of employees is considerable; the lower circuit thus provides employment for both the urban poor

Table 2.2 Characteristics of the two circuits of the urban economy in
              underdeveloped countries

	Upper circuit	Lower circuit
Technology	capital-intensive	labour-intensive
Organization	bureaucratic	primitive
Capital	abundant	limited
Labour	limited	abundant
Regular wages	prevalent	exceptionally
Inventories	large quantities and/ or high quality	small quantities poor quality
Prices	generally fixed	negotiable between buyer and seller (haggling)
Credit	from banks, institutional	personal, non-institutional
Profit margin	small per unit; but with large turnover, considerable in aggregate (exception = luxuries)	large per unit; but small turnover
Relations with customers	impersonal and/or on paper	direct, personalized
Fixed costs	substantial	negligible
Advertisement	necessary	none
Re-use of goods	none (waste)	frequent
Overhead capital	essential	not essential
Government aid	extensive	none or almost none
Direct dependence on foreign countries	great; externally orientated	small or none

and unskilled migrant workers.

The upper circuit employs many foreigners: the number varying with the country's degree of industrialization and modernization. In the lower circuit, jobs are allocated locally. Occasionally, however, other nationalities such as the Lebanese in West
Africa, the Chinese in certain parts of Asia, or the Indians in East
Africa work in this circuit as independent traders.

In the upper circuit, prices are generally fixed. Even in cases of
oligopolistic competition, the lower price limit cannot be much
below the market price without endangering the future of the

firm. In the lower circuit, haggling is the rule and price fluctuation margins are very large (Uchendu 1967). In the upper circuit, price movements take place on the assumption that the rate of profit is known in the long run, whereas in the lower circuit, short-term considerations are paramount; the notion of profit is thus different in each circuit. In the upper circuit, the goal is to accumulate sufficient capital to permit a reproduction of economic activity commensurate with the demands of technical progress. In the lower circuit, capital accumulation is of little, if any, concern: the major objective is firstly to ensure the day-to-day survival of both business and family and secondly, where possible, to have access to some 'modern' consumption goods. The volume of profits in the upper circuit is high whilst its profit-margins are relatively low. In the lower circuit the reverse is true. This is explained not only by the numerous middlemen operating between the initial supplier and the final consumer, but also the widespread use of private credit (usually at the usurious rates necessary to support the vast number of money lenders); unfortunately this complex phenomenon has not been sufficiently studied.

Upper circuit activity is largely based on advertising, one of the tools used to mould tastes and distort demand. In the lower circuit, advertising is not necessary because there is frequent customer contact; nor is it possible, because profits supply the everyday needs of the individual and his family. Upper circuit activities have high fixed costs, which usually increase in proportion to the size of the firm.

Lower circuit activities have almost no fixed costs, neither are direct costs very high.

In the upper circuit, the re-utilization of durable consumer goods is almost non-existent, whilst the lower circuit activities are often based on precisely this re-utilization, a fact well illustrated by the large number of small-scale clothing, appliance, automobile, etc. repair shops to be found in any Third World city.

Upper circuit activities benefit directly or indirectly from government assistance; lower circuit activities however tend to be the recipients only of government harassment.

Upper circuit activity depends largely upon overhead capital, often provided by the State, a condition unnecessary for the establishment of lower circuit activities.

The upper circuit responds to the needs of a capital-intensive *production*, which may be either local or external. Consumption is

academic cowardice? see p. 10.

purchasing power and is therefore selective; however, upper circuit enterprises can use advertising to expand their activities through the creation of new tastes and the manipulation of demand. The lower circuit is *created* by demand, whether 'pure' or distorted by demonstration effects; in reality, it is highly dependent on consumption.

Upper circuit activity tends to dominate the entire economy, particularly in the primate city. Control is exercised either directly or through State intervention. The lower circuit, however, tends to be controlled, subordinated and dependent.

Another basic difference between the two circuits stems from the fact that the lower circuit is locally integrated, while in the upper circuit, local activities are integrated with those of another higher-order city within the country itself or abroad. Even a metropolis that is relatively self-contained in economic terms will exhibit some measure of external dependency with respect to technology, access to information, capital and raw materials.

In summary, then, the lower circuit finds the elements of its articulation in the city and its region, while the upper circuit usually seeks this integration outside the city and its region.[6]

Three classes – two circuits

The division of the urban population into social classes recurs as the principal theme in the work of many sociologists, though not without certain problems; indeed each city seems to require a different sociological classification. Le Chau (1966) for instance, distinguished three sectors of the Ivoirian urban economy: the *traditional* sector (the primary and artisanal subsistence production which occupies 80 per cent of the labour force), the dominant *non-integrated* modern sector comprising export crop-production and its modern ancillary services, and the *mediating* sector, consisting mainly of the service and transport industries, acting as a mechanism of inter-relationship between the other two sectors. Alternatively, for a region of Brazil, Leloup (1970:198–9) points to the existence of three urban economic circuits: the circuit of the *privileged* classes, that of the *middle* and *working* classes, and finally the circuit of the *marginal* classes.

The definition of poverty has also caused problems: classifications, typologies and subdivisions abound, often without achieving any more than the proliferation of euphemisms (Medina 1963:72). However, for the purposes of this study, the poor in a given society are defined as those without regular access to what would be generally considered the minimum level of consumption; they seldom have access to institutional credit and thus figure significantly among the clients of the small traders and craftsmen who offer personal credit at exorbitant interest rates. They are the non-employed, the underemployed, and the low-income wage-earner.

The upper classes exert control over the urban, regional and even national economies either directly as owners or indirectly as intermediaries. The middle class can be defined in a residual manner occupying an intermediate position between the lower class (poor) and the upper class (rich). It comprises all those earning wages in excess of subsistence as well as landowners and entrepreneurs with incomes insufficient to allow them upper-class status. The social prestige attaching to various economic activities can also be incorporated into the definition (McGee 1971a:175).

The exercise of control separates the upper fraction of the middle class from the upper class itself. Though the middle class benefits from the urban economy, it has little control over it. However, the fact that Third World urban society can be divided into three classes does not imply the existence of an identical number of urban economic circuits.

As far as some prestige consumption goods are concerned – housing, cars, holidays, etc., the middle class tend to imitate the upper class. However, for other consumer products (e.g. current consumption such as food) the middle class tend to use the lower circuit and the neighbourhood personal credit facilities, thereby making available purchasing power for the purchase of goods normally reserved for the upper circuit. In other words, by shifting its consumption the middle class participates in circuit. *In no case does it create a third circuit.*

Polarization, not dualism

It is essential to clearly distinguish between dualism, as defined, for example, by Boeke (1953), Lewis (1954), Hirschman (1964:210), Turin (1965), Belshaw (1965:96–7), Furtado (1966:126), Lambert (1968a), Barros de Castro (1971: Chapter 7), and the two circuits of the Third World urban economy. The 'modern'/'traditional' dichotomy, prevalent and perhaps valid in the past, has no place in a world now dominated by innovation-diffusion and rapidly changing consumption patterns. Many so-called traditional activites either had to be modified, decline in scale or significance or disappear altogether. They lost the dominant position they had held in the precolonial economy and many found their markets restricted to the poorest consumers. Exceptions to this rule have occurred, as in the case of artisans producing for the tourist market.

The principal error of many 'dualists' is their very partial approach to the study of Third World economy and society, focusing almost exclusively on *production*. Many writers speak of a capitalist and traditional sector, basing their distinction on the co-existence of technologies of different epochs. This seems to imply that technology is independent and unaffected by the specific conditions of society and the economy. The problems of an economic society cannot be studied piecemeal; besides production, we must also analyse the distribution and employment aspects, in other words, the entire system.

Peattie (1968:38) astutely puts quotation marks around the expression 'dual economy'. It appears more reasonable to generalize a concept that she developed with reference to Venezuela and speak, rather, of a 'bi-polar' economy (Peattie 1968:39). This is also the opinion of Stavenhagen (1969:104) for whom the relations between the two sectors 'represent the functioning of a single society in which the two poles are integral parts, these two poles originating within the same historical process'.

An alternative concept of dualism, in which two historically distinct activities come into conflict, also seems outmoded (Havens and Flinn 1970:7). Even the theory of transition (Smelser and Lipset 1966) between two such situations is difficult to accept; otherwise one would have to accept that the contemporary realities in underdeveloped countries are nothing but stages toward the current situation of the developed countries. This paradigm has already distorted the analysis of Third World urbanization to such an extent that its further utility is in doubt (Wheatley 1969; Silvany 1971).

It must be recognized that the much-abused term 'dualism' has become convenient in designating the co-existence of various forms of production, distribution and consumption in underdeveloped countries. The drawback of this term is that it is based on the idea of a dichotomized or fragmented urban economy, as Mabogunje (1965) has suggested. This approach often leads to separate treatment for each supposedly separate sector of the urban economy.

The concept of a specifically *urban* dualism also becomes meaningless when it is realized that both circuits of the urban economy owe their origin and existence to the same causes – those we have called *technological modernization*. Though the two circuits are apparently independent, the linkages between them are considerable and are characterized by the dependence of the lower upon the upper, in the same way that traditional activities are dependent upon modern (Havens and Flinn 1970:8). Thus the 'dualism' identified by so many authors is nothing more than the general manifestation of the upper circuit's hegemony, which can be seen in more striking terms in the guise of monopoly, on the one hand (Mason 1967:79), and underemployment on the other (Singer 1970:66–7; Eckaus 1955:554–8; Dasgupta 1964:177).

Thus, to analyse the two circuits of the urban economy from a dualistic standpoint is to deny the historical dimension indispensable to a valid conceptualization of the reality of contemporary underdeveloped societies.

It appears that he is saying that the two circuit approach is not dualistic in that it provides for a linkage between the two. However, in this sense dualistic must be taken to mean two separate entities with no linkages. It seems that this point is not only realized but is relatively old in the pertinent literature.

3

The colonial urban economy: two circuits?

At this point we shall attempt to indicate the specificity of the two circuits of the Third World urban economy, and, in doing so, avoid three common errors. The first consists in believing that valid comparisons can be made between the urban economy of the European nations during their industrial revolutions and that of the contemporary underdeveloped countries, despite the fact that the two circuits of the latter are clearly the result of more recent technological modernization, and should be analysed as such. The other two errors are quite similar; one posits the ghetto as part of the lower circuit, whilst the other attempts to identify the shantytown with the lower circuit. Neither of these relatively limited frameworks is appropriate, since they merely represent manifestations of the more pervasive dependent nature of a whole economic system.[1]

During the process of Western industrialization, contemporary developed countries did not experience a gradual and proportional decline in the economically active population, a trend which certainly characterizes the same process in most underdeveloped economies (Clarke and Clark 1969:44). The developed countries' industrialization required rural labour to supplement inadequate urban supplies: in the Third World, the process of capital-intensive industrialization attracts far more labour than it can possibly absorb.

Thus, since their earliest industrial beginnings, Third World cities have been characterized by a tertiary sector numerically larger than that of the manufacturers in contrast with developed countries, where the urban expansion of the tertiary sector occurred later. In any case, the tertiary sector of poor countries is 'primitive' compared with that of developing countries (Beaujeu-Garnier 1965). Lambert (1965) describes it as being a 'refuge' sector.

Another distinguishing factor is that in nineteenth-century Europe, levels of productivity were roughly similar in manufacturing and services: clearly a very different situation exists in the contemporary Third World.

The ghetto and the lower circuit

Is it either valid or desirable to compare the poor of the Third World with the underprivileged of the developed world? Some have attempted to draw a parallel between the 'ghetto'[2] of the wealthy countries and the shantytown of the underdeveloped countries' urban centres, both in terms of the problems themselves, and the solutions deemed appropriate.

Firstly, in industrial countries, the urban poor are relatively few in number. They comprise groups who have been historically the object of discrimination, for whom upward mobility has been most difficult, such as the immigrant populations recruited to perform those essential low-status jobs shunned by nationals. The urban poor in underdeveloped countries, relatively greater in number, originate in both the middle and lower classes, with both rural and urban roots, and *less* social mobility than the more recent migrants.

Similarities certainly can be found between these two groups: both ghetto and shantytown resident finds permanent employment relatively difficult to come by. Yet the job mobility of the former is limited, whilst the labour of the Third World urban poor is characteristically flexible and adaptable. This is the basic difference between the urban economy of industrial and underdeveloped countries. Elliot Liebow (1967:57) points out that for those who are often without work, any opportunity is seized, since 'a job is a job'. This comment has still greater validity in Third World cities, where the availability of occupations enabling poor and unskilled workers to earn a living is much greater. Employment mobility among ghetto residents is limited, physical mobility often being as restricted as job opportunities. The employment available in comparable districts in underdeveloped countries is much greater, and the number of activities tends to expand with population through a 'self-inflationary' process (McGee 1971a:74). In developed countries, the number of these activities tends to decrease.

Unemployment compensation paid, in the United States and Western Europe, to anyone without work (Becker 1968; Caplovitz 1963), may permit the individual's existence to be a little better than 'hand to mouth' and 'day to day'. In underdeveloped countries where such measures are not found, the search for the means of subsistence is continuous, prompted by the combined pressures of debt payment, credit maintenance and survival. Thus, poverty with relative security and the virtual absence of a lower circuit in developed countries contrasts with a much more insecure poverty in underdeveloped countries.

As Joan Nelson (1969:9) accurately observes, constant comparisons between American ghettos and squatter settlements of cities in developing countries are suspect, for 'conditions differ in many respects'. Even if some of the characteristics of the lower circuit can be recognized in cities of developed countries, this, in itself, is not sufficient to establish a valid comparison.

Shantytowns and the lower circuit

Just as we have criticized the parallels drawn between the ghetto and the shantytown, we find the identification of the shantytown and the lower circuit equally spurious. Studies of urban poverty which contrast the shantytowns or slums with the city centre constitute a serious misrepresentation of reality. While such an approach could provide technically acceptable results (Frankenhoff 1971), it is doubtful whether it could itself lead to the construction of a valid theory. Poor housing and low income districts will certainly vary in character within and between countries; different types of slums may even be identified within the same city, differentiated by location, appearance, the origin and activity of the population and individual and family income distribution. Indeed, the shantytown will not include all the poor of a city, nor will it embrace all those who could be defined as 'poor' according to a common criterion. The knife-grinder who lives from irregular income, the wage-earner in services or industries, and even small-scale entrepreneurs may all live in the same poor district (dos Santos 1971). Anyone who has visited a Latin American city will recall the forest of TV aerials to be seen above even the poorest slums and *favelas*.

Thus the contrast to be made is not that between shantytown and the city centre but between the lower and upper circuits. Whilst some shantytown residents may partially escape the lower circuit, residents of other districts may, on the other hand, be completely attached to it. The dangers of ignoring these factors are many and varied.

The debate concerning the existence of 'urban ruralization' has continued despite an apparently conclusive refutation in studies by Leeds and Leeds (1970). Even today, new urbanites are frequently called 'rurals in the city'. Frankenhoff (1971) has made the suggestion that the major function of the shantytown labour force is the provision of manpower to the 'centre', and that this factor controls existing relations between the two entities; this appears to be as debatable as the 'theory of urban exports' from which it is derived. McGee has shown that there exists considerable differentiation between the commodity flows which link together the two subsystems of the urban economy. Moreover, both the lower circuit and the shantytowns generate economic activity. The mere presence of individuals not permanently engaged in the economy of the centre creates activities which operate independently of 'central' demand. New needs imposed by technological modernization will, at the aggregate level, produce the appropriate responses from the poor.

The contemporary nature of the two circuits

According to our definition, the two circuits of the urban economy are both products of contemporary technological modernization; whether industrialization was initiated before the First World War or more recently, the two circuits did not previously exist in underdeveloped countries. Similarities between the colonial and the contemporary Third World city could perhaps be established on the basis of isolated factors; however, a valid parallel between the 'traditional' (Wheatley 1969:4) and the contemporary city cannot. Colonial cities constitute a link between two distinct worlds, one of which produces raw materials, the other transforming these into marketable manufactured goods. In the colonial city, these products were consumed by a small minority of merchants, civil servants and wealthy landowners.

The urban economy had no real export industry nor specialized services. The wholesaler mediated in virtually all relationships, whether at a local, inter-regional, or international level, thereby usurping the functions and retarding the evolution of an authentic industrial and/or financial class. No distinction between small-scale and 'specialized', 'integrated' trade was in evidence. The 'bazaar' served both the wealthy and poor with virtually everything they required.

Consumption was much more limited in terms of both volume and choice; advertising was embryonic and there was little evidence of the demonstration effect. Since the colonial town housed mainly civil servants, merchants and wealthy landowners, income disparities were relatively small. Household servants' and other underemployed workers' consumption was minimal and was mainly satisfied by the activities of artisans who were yet to be confronted by industrial competition and could thus provide considerable local employment.

Where industrialization began early, the initial effects were not conducive to the simultaneous development of two urban circuits. Rural-urban migration was insignificant compared with today; people were *pushed* (by adverse local conditions), rather than *pulled* via the demonstration effect. Such subjective perceptions of poverty only evolved later. Also, since industrial activity was not as concentrated as it is today and used technologies which guaranteed both an absolute and relative expansion of employment, job opportunities in towns were assured. Modernization of production and marketing did not lead to the creation of very large-scale manufacturing or commercial units, and the existence of *relatively* large enterprises could not be held responsible for the disappearance of smaller sized units.

Since industrial expansion was linked to that of the market (Furtado 1968), the relatively stable price stucture tended to stimulate consumption. Increases in production did not necessarily require, as they do today, the utilization of the most up-to-date technology; thus a 'positive feedback' was developed in all urban activities, with production and employment increasing simultaneously.

Activities complementary to modernization (e.g. railway and port construction) also generated employment. Distribution and other tertiary activities were mechanized to such a minimal extent that they also opened up job opportunities. Government activities also tended to expand rapidly so that considerable public service employment was ensured. Since national efforts toward industrialization and infrastructure development were based on its export capacity, cash-crop zones were enlarged and new areas developed, the surplus population of rural areas moving both to the cities and the new areas of commercial agriculture. Consequently, it is not surprising that the emergence of shantytowns did not become generalized until the 1940s.

In the colonial period, the foreign presence took several forms, manifested, for example, in both the arrival of immigrants and the penetration of foreign capital. Equally so, migrations have taken place under different historical forms: one wave was initiated by sheer poverty, another by the desire to 'strike it rich'. In Argentina, the proportion of the population of foreign birth was 12 per cent in 1869, 26 per cent in 1895 and had risen to 30 per cent by the beginning of the First World War (Germani 1966:386, Table 3). Another type of migration could be described as 'technological', involving those whose skills were more valuable to a developing economy than their own; this contrasts with the exodus of workers marginalized in their own countries by the introduction of labour-saving technologies.

Previously, industry was not required to produce consumption goods for privileged members of colonial urban society; in any case, these latter were too few in number to warrant such development. Equally so, this stratum preferred cosmopolitan consumption and consequently imported many of the goods it desired, leaving local production to serve the interests of the urban masses. The banks were mainly interested in import-export activities and the large profits to be earned thereby; such industry as existed was forced to rely on pre-existing networks of credit and capital.

The size of colonial urban areas (small by today's standards), a less marked inequality in urban incomes, and a primitive transport and communications infrastructure, all contributed to the preservation of artisanal production. Thus there is little evidence to suggest the co-existence of an upper and a lower circuit in the colonial urban economy.

PART II

4

The upper circuit

The import motive

Changes in a country's consumption patterns, brought about through the demonstration effect, entail concomitant changes in the balance of trade. Import demand depends largely on the level of national development and the extent to which the population is exposed to new patterns of consumption. Modernization and industrialization require throughout their evolution that large amounts of commodities be purchased on the world (rather than national) market; the first stages of industrialization require equally large expenditures on capital goods. The countries of the Far East, somewhat tardy in their industrialization, give ample evidence of the degree of external dependence involved:

Table 4.1

Country	Year	Capital goods imports as % of total imports
Burma	1958	40.8
Cambodia	1963	27.6
Indonesia	1958	27.3
Malaysia	1958	13.0
Singapore	1963	21.1
Philippines	1963	44.6
Thailand	1963	44.2

Source: United Nations (1965) 'Industrial Development in Asia and the Far East', December.

As import-substitution begins, the very structure of imports is naturally transformed; new lines of production entail new demands for equipment, but these latter are amplified by the current phase of technological development, which demands a continuous renewing of capital equipment. For the already industrialized, domestic production can satisfy part of the demand for equipment; for those still attempting to industrialize, external dependence and the level of imports will both tend to rise. Imports of new technology often require complementary purchases of raw materials and intermediate goods which will only be available on the world market; dependence of this sort is clear evidence of the lack of integration of locally based industry in the Third World.

In order to maintain the necessary level of stocks, import firms need access to large-scale finance, all the more so if credit must be extended to clients. Given the possibility of changes in exchange controls and tariff levels, only the most powerful companies will be able to maintain their position in the market. Additionally, the small foreign exchange reserves of the poorer countries are further diminished by the purchase of relatively large quantities of armaments. Between 1950 and 1970, Third World imports of combat aircraft, warships, missiles and armoured vehicles rose from $300 million to $1100 million ($1400 if Vietnam is included) (Myrdal 1972:21). The average rate of growth of underdeveloped economies' G.N.P. over this period was 5 per cent compared to a 9 per cent increase in arms purchases. Such transactions are doubly advantageous for the developed world: arms rapidly become obsolete, and old stock can be dumped on the Third World. Also, as Bognar (1968:557) suggests, modern weapons require progressively smaller amounts of raw materials inputs and more technological effort, and thus increase Third World dependence on the central developed economies.

Import-substitution industry

Third World industrialization is increasingly constrained by the need to acquire modern technologies which are in a state of continual transformation. This entails a growing dependence on external sources of equipment, raw materials, capital and 'know-how'. Three forms or paths of industrialization can be discerned (though the following only represents a sort of continuum) from the available evidence: (i) various degrees of import-substitution, producing mainly for domestic consumption, (ii) the exporting of a certain portion of the national mineral or agricultural product, and (iii) the more recent creation of a manufacturing sector producing commodities almost exclusively for consumption in the developed countries, and constituting little more than the transfer of certain lines of production from the rich to the poor countries. In underdeveloped countries, these latter activities are usually called 'transformative' or 're-exporting' industries.

Industrialization through import-substitution creates much the same dilemma in all underdeveloped countries. Infant industries will inevitably require protection against foreign competition whilst import-*substitution* will also involve increased *dependence* on imports. But there are other drawbacks: the market may shrink as local production replaces imports; foreign exchange reserves will decline as capital goods, raw materials and services need to be purchased. This provides a fertile breeding ground for the monopolies[1] that will restrict the market even further.

Tariff protection granted to an industrial sector may be tantamount to the protection of a monopoly, for the first firm to be established can rapidly gain control of the market (Mason 1967:102). Such a process may distort the production structure and this will have repercussions on national development.

Though import substitution under given circumstances may appear to be a dynamic process, it inevitably develops internal contradictions such that imports may *increase*. As Tavares (1964, 1973) has pointed out, the initial requirements of new industry often put pressure on import capacity; if the imports required to maintain current production in the consumer goods section continue to be replaced without leaving a sufficient margin for the entry of the capital goods indispensable to the expansion of industrial capacity, then the 'import capacity' of a country can be detrimentally affected, with the result that either industrial growth is impaired, or the economy is further burdened with debts.

As the poor countries become capable of satisfying more of the local demand for manufactured goods[2], a modification in the world division of labour takes place: rich countries are now able to concentrate on more dynamic types of product.[3] Thus import-substitution in dependent countries corresponds to the export-substitution of dominant economies, within the relationship that

Maza Zavala (1969:74) described as 'secondary neocolonial imperialism'.

Many hypotheses have been advanced in support of import-substitution as a vehicle of Third World industrialization and development. E.A. Johnson (1970:259), Lewis (1967:31), Manne (1967) and Chauleur (1970:8) are all for various reasons optimistic about such a process being successful. Economies of both scale and agglomeration are always useful, as are externalities; but it does not necessarily follow that industrial growth will be thereby produced. Modern industries are not *per se* complementary; as Jalée (1969:174) has said, 'to create industries is not to industrialize', since the industries which so often emerge 'do not become an integral part of the host country's development programme but combine with the strategy of the imperialistic monopolies who, often with the collaboration of local private and/or public capital, control them.'

Export industries

Whilst the Industrial Revolution was unfolding in nineteenth-century Europe, the role of the colonies as suppliers of raw materials for that very process of industrialization was considerably strengthened. Changes taking place in these colonies largely reflected the changing needs of the colonizers.

As European, and later American, standards of living improved during the process of industrialization, the volume of largely unprocessed food and mineral imports from the Third World increased. Those who began to export first, also appear to have taken the initiative in import-substitution too (e.g. Argentina and Brazil). Nevertheless, large exporters who became politically independent only recently, such as India, thereby suffered considerable delay in their attempts to industrialize.

The textile industry was the first to be located outside the developed countries, but other manufacturing industries have also moved towards the poor countries. As a result, today most of the underdeveloped countries have freed themselves from the need to import textiles and clothing and they have become important exporters of these products to the rich countries. This trend can only continue to grow in the second stage of the present technological period.

The two phases of the technological era (through the second of which we are currently passing) entail characteristic strategies on the part of both poles in the system, namely the developed and the underdeveloped countries. Such an historical subdivision or periodization becomes vital when we consider just how inter-related is the history of underdevelopment and that of the evolution of the international division of labour.

The first historical phase has been described as the inter-nationalization of the division of labour; part of the industrial apparatus of the developed world is transferred under specific circumstances and with various guarantees to the underde-veloped countries, where use is made of the 'external proletariat', whilst the tertiary sector remains firmly in the hands of the dominant economies.

In the second phase of this technological era the situation of the underdeveloped countries changes: 'growthmania' (Mishan 1967:3–8) leaves in its wake a stunted and unsatisfied internal market as well as a growing need to export. The terms of trade deteriorate, and the contradictions inherent in the complement-ary need to both import and export tends to reduce the value of Third World currencies on the world market. A new tendency emerges as Third World industrialization commences; externally-oriented industries migrate from the industrialized countries to profit from locational advantages, fixed external economies, cheap labour, and specific government enticements. These new 'colonial' industries are not necessarily connected with the export of local, unprocessed products but instead are linked to the developed countries' import requirements of finished and semi-finished products. This type of industry has certain charac-teristics in common with the export of agricultural produce: dependence on a restricted market, an orientation towards fore-ign requirements, and a need for tariff protection. The charac-teristic strategy of this period is clear: capital accumulated in the developed countries is transferred to the Third World.

The period in which the Third World develops a potential for exporting manufactured goods can be divided into two distinct phases: the first is somewhat problematical for the developed world and is initiated by the underdeveloped countries them-selves. The second phase consists of the developed economies' decision to transfer part of their production to poor countries, thereby making cheap imports available in the future. Underde-veloped countries have recently experienced both an increase in their exports of manufactured goods and their imports of numerous commodities from developed countries. This is particularly so in the textiles and clothing sector, where growth has been both rapid and substantial:

Table 4.2 Third World exports to developed countries
($ millions)

	1965	1968	%
Textiles	763	875	14.7
Clothing	410	473	15.4

Source: United Nations (1971).

Table 4.3 Developed world imports from the Third World
($ millions)

	Textiles			Clothing		
	1965	1968	% increase	1965	1968	% increase
United States	300	338	12.7	190	399	110.0
United Kingdom	140	156	11.4	77	119	54.5
Sweden	10	12	20.0	19	31	63.2
France	84	96	14.3	69	76	10.1

Source: United Nations (1971).

Progress has also been made in Third World export performance in metal products, machinery and several other commodities (Table 4.4).

Whilst running the risk of being labelled neocolonialist, many developed countries are exporting semifinished goods (car components, ready-cut cloth patterns, etc.) to underdeveloped countries for assembly. Though imported manufactures constitute an average of 8 per cent of total imports by developed countries, some countries import much more (e.g. Belgium, Britain, United States and Japan); but in absolute terms the United States itself imports half of all Third World exports of electrical and electronic equipment (particularly from US subsidiaries in South Korea, the Philippines and Taiwan) 33 per cent of Third World chemicals exports, 70 per cent of wood, more than half of all clothing exports and about 60 per cent of the Third World's other consumption goods exports. Additionally, in both the UK and the USA, half of the clothing imported originates in underdeveloped countries. A similar trend has already developed in the trading patterns of the Soviet Union.[5]

Table 4.4   Imports by developed countries from the Third World
($ millions)

	1965	*1968*	*% increase*
Ferrous ores	2213	2393	8.1
Nonferrous ores	965	1016	5.3
Nonferrous metals	1875	3036	61.9
Foodstuffs	7952	8980	12.9
Raw materials	7064	7466	5.7
Primary industrial products	3695	5525	49.5
Machinery	176	424	140.9
Other industrially processed products	727	1378	89.5
Total manufactures	5003	7818	56.3
Wood and cork	757	1025	35.4
Wood and cork products	133	249	87.2
Leather products	105	156	48.6
Clothing	410	473	15.4
Thread and textiles	763	875	14.7

Source: United Nations (1971: 234–35, Tables A25–A27 and Table 49).

Table 4.5   General situation 1960–9; imports by developed countries of
Third World products (1959–61 average index = 100).

Import category	*1960*	*1969*
Foodstuffs	100	105
Raw materials	104	93
Fuels	99	93
Manufactures	101	140

Source: United Nations (1970: 318, Table 49).

The fact that most underdeveloped countries have a limited number of exportable commodities means that dependence rather than the sort of development envisaged by the proponents of the 'free play of market forces', has become the general rule (Pinto and Sunkel 1966:82). This dependence is amplified by the fact that exports are often destined for a single developed country or bloc of countries. Dependence on agricultural exports ironically often coincides with heavy food import bills; the expansion of agricultural production for industrial transformation and eventual export often leads to the disruption of subsistence agriculture. The process of urbanization merely exacerbates an already high import requirement, particularly in the case of foodstuffs. However, agricultural products are not always exported in their raw form; sometimes the developed countries find it more profitable to locate the preliminary processing of raw materials in the countries in which these products originate. The typical export-oriented industry clearly has a level of production which dwarfs the needs of the local market; for example, 84 per cent of the production of Dakar's groundnut oil mills and 99 per cent of that of its fish canneries is for export. This form of industrialization can have little social benefit for the underdeveloped country, aggravating as it does the limited degree of industrial diversification and integration.

New techniques of production and new (chemical rather than natural) inputs have also had a profound impact on the Third World: the rich nations, particularly the United States, have moved rapidly into the production of numerous synthetic substitutes for conventional raw materials.[6]

Table 4.6   Developed countries' production of synthetic materials

Period	Product	Increase in production
1953–68	plastics and resins	3.5–fold
1953–68	noncellulosic fibres	30–fold
1937–68	rayon and acetate filaments	64–fold
1937–68	synthetic rubber	4.3–fold

Source: Adapted from United Nations (1959, 1966, 1969).

The availability of these new products has had at least two consequences for the Third World: (i) their production of certain basic raw materials either stabilized or fell, seriously damaging their foreign exchange earnings,[7] and (ii) they were forced to buy either these new materials or the equipment to produce them (depending on the local level of industrialization) thereby damaging formerly remunerative external and domestic markets.

Export-oriented commerce and industry both have a tendency towards concentration[8] and monopoly, thereby facilitating a collusive setting of producer-prices by exporters. Thus the export-orientation of underdeveloped economies acts as a mechanism of transfer working to the advantage of multinational corporations and to the detriment of the direct producers. The capacity of a nation to produce will clearly determine its ability to export; its capacity to import, however, should be directly dependent upon export and other earnings from national production. The existence of a market is not sufficient to provide the impetus to industrial expansion; material and institutional conditions must also be fulfilled (Maza Zavala 1969:67). Economies dependent for the most part on exports are at the mercy of cyclical fluctuations in the world market prices of their products, over which they can exercise little or no control; consequently, they are doomed to become more externally and less domestically oriented (McKee and Leahy 1970a:84). They will also suffer significant structural changes, even in their infrastructural development, a phenomenon which Desmond (1971:73) considers to be quite often the greatest threat to development. For example, even though Venezuela managed to increase the volume of its exports between 1950 and 1963, from 1957 onwards both its net terms of trade and its propensity to import suffered a downward trend. To export more, more had to be imported; to do so required the foreign exchange which only more exports could bring. In this way the Third World is forced to buy more technological inputs from abroad in a seemingly vain attempt to pursue an export-oriented policy; it is, of course, the poorest classes who foot the bill. Indeed, they are forced to pay twice over, once through a fiscal system which depends predominantly on indirect taxes (which affect the poor most of all), and once again because the contradiction between the need to export and the need to import makes it virtually impossible in the context of monopolized markets to pursue a strategy of expanding production for basic domestic needs. In other words independent national industrialization and development also become a dream.

The marginal upper circuit

There are two organizational forms of manufacturing activity in the upper circuit: the upper circuit proper and the marginal upper circuit – the latter being composed of less modern forms of production. The marginal upper circuit either emerges out of the remnants of anterior organizational forms or as a response to demands which do not necessitate the most modern forms of activity. Such a demand may come from modern activities as well as from the lower circuit. The marginal upper circuit thus has both a residual and evolutionary character; in the intermediate city, the evolutionary aspect is dominant.

There is no 'marginal' commerce in the upper circuit because modern trade must conform to strict codes of practice with respect to the regularity of payment of salaries, accounts, taxes and rents. If a merchant defaults in some way he can switch to the lower circuit, but must change his business practices accordingly.

Other classifications have been made (e.g. Ramos 1970:151) to differentiate manufacturing enterprises according to their intensity of activity. A simpler taxonomy, more amenable to the study of the two circuits of the urban economy, both enables the distinction to be made between the different types of manufacturing, as well as facilitating the study of their spatial effects. This perspective is broadly comparable to that of Jones (1971:20).

In a study of the Mexican city of Guadalajara (Santos 1968), apart from the artisanal sector, two modern manufacturing sectors were identified; first, enterprises 'mature' from their very inception and second, a sector in which competition still exists between enterprises with different levels of technology, capital, plant size, and labour-utilization. The inequality between these sectors will be quite large; some branches of industry will have successfully achieved 'modernity' comparable at an international level, whilst others, due to rapid population growth and low standards of living, will retain a less modern form.

Mason (1967:94) studied the case of Greece, where in some industries 'two or three large firms co-exist with a much larger number of smaller, high-cost competitors'. For some small enterprises, the conditions for price formation and the degree of returns to scale will be determinant (Utton 1970:21) whilst for others the crucial variable will be capital requirements. However, the levels of technology and managerial competence will also be important; in Burma, in four out of seventeen industrial branches, fixed capital per worker was found to be higher in the smaller-scale enterprises; though in India and Pakistan the reverse is more generally found, the gap is often much smaller than might be expected (Kus'min 1929:21–3).

Though it is difficult to share the optimism with which Ranis (1962:345) views the apparent advantages of small-scale production, it is true that social insurance contributions and tax payments may be more easily avoided, and wages lower than those of one's larger competitors can be paid, if one is a small-scale operation. Large firms have high capital-labour ratios and therefore assist in the maintenance of low wages. Smaller enterprises pay salaries at basic rates only, without the need to add legislated insurance, housing, other payments and perquisites. Advertising expenditure is also small or even non-existent, yet inferior quality products often benefit indirectly from the advertising of superior substitutes. These advantages ensure that the marginal upper circuit remains in business. Sometimes even productivity is above that of the upper circuit. 'The myth of higher productivity in large enterprises must be reduced to its real dimension. Production capacity does not accurately correspond to productivity indices' (Messner 1966:243).

While monopolistic capitalism is dominated by giant enterprises, one must not forget, as Baran and Sweezy (1968:63) point out, that the medium and small firms, operating with relatively little capital, also demand to be taken into account 'in the calculations and strategy of large capital'. The maintenance of high prices is one of the elements of such a strategy, assuring that the marginal upper circuit continues to work on behalf of an upper circuit which can produce at lower cost.

Modern retailing

The modern retail sector comprises a wide variety of units ranging from department stores and supermarkets (offering many and varied products to a large clientele), to boutiques selling a small number of luxury goods to personal clients. But most of the modern retail sector consists of medium-sized or small specialized traders selling durable or non-durable goods ranging from food, clothes and drugs to electrical appliances and books.

The department stores and supermarkets are strongly supported by the banking system. Indeed they may even control the banks, in which case a new type of commercial capital, similar to the financial capital of big industry, makes for a certain autonomy among retail establishments. In underdeveloped countries, the development of supermarkets and department stores is linked to an expansion and diversification of demand and the payment by cash, credit cards or on personal account.

Buyer-seller relations are essentially impersonal in this type of 'super-commerce'; consequently the number of supermarkets varies according to both the size of the middle and upper class and the number of salary-earners in the economy, whilst their scale of operations is related to the density of the well-to-do quarters. Boutique customers, through a more personal relationship with proprietors, may have access to individual credit (though not necessarily that of a 'bureaucratic' nature, i.e. credit cards).

Upper circuit distribution and retailing is highly dependent on either imports or local production; the direction of this dependence will be determined largely by the level of industrialization in the country in question, its ability to import, the availability of appropriate transport, and, of course, fashion. The dominant role played by imports will continue until a new stage of import-substitution is reached.

The introduction and distribution of new commodities is not necessarily undertaken by local entrepreneurs, since often they lack the necessary capital; in many countries, foreign traders have much better access to bank credit. Indeed, there is evidence to suggest that the extent of foreign domination of local commerce is a function of the level of economic development in the underdeveloped country.[9]

Foreign capital

Foreign capital gravitates to those branches of industry which can provide the most profitable environment; its penetration varies with the level of industrialization and infrastructural development of the host economy, the speed with which investments can be amortized, and the facility with which profits can be repatriated. The magnitude of profits will depend upon absolute levels of output and the political stability of the host economy, among other factors.

Where formerly ports and railways acted as the magnets for foreign investment, international financial and banking institutions (closely controlled by the super-powers) now provide the major channels for profitable activities. Involvement in mineral extraction is still a highly prized investment, since developed economies need to exercise control over the production of raw materials upon which their own economic growth is so dependent. But the exploitation of such raw materials is undertaken with the consumption and inventory needs of the developed world as its major criterion; such control enables prices to be manipulated in favour of consumers rather than producers. More than half of United States foreign capital was invested in various forms of extractive industries by 1966.[10] Both commercial and service activities in the Third World are substantially in the hands of foreign capital. Processing industries established in underdeveloped countries followed the same metropolitan profit maximization rationale.

More recently, the revolution in consumption patterns encouraged foreign capital to be invested in the production of commodities destined for consumption by the rising middle classes of the Third World, as and when the level of industrialization and modernization demanded. Foreign capital also tends now to locate itself in those strategic lines of production which are nevertheless oriented towards the domestic market, such as chemicals, iron and steel, etc. Thus Japan has become involved in Brazil's shipbuilding industry and its production of basic metals; in 1966, Brazil's major industries had the following distribution of foreign capital from the major developed countries:

Table 4.7   Distribution of foreign capital in Brazilian industry

Sector	Foreign investment (%)				
	United Kingdom	United States	France	West Germany	Japan
Foodstuffs	31	8			
Textiles	20		10		
Petrol retailing	17	7			
Insurance	8				
Cars		23		45	
Chemicals		14	28	21	
Machinery		10			
Pharmaceuticals		8			
Rubber products		5			
Metals production			10	6	44
Shipbuilding					14
Banking			8		
Glass			8	15	
Others	24	24	40		42

Source: Martin (1966).

The situation is similar in Venezuela, where foreign capital has

sought out the most profitable sectors, namely automobile manufacture, chemicals, cement, rubber, foodstuffs and petroleum
products. More recently, the developed countries have focused
their attention on a number of light industries (such as textiles)
the products of which are marketed mainly in the countries from
which the investment originated; between 1959 and 1969 over 21
per cent of foreign investment in Thailand was destined for the
textile sector.

The major result of this foreign investment has been the transfer of capital to the developed countries; many poor countries
have attempted to increase their export capacities to offset this
outflow of capital, but high freight and insurance charges, along
with the heavy burden of debt repayment, have largely nullified
this strategy.[11] Official data from the World Bank and International Monetary Fund indicate that Latin America attracted
$11,493 million whilst transfers out of the continent amounted to
$14,741 million; if payments for services are also included, the
net transfer is even larger. Similar data can be presented for
individual countries such as Colombia (Havens and Flinn 1970: 5)
and Peru (Jones 1971: 109-10).

These resources, repatriated in order to finance investment in
developed countries, could have otherwise formed the basis for
infrastructural development and capital accumulation in the
countries which gave rise to them (Baran 1971: 306). This frantic
policy of repatriation is exacerbated by a fear on the part of the
multinationals that devaluations and/or political upheavals might
jeopardize the profitability of their investments. These fears are
usually crystallized in the harsh conditions laid before the potential recipients of foreign investment (Fuch 1959: 101-2; Ikonicoff
1970: 682); and yet the rate of re-investment in the developed
countries in Third World industrialization continues to represent
a relatively small proportion of total capital flows. Profits repatriation nevertheless remains high, indicating that such investments are very profitable, though not, of course, to the Third
World economies from which the surplus value is expropriated.
In this context Baran (1957: Chapter 6) was forced to ask whether
re-investment or *new* investment constituted the greater threat to
the development of the Third World. It seems strange to relate
that Marxist scholars long considered 'underdeveloped countries
as merely the outlet for the surplus capital of the metropolitan
imperialists; only recently have they examined reality in the light
of the reverse proposition' (Jalée 1969:158). In fact, the under-

developed countries merely represent the land on which the
seeds of foreign capital bear fruit; however, the fruit is sent back,
along with most of the seed, to the metropolis.

The mediating role of the banks

The influence of the banking system is felt throughout the upper
circuit of the economy, the monetarization of underdeveloped
economies quite naturally producing a proliferation of banks.

Table 4.8 The expansion of banking
in Thailand

Year	No. of bank branches in Thailand
1953	100
1965	400
1968	500

Source: Rozental (1968).

Generally, however, private banking activity is preceded by
public financial agencies such as the post office, savings banks,
and even government banks, as was the case in Sierra Leone
(Riddell 1970a). Private banks play only a pioneering role in
collecting savings in areas where wage-earning activities have
developed or where there is a high level of income.

Private banks generally prefer to finance trade activities, for
such activities have a rapid turnover of capital, tending to produce larger profits at low risk, whilst assuring the banks a large
measure of control over the business. The banks thus indirectly
finance agricultural activities, particularly those producing either
raw or semi-processed materials for export. For example, agricultural activities may receive seasonal credit to finance harvesting
(Engberg 1967:68). These are simple and relatively risk-free
banking operations; it is often a means of assisting the very
foreign manufacturing industries to which the banks themselves
may be directly or indirectly linked.

Foreign banks prefer to operate within the externally oriented
sectors of the economy, adopting such a rigid and conservative
operational framework, that few local businessmen, even the

most powerful, can satisfy the basic conditions for loans (Myint 1965b:73; Bauer 1954b).

Banks usually do not deal directly with rural producers but operate through import-export firms and other intermediaries, thereby further reducing local access to capital. Also, since credit is granted only for short periods of time and for specific purposes, the banks may play a negative role from a regional point of view. They act as financial agents, collecting and sending capital to the larger cities, whence a large portion finds its way abroad. Thus banks foster a perverse flow of credit; instead of directing capital from the rich countries to the underdeveloped countries, the flow is exactly the reverse (Myint 1965b: 73-74). A comparable process takes place between the prosperous and depressed regions of a country.

Whilst discouraging local initiatives, banks channel foreign capital toward the creation of modern externally oriented activities outside the control of the local economy. Thus, in no way does the bank play a pioneering role in the evolution of local activities. On the contrary, by draining capital out of the region for joint investment, it deprives small and middle-sized cities of the capital which would allow them to initiate modern activities to serve local needs; thus the bank acts as a tool of regional imbalance.

Efforts to correct this situation are seldom effective; the national banking system only plays a dynamic role if the country has a high level of national savings. Dependence on foreign banks is in reality just one element in a world-wide economic structural imbalance. The bank is a link in an unequal relationship, favouring the economic activities of the upper-level cities and discriminating against those of lower-level cities. Some local banks have remained independent of the big banks, but they are not numerous enough to contradict the general rule; i.e. the existence of a pyramid of dependence whose summit is located within the international banking system, *outside* the underdeveloped country.

The multinational corporation and dependency

The large multinational corporation[12] has been characterized by Houssiaux (1966:296-9) according to three criteria: administrative homogeneity, the international conception of the enterprise's development, and the international character of its environment and institutions. Furthermore, they are characterized by a continuous yet transformative structural extension of control to formerly national corporations; transfers and collective services are also organized according to an all-embracing, centrally established and executed policy. Their activities are extremely diversified and their sphere of influence is global – an additional safeguard against unfavourable trends in the business cycle. The international conglomerate forms a transnational productive structure with a corresponding superstructure; that is, the system of bilateral and multilateral relations (Sunkel 1970:39).

While the number of multinational corporations producing less than 15 product categories is diminishing, the number of enterprises producing more than 15 product categories has increased (Furtado 1968:325). This trend is sufficiently rapid to suggest that 'in a generation 400 to 500 international corporations will own two-thirds of the world's fixed assets' (Barber 1968:7). At the same time, the activities of large corporations in the underdeveloped countries are expanding. Some economists, however, have retained a wholly classical posture despite the profound changes in the operating conditions of the economy brought about by the burgeoning of multinational corporations. They retain a microeconomic approach and analyse the entrepreneur's role in a dependent economy (Harris and Rowe 1971) as if the entrepreneur were an independent individual. Thus they neglect, either deliberately or through naivety, the role of the modern business enterprise and, above all, that of giant multinational corporations 'as well as most of the mechanisms which underlie the enterprise's activity' (Caire 1971:895).

The establishment and maintenance of unfavourable terms of trade between the Third World and the developed countries has been facilitated by the cheapness of labour in the periphery. The case of Taiwan is typical: there, labour is at its cheapest, wages averaging one-third less than in Japan, and two-thirds less than in Hong Kong. Relations with the United States, stable until relatively recently, provided the appropriate conditions: as Taiwan's major trading partner, the United States has provided $1500 million of 'aid' over ten years and has established many export-oriented manufacturing industries (Simon 1971), thereby permitting Taiwan to attain rates of growth of 10 per cent, comparable with the best achieved by Brazil and Japan. But this growth was achieved at the expense of giving foreign enterprises a wide range of advantages: tax exemptions on most factor imports, unrestricted profits repatriation, the retention of full control and ownership by shareholders, tax holidays on turnover tax, low interest loans for up to 70 per cent of plant cost, and free transport to and from the ports (*Business Week* November 1970). It is hardly surprising that the prices charged by multinational corporations in their own countries are considerably lower than national capitalism can afford to ask; thus the United States, for instance, was able to earn much higher profits abroad than at home:

Table 4.9 United States domestic and foreign rates of profit (%)

Year	Domestic	Foreign
1954	11	16
1960	9	14

Source: Bognar (1968: 183).

American production abroad grows at double the rate of its domestic production; in the world 'league' of industries, it is third behind United States and Soviet domestic production (Sunkel 1970: 36). Such a situation is made even more profitable by the fact that a large part of the business concerned is undertaken between subsidiaries, thereby minimizing the leakage of profit to other parties.

The orientation towards exports and the 'conquest' of foreign markets by Third World economies is necessitated by the narrowness of the domestic market, itself a product of partial, peripheral industrialization (Maza Zavala 1969:74); local demand is largely an irrelevance, since most of the intermediate and other goods are shipped to the developed countries, usually that which has made the initial investment. Access to such inputs, made in the periphery, reduces the costs of production, particularly in the dynamic industries of the central economies (McGee 1971b). The effects of 'new style' industrialization are hardly advantageous to the Third World: domestic agriculture is distorted and stultified[13] due to the replacement of local raw materials by imports; additionally, crises are always imminent, since the Third World governments can exercise so little control of the industries operating within their national boundaries.[14]

Nevertheless it is suggested that, were the developed economies to adopt more liberal trade policies, the Third World's exports of manufactured goods would rise (Jones 1971: 24) and the underdeveloped countries would simultaneously be liberated from a dependence on domestic markets and launched into industrial development (McNamara quoted in S.E.R.F.H.A.U. 1971). Even socialist economists (Bognar 1968:555) join the chorus exhorting the developed countries to reduce the tariff barriers which exclude Third World industrial products from the markets of the developed world. It seems that both camps are defending the same technological interests: Bognar is suggesting that the socialist world should follow in the liberal footsteps of world capitalism.

The 'poorest of the poor', the 'nonviable' economies, which have *per capita* incomes averaging less than $100, limited industrial growth and high rates of illiteracy, are likely to feel the impact of foreign industrial intervention more deeply than any other. New export-oriented industries will be implanted, requiring only minimal local infrastructure and external economies; a low standard of living will ensure a plentiful supply of labour, whilst low literacy and educational attainment will insulate labour relations from economic and political conflict. A few more wage-earners will be created, each one having the production skills and consumption patterns of the developed world; a lower middle class will emerge, jealously guarding its newly won privileges, whilst the mass of the population will continue to experience relative impoverishment. Nevertheless, G.N.P. would rise each year, though the largest part of national surplus would accrue to the multinational corporations which had previously 'come to the aid' of the poorest Third World countries.

A major factor in maintaining the hegemony of the large multinational corporation is research. In essence, a double monopoly exists, first, between developed and underdeveloped countries, and second, between multinational and other corporations and poor nations, whatever the latter's degree of industrialization. According to UNESCO statistics, developed countries have 95 per cent of the scientific capacity required for economic expansion; this is all the more serious when it is realized that technological transfers are difficult.[15]

The State may finance private enterprise research directly: 'in the United States about 54 per cent of public research funds were used by private enterprise (this rate increased to 69 per cent in 1968), in Great Britain 48.5 per cent, but only 28 per cent in

France and 23.5 per cent in Germany. France spends most of its public research budget on State research, while West Germany spends almost half of its funds in the university research sector' (Jalée 1969:110). Of course, multinational corporations themselves carry out research, but almost exclusively in their countries of origin. In many underdeveloped countries, research institutes do not attempt to study new problems (Ree 1968: 40), thereby preventing a more accurate understanding of these countries' needs. Researchers in underdeveloped countries, usually trained in American or European universities, often base their research on models transferred from developed countries, without taking local realities into account. In short, the centralization of research in the rich countries acts as a drain on national resources, a means of polarization and a source of dependence.

The consequences of dependency

Modernization results in the centralization of decision-making and in various forms of dependence. In cities, this leads to the non-integration of upper circuit activities. Investments are made in totally unconnected industries but an economic integration at a level of complexity seldom found in underdeveloped countries themselves takes place at a higher economic level outside the country. This situation applies to large and small countries alike. In the principal cities, however, this external orientation is most acutely manifested in technological dependency. In simpler terms, non-integration means that the possibilities for an endogenous growth of the upper circuit are minimal throughout the Third World.

The policies pursued by large enterprises are related to planned development, for they are externally formulated according to the corporation's objectives. Harmonious growth of the upper circuit can only take place when policy is formulated in the context of national and urban space. When economic activities become locally integrated, *local* linkages are created and intensified. The city thereby recovers some of the decision-making power that formerly eluded it. Such integration is nevertheless rare, because any country wishing to obtain credit or foreign investment must adopt the rules imposed from outside. Except in countries where economic or military considerations are strategically imposed, the capital-providing countries may choose between several nations having the same material resources.

Hence, countries on the capitalist periphery adjust themselves to growth models which principally benefit the rich countries.

E.A. Johnson (1970:258) believes that the State has at its disposal the necessary power to establish a spatially unified and interlinked industrial structure. In reality, there exists a world system of relations, dominated by private interests which intrinsically oppose, by all possible means, any effort at local integration, consequently blocking all initiatives in authentic national development.

pessimistic at best.

5

The State and the upper circuit

The study of the relationship between modern business activities (as exemplified by the monopoly) and the State is indispensable for an understanding of the economic and social realities of underdeveloped countries.[1]

In most underdeveloped countries, the co-existence of a high degree of technological dependence and the genesis of industrialization results in the establishment of firms already controlling a substantial share of the market, able to bypass the atomistic competition which characterized the industrialization of the West. This phenomenon is found in all Third World countries, not just those currently industrializing, and is a consequence of the technological progress of the rich countries and its implications on the organization of modern production. Although the present scientific and technological revolution is not the first of its kind, as Jalée has pointed out (1969:103), the emergence of technology as the autonomous and key variable distinguishes this period from all others.

Concentration is inherent in the internal logic of monopoly; the increasing indivisibility of investment contrasts with the flight of capital to developed countries. This capital returns, technologically 'enhanced' by the monopolies, who, by administering prices, free themselves from the potential hazards of a limited market share. The size of such enterprises gives an additional guarantee of market control. Certain writers, such as DeVries (see Mason 1967:94) believe that the smaller the country, the greater is the potential for concentration, but this opinion is not widespread. For others, the possibilities of price war appear greater in the largest countries, for firm-size tends to increase and price equilibrium becomes more unstable when no agreements exist between producers.

Economies of scale do not retain a decisive importance for industrial location when output has an apparently assured external market; when this happens, the domestic market is no longer even considered by certain industries. The key factor becomes the costs of raw materials, transport, and the maintenance of privileged relations with the countries in question. For domestically oriented industry, however, the problem of economies of scale – a direct result of the technological revolution – aggravates the dependence of those underdeveloped countries required to attract increasing amounts of foreign capital.

Economic concentration is exerted in all spheres according to the level of industrialization of both country and economic sector. No country escapes this tendency which, moreover, originated in the developed capitalist or socialist countries.[2] The problem is primarily technical; other variables intervene, but technology stands out as the dominant and dynamic factor, having profound quantitative and qualitative effects on both developed and underdeveloped countries. Although data on underdeveloped countries are not always readily available and sometimes of questionable value, the existence of a comparable degree of concentration, in a wide range of economic sectors can be seen in both developed and peripheral capitalist countries (Table 5.1).

Concentration and the monopolies

Although industrial concentration is frequently associated with the emergence of monopolies, these two phenomena are not necessarily synonymous. According to Kiskor and Singh (1969: 391), the monopoly is a manifestation of the structure and behaviour of markets while concentration is a reflection of the structure of economic organization. But is such a distinction valid for the present period where the structure and behaviour of markets are a corollary of economic organizations now controlled by new technological conditions? The distinction drawn by Kiskor and Singh would be of greater value for the period prior to the Second World War.

Concentration and monopolies have the same origin. Accor-

Table 5.1 Industrial concentration trends in selected developed and underdeveloped countries (%)

Country	Food		Leather		Chemicals		Metals		Transport		Machinery	
	% firms	% output	% firms	% output	% firms	% output	% firms	% output	% firms	% output	% firms	% output
Columbia	3.4	50.7	1.5	44.5	8.6	55.7	12.9	79.8	3.1	50.0	3.4	56.5
Philippines	1.3	47.3			4.5	52.5	14.7	75.0	2.9	46.3	10.7	53.9
El Salvador	3.4	65.0				52.8	33.3	90.7	11.1	57.2		
Malaysia	4.6	55.8			8.9							
West Germany	3.3	53.3	4.1	49.2	2.5	66.6	3.6	67.5	6.6	86.3	3.1	46.3
United Kingdom	2.8	49.6			2.9	46.9	5.5	62.3	2.3	52.2	4.6	53.2
United States	2.9	46.0	10.1	55.3	2.2	54.1	3.0	60.2	2.0	60.0	1.7	50.1

Source: Merhav (1969:46, Table 1.5).

ding to Schneider (1967:213) technological progress in developed countries does not necessarily produce a trend towards larger production units. However, this is not so in underdeveloped countries, which are more responsive to technological change and where industrial concentration takes place whether the country is large or small, recently or previously industrialized, and regardless of its historical development.

Merhav considers the 'conditions of entry' (Bain 1956) to be the key concept in a new theory of oligopoly. Entry conditions can be defined as those advantages enjoyed by the firms relative to those of potential competitors in the same branch; this implies the ability to inhibit competition. Bain believes this is a structural concept, 'defined in relation to the average minimum cost that can be obtained with the firm's most efficient scale and at an optimum rate of capacity-utilization'.

In effect it is the 'conditions of entry' confronting new firms which determine the development of monopoly. Bauer and Yamey believe that the obstacles to market-entry facing new firms vary according to the situation. They identify three types of restrictions (Bauer and Yamey 1957:185-6): barriers that can be created and/or removed by legislation; those created by monopolists themselves; those created independently of both public powers or already established monopolies, such as the demand for workers with skills in short supply, or the need for large investments (see also Lean 1969:8). In these cases, technological progress once again emerges as a basic and determining factor in the creation of monopolistic structures, especially in underdeveloped countries.

Investment, for both multinational enterprises and monopolies, is no longer determined by market size but has become 'autonomous'.[3] Forecasting in this field is possible because corporations either control the size of the local market or are independent of it (e.g. export industries). For this reason it is difficult, under present conditions, to accept Myint's postulate (1965b: 157) that the rate of growth of the domestic manufacturing sector depends on the ratio of the size of the local market for each imported good to the output of the smallest-sized firm which can be established to produce them. On the contrary, lack of investment weakens the market while the presence of new activities produces a multiplier effect.[4] This, moreover, helps explain how monopolies contribute to the stagnation of economic growth.

'Creative destruction' for whom?

The monopolistic situation in underdeveloped countries, according to the Schumpeterian model of 'creative destruction' (1950:
Chapters VII and VIII), is merely transitional, for market conditions erode the monopolies' position and lead to the return of
competition. According to Schumpeter (1950) the monopoly is
doomed to destruction, yet its creation is essential to the
development process for two main reasons: first, entrepreneurs
being few in number, must be allowed to use all available
resources in the most efficient manner, even at the risk of concentrations; second, entrepreneurs require market power, the protection necessary for success innovation (Mason 1967:88-9).

The process of 'creative destruction' could operate more effectively in underdeveloped countries with rapidly growing markets
if monopolies were not so quickly and heavily protected by
government. In such a situation monopolies cannot be eroded
easily by subsequent competition due to the lack of a capital
market, labour immobility, the protection afforded by the high
transport costs of raw materials and finished products, and limits
in the choice of techniques.

'The temporary advantages that some firms create over their
competitors through innovation and increases in the scale of their
production often become permanent and irreversible.' Once
established, the monopoly tends to emerge as a stable structure
(Merhav 1969:32-47). Such a process occurred in Pakistan and
India as a result of the historical development of commercial
activities and various inequalities in the access to capital (Ranis
1962:345, quoted by Mason 1967:98-9). This clearly constitutes a
generalized situation throughout the Third World.

**The characteristics and consequences
of monopoly power**

In an underdeveloped country, once a monopoly is set up it
enjoys excessive and accumulating economic power. The large
firm assumes two fundamental roles in the modern economy:
'determining the quantity and price of supplied goods and services', and 'deciding how, where and when existing and potential
resources' should be allocated (Chandler and Salisbury 1966:
101). The problem posed by the monopoly can be summarized in
terms of the following variables: (i) the relationship between

output, price and domestic consumption; (ii) the relationship between market size, conditions, other firms and the conditions under which new firms may enter the market, at what scale, and in which particular branch or process; (iii) the relationship between, on the one hand, the way in which surplus is distributed between giant enterprises, the State and households, and on the other hand, the possibilities of consumer access to different products. This introduces three basic problems, each of which will now be discussed: the determination of the firm's level of capacity-utilization, the rationale behind pricing policy, and how inventory and input-utilization levels are decided.

A *Excess capacity*

In the 1950s and early 1960s excess capacity and limited market-size was conventionally assumed to be linked (Borde 1954; Almeida 1965), mainly because of the immaturity of development theory and a failure to recognize the effect of monopoly. As a result, excess capacity was seen as a bottleneck to economic growth; thus the limited market was frequently held responsible for the export orientation and consequent dependence of less-developed economies.

Many industries in underdeveloped countries operate well below capacity, yet achieve significant profits because of their ability to fix prices independent of production costs (such as raw materials, labour and power). As a result, a higher rate of profit can be made on invested capital. State protection can also be a favourable factor.[5]

Moreover, monopolies often find that it is more profitable to maintain excess capacity up to the break-even point, in order to block new competition.

Excess capacity is certainly in evidence in planned economies such as Algeria,[6] but the effects are quite different because the choice of technologies, though subordinate to international conditions, is not made exclusively by business interests, but constitutes part of the national development strategy (Destanne de Bernis 1971). Moreover, prices are fixed by the State as a function of its own growth ideology; the profits that make up depreciation and reserve funds in the underdeveloped countries of the capitalist periphery are, in this case, retained by the State, which now has control over new investments. The suppression of the firms' financial autonomy has been devised in order to prevent large modern industries, especially those in private and foreign hands, from gaining control over the country's present and future industrialization.

B *Price policy and advertising*

Prices are a source of power for conglomerates and monopolies; Adam Smith in *The Wealth of Nations* (Chapter 8) was the first to state that a small number of producers could fix prices, this factor being one of the fundamental characteristics of monopoly.

Compared with the period described by Smith, contemporary monopolistic structures are to be found in most production and certain commercial sectors – a situation inherent in the nature and operation of the system, and the exigencies of permanent technological progress.

It goes without saying that price fluctuations in one sector effect changes in others, necessitating a concerted price policy for the entire system; 'the price system is a one-way street – upward' (*Business Week* 1957: No.15). Technological progress leads to modest wage increases and sometimes to limited price reductions (Sylos Labini 1969:123). This is largely because of a conditioning to artificial demands whereby the consumer readily submits to the higher prices asked for only slightly modified goods. Demand-creation has now become a widespread practice; foodstuffs are probably the most conditioned sector.[7] The effects are disastrous[8] in underdeveloped countries where the traditional and locally based consumption patterns have rapidly been destroyed by the advertising efforts of multinational corporations (Furtado 1970: 194).

C *Forecasting for stability*

Forecasting is fundamental to the equilibrium of modern enterprises; long-term projection ranks second to size as the dominant characteristic of large enterprises (Demonque 1966:73) because a multinational enterprise's behaviour is linked to world-wide factors, such as changes in demand and income (Houssiaux 1966: 293). In order to maintain 'regular and profitable' operations the large firm is now forced to avoid instability and to adopt a policy of forecasting (Baran and Sweezy 1968:67-8). One of the bases of forecasting is the replacement of bank capital by financial capital, a transition vital for the independent pursuit of a firm's objectives. This was not so before the current technological era, i.e. before monopoly became the 'normal' organizational form for the upper level of the capitalist economy and could accumulate surpluses without taking account of market-size. The advent of the technological era introduced widespread advertising and allowed large firms to maintain a permanent gap between cost and price, thereby permitting increases in profits.

Technology develops very quickly and the firm must ensure that it always has access to funds sufficient for the replacement of its fixed capital reserves. Thus it creates the depreciation and re-equipment funds essential to both financial independence from other firms and the banks and also to its survival in the rat-race of technological development. Financial independence is not restricted to multinationals and can also be found in the newer Third World industries, especially those operated by foreign capitalist ethnic minorities (Afana 1966:139).

In the United States, prior to the Second World War, 50 per cent of the capital for corporate expansion came from reinvestments, but presently 90 per cent of new investment is from reserve funds (Furtado 1970a:189), a change also found in underdeveloped countries. In this respect the United States was overhauled by Brazil between 1962-5, at a time when the average direct American investment was $10 million per annum whilst investments from reserve funds (not including depreciation funds) approached a rate of $90 million (Furtado 1970a:193).

Yet control over the future does not rest only on price control and the concomitant capital accumulation. Investment diversification as a means of 'ensuring a strategic domination over the economic conjuncture', through agreements among firms, is also a significant and prevalent factor (long ago identified by Veblen 1904:24) which has manifested itself as new technology has been introduced and rate of its obsolescence accelerated.

Such diversification is necessary for the maintenance of the firm's equilibrium but requires a rapid shift of funds to those sectors that offer high profits for large investments – even at the risk of throwing the whole economy into crisis. Capital thus accumulated can be reinvested in the same activity, but this is becoming a rarity. It may equally be used to finance new plant.

One of the most efficient forms of controlling the direction of economic development is the creation of conglomerates and multinational firms, which, by virtue of their international influence, make for a form of monopoly which is more powerful and yet more difficult to analyse. Such enterprises can impose conditions (at the international level) and sometimes (at the local level) establish an alliance with the State to the detriment of national economic growth and a more equitable income distribution. This is ultimately to the detriment of public authority itself.

Monopoly in a Third World context

Excess capacity reinforces monopoly and is consequently an obstacle to national growth. The combination of monopoly and preferential access to technical progress gives large firms greater profits which are not reinvested. 'Technology intervenes in order to create a greater underdevelopment in the satellite countries. Its importance stems from the fact that it is rapidly emerging as the new base for the centre's domination over its satellites' (Gunder Frank 1968). The classical conditions of development are blocked by the development of monopolies and can no longer be met;[9] thus the economy is soon condemned to stagnation.[10] Moreover, this blockage by the monopolies is twofold; it not only affects the growth of other industries but also that of their own enterprises (Baran 1957: Chapter 6). If, as Myrdal suggests production generates its own demand and market size is contingent on production volume, then the situation becomes doubly problematical. Modern industry which tends to eliminate craft activities and under-utilize its own resources produces a double negative effect on production. Therefore, market size and consequently the rate of growth are diminished. The lowering of wages leads to a relative drop in consumption and acts as an additional stumulus to the weakening of both the traditional sector and a part of the modern sector.

The often violent contraction of artisanal production makes an underdeveloped economy not only more dependent but also more vulnerable. Large-scale modern industry asserts its power over a doubly dependent market; artisans must buy from modern industry at very high prices and also face the possibility of both quantitative and qualitative reverses. Therefore, both the standard of living and the potential for national growth are put at risk. This is typical of the monopolistic situation provoked by rapid industrial concentration. 'Profits from the monopolies are increasingly accrued to the firms themselves, creating an obstacle to a more equitable income distribution and in no way favouring capital formation' (Sturmtal 1955:194).

Raul Prebisch (1972:47) is mistaken when he attributes unemployment and labour surplus in Latin America to insufficient growth. On the contrary, these two problems result from the monopolistic structures that influence *all* sectors of national life – both the private (especially the more dynamic branches) as well as the public sector. For example, when corporations and monopolies control basic inputs, they can manage national resources in a certain manner because they administer the prices, thereby intervening in both private and public consumption. Their presence restricts domestic demand, restricts economic activities mainly to export production (Griffin 1971:5) and aggravates their dependence on foreign markets.

Corporate decisions regarding wages, prices, dividends and investment directly affect major State objectives such as economic growth, full employment and price stability. These decisions are made in the interests of the firm and not of the economy (Reagan 1971: 3, 141); the effects are much more damaging to the underdeveloped than to the developed economy.

Monopolistic industries, though already closely associated with governmental organization nevertheless feel it necessary to further ensure both their survival in and domination over the market: through administered prices, economic power can be wielded. Their goal is an annual increase in technical reserves at the expense of the population's savings. Such action is equivalent to reducing State capital-formation, thereby reducing investment capacity. This decline in investment affects both the private and public sector, whilst the results are cumulative and exacerbated by the fact that the State, as it becomes relatively poorer, loses its freedom of investment decision-making.

Third World industrialization and development policy

No contemporary Third World state, however small or impoverished, can remain outside the current wave of new conditions, since the latter have global repercussions; nevertheless, in their attempts to industrialize, governments are likely to follow one of three basic models. In the first instance, an underdeveloped country could accept externally imposed dependence because of either the weakness or complicity of its ruling classes. Second, there exists the possibility of the domestic elite actually soliciting and planning for such foreign domination; third, an underdeveloped country might seek to establish an autonomous development process. Each model will, of course, be found in numerous historical and conjunctural variants.

Most Third World countries correspond to the first model, though it is often difficult to distinguish between this and the second policy: governments rarely have room for unimpeded decision-making in the face of international pressure. However, certain obvious examples could be cited, such as Malaysia, Burma, or Brazil. In Malaysia, two policies, supported by international organizations such as the World Bank, were introduced in order to attract industry: a package of privileges was offered to 'pioneers' of industrialization, which consisted of tax, customs and exchange exemptions, whilst 'joint ventures' between local and foreign capital were similarly solicited. Thus the ground was prepared for the eventual destruction of Malaysian manufacturing industry; the gap between rural-urban migration rates and the expansion of employment widened, external dependence deepened and the penetration of foreign enterprises was further facilitated by the provision of local capital.

In Burma, after the 1962 coup, three sectors of industry and their future control were delimited (Table 5.2).

Table 5.2 Sectoral control of Burmese industry after the 1962 coup

Sector (and nature of capital involved)	Industries controlled
State industries	arms, metals, energy
Foreign industries	gas, fertilizers, paper, cotton spinning, nylon, strategic chemicals
National industries	food, drinks, tobacco, other chemicals, textiles

Source: Angrand (1968).

This distribution gave over the more dynamic and high productivity branches of Burmese industry to foreign control (i.e. multinational corporations), whilst basic industries were reserved for the State and traditional manufacturing activities were left for Burmese capitalists.

The case of Brazil is somewhat different. The economy remains underdeveloped despite its considerable industrialization; Marini (1972b) describes Brazil as 'subimperialist'.[13] The export of manufactured goods has increased, whilst a considerable upward trend in domestic demand for capital goods has also been experienced. Technological progress and economic development have required increasing amounts of government expenditure on development infrastructure such as transport and energy. The high price of these advances has included the virtual sacrifice of all significant industry to foreign interests and the acceleration of monopolization of these sectors. Such a structure of industry was deemed necessary for survival in the world market; nevertheless, certain strategic branches of production (nuclear power, aviation, etc.) are jealously guarded by the metropolitan economies, thereby blocking development in the periphery. Government policy has caused the destruction of numerous small and medium Brazilian firms, whilst real wages have declined. Brazil has obtained levels of economic growth equal to those achieved by Japan, but at what price? The mass of the Brazilian population remains in chronic impoverishment.

On the other hand, countries like Peru, Yugoslavia and Algeria have attempted in their recent past to industrialize without a loss of sovereignty. The latter country still has much private enterprise in its most dynamic branches of production, yet the State reserves the right to fix prices, and establish depreciation and reserve funds to be used in the general national interest. In this way, Algeria has avoided the domination of its economy by conglomerates and monopolies, and has ensured that industrialization serves the national, rather than sectional or foreign interests.

Peru's recent orientation involved a policy of transforming the urban industrial sector into the leading sector of the economy; in many cases, the government had the right to control basic industry and lent its weight to the encouragement of industries producing mass consumption goods. Less priority was given to non-essentials and luxuries (Quijano 1971a:70-1). In order to situate itself effectively between Peru's undoubtedly dependent economy and the world-wide structure of imperialism, the Peruvian state attempted, in its 1968 revolutionary changes, to participate actively in capitalist accumulation whilst establishing control over its own internal economic affairs. This was to be achieved by the strengthening of administrative power, a fiscal reorganization in the economy, the extension of State capitalism, and the expansion of State planning of the economy.

The State and the upper circuit

In underdeveloped countries, the State allies itself with the upper circuit of the economy in order to achieve the technological modernization it so desires. Whether support is overt or more covert, it invariably results in an aggravation of the external dependence of the country, submitting the population to heavy fiscal pressure without an improvement in either the employment situation or the level of social welfare. Official generosity towards firms of the upper circuit is carried out to the detriment of the population, particularly the most underprivileged classes.

Several forms of State support are given to the development of the upper circuit which reduce the investment capacity of the State in sectors directly benefiting the population: protection is granted to enterprises with a large degree of monopoly; direct or indirect financing of large firms takes place through the provision of expensive infrastructure; professional training; promotion of basic industries; subsidies for production and export; finally, different types of agreements are made with the dominant enterprises in the economy (discriminative fiscal legislation, investment codes and development plans). This list of official favours is not exhaustive: many other forms of State discrimination exist which profit particularly the larger-scale activities in the upper circuit.[11]

Many countries, such as Brazil (Arraes 1969:212), acquire domestic credit problems through their anti-inflation policies. This situation necessitates the very external credit which will facilitate the penetration of foreign capital, and immediately produce both greater concentration in and foreign control of the economy. It should be added that the State bureaucratic apparatus is another instrument in the service of the bourgeoisie whether national or international. There is both a financial and a political price to be paid by the State for the protection afforded to the upper circuit of the economy. Since the State is increasingly forced to allocate its resources to cumulative modernization, it suffers a reduction in its decision-making power, a consequent reduction in its role as a State, and thus becomes less and less independent.

A *State finance and big business*

Direct State intervention in the economy may take place through

If the State can finance or establish a monopoly why won't the same conditions hold as regards multinational monopolies.

investment, with the State either participating in private industry, or creating publicly owned and financed basic industries. While such a policy is intended to encourage industrialization, it is often tantamount to a public financing of private local or foreign industry. When the State takes responsibility for the creation and operation of basic industries, private light industry benefits from a reduction in their operating costs. Direct or indirect financing through public investment contributes to stunted and/or distorted forms of national industrial and economic growth.

Thus in 1966 in the Ivory Coast, the State's special investment and equipment budget contributed 500 million CFA francs to the establishment of the Krupp paper mill, stating that the government wanted to not only be involved in activities profitable to the nation, but also hoped for the opening up of opportunities for competent Ivoirians to have access to profitable investments.[14]

A more discreet yet still visible form of State-financing of large foreign or national firms is the practice of a particular type of international division of labour, whereby the State takes charge of heavy industries while permitting investment by multinational firms in the more profitable sectors. The following example shows the inequality in the international division of industrial labour between Japan and certain Asiatic countries.

Table 5.3 Distribution between heavy and light industry (value added *per capita* in 1958 US $)

	Light industry	*Heavy industry*
Philippines 1961	72.1	27.9
Burma 1961	73.0	27.0
Indonesia 1958	71.4	28.6
Malaysia 1958	74.6	25.4
Thailand 1961	85.1	14.9
Japan 1961	27.7	72.3

Source: United Nations (1969–70: 207, 209, 215).

B *State provision of infrastructure*

Public works which take up such a significant proportion of a country's already limited resources, now constitute one of the essential elements of the domination of underdeveloped by developed countries. The construction of infrastructure is a way of indirectly (and sometimes directly, depending on the degree of corruption of planners or civil servants) financing the establishment of modern industries. But a distinction must be made between infrastructure indispensable for the State to merely assert itself as a modern entity and that established with the deliberate goal of attracting investment. Yet in both cases, the results are almost identical. Excluding infrastructure of a strategic nature, governments are strongly influenced and even pressurized into providing for the precise needs of large corporations.

In countries which have only recently acquired political independence, the colonial powers had previously managed transport infrastructure according to a policy controlled by private entrepreneurs constantly pressing for State initiatives. Large corporations either directly influence public decisions, or indirectly through international financial organizations. Even in the rare cases of private investment in transport, the State is forced to follow the pattern imposed by special interests in order either to link the private to the national network, or to assume responsibility for maintenance. The creation of private transport networks tends to distort not only traffic costs, routes, density, and the allocation and use of factor inputs, but the effects extend to the entire economy (Caire 1971:894).

Although the private sector may sometimes assume responsibility for the provision of certain types of infrastructure, this task is increasingly reverting to the State.[15] For example, in the Ivory Coast the percentage of private investment in infrastructure dropped from 30 per cent during the period 1950-60 to 27 per cent between the years 1961 and 1965, while during the same period private investment in the industrial sector rose from 12 per cent to 30 per cent. This development is not at all paradoxical for it indicates the extent to which inducements are given to mainly foreign investment whilst the public budget is burdened with the financing of essential infrastructure. Such circumstances should be considered as part of the unequal international division of both labour and costs. Such infrastructural development increases domestic G.N.P. but increases even more that of the metropolitan economy; again we are forced to question the utility of G.N.P. as an index of development.

The following example illustrates the point: in Mauritania, the proportion of the budget allocated to equipment diminished between 1964 (19.8 per cent) and 1967 (9.8 per cent), due to the fact that between the years 1961-4, the State, already overburdened with heavy expenditures, had been required to make available funds for the plant and infrastructure required for the establishment of MIFERMA (Société des Mines de Fer de Mauritanie), a multinational firm exporting iron ore (Tiercelin 1968: 101).

The generation of electricity is another case in point: its production generally increases at a faster rate than that of other sectors and is generally offered to foreign enterprises at a price lower than that of the developed countries. The State takes charge of electricity generation and distribution since one of the conditions for obtaining foreign loans is the sale of cheap energy to the country's multinational and large enterprises, whilst the population is left with little more than a token service.[16]

It is difficult to accept Maddison's analysis of Mexico (1970: 165) in which he identifies the nationalization of the railway system and electricity generation with a concern for economic independence. Perhaps that was presented as the goal, but the results were quite different. Consequently, when referring to the fiscal benefits accruing to countries with large-scale industrial enterprises (especially those involving mining) the first priority must be to know the ultimate destination and use of the resultant funds. It is not surprising that public services, such as the post office, telecommunications, and urban and regional transportation, are usually in deficit, for they are part of the State's indirect financing of modern capitalism.

The social overhead capital developed in the large cities provides another ironic and paradoxical subject for analysis. Due to the pressing demands of the urban popluation, the State feels justified in this expenditure which ultimately aids the expansion of upper circuit activities at reduced costs while funds available for other capital projects diminish (McKee and Leahy 1970a: 487). The use of public resources to create overhead capital helps reduce production costs but not prices, thereby actually preventing social *investment* (Robirosa 1971:47, 48). This explains why Frankman (1969:13) advises minimal expenditure on overhead capital, in order to eliminate excess capacity in this field. He suggests that the State should respond only to 'real needs', so that surpluses remain for use in other social capital projects; this implies the ability to forecast growth for each sector as well as new needs.

The ideology of growth plays an important role in the authorities' investment decisions. The people accept as quite reasonable that governments need to lay the foundations for new and additional industrialization, and healthy G.N.P. figures reinforce their faith. However, the effects of public expenditure, already seriously limiting economic growth, also block social development because the residue available for State social investment tends to be reduced. There are also implications on spatial organization (see Chapter 13).

It is interesting to compare the growth of total G.D.P. with the growth of 'infrastructural' G.D.P.[17], because this shows where most national investment efforts are located. In Venezuela, for example, the growth of G.D.P. has been accompanied by a larger increase in infrastructural G.D.P. Thus a deepening dependence on foreign countries and an increasing domestic neglect of policies for income redistribution and increase in popular living standards are simultaneously experienced.

State bankruptcy, mass poverty and economic backwardness

The State's equipment budget is burdened by the cost of infrastructure designed to attract investment, whilst the arrival of new firms encumbers the administrative budget by making necessary much additional bureaucratic machinery.[18] According to certain official interpretations, the poorer the country, the more civil servants it employs to solve its employment problems, a policy which reduces its investment capacity. In reality, the bureaucratic hypertrophy found in underdeveloped countries[19] is a consequence of modernization and largely serves the modern sector, as well as providing the conditions for improved profitability, many of the benefits of which are exported. The State is forced to seek loans in order to pay all its civil servants, whilst the population of the rich countries, misled by the mass media, is convinced that 'aid' and the activities of multinationals helps the poor countries, when in reality, the economies are enriching at the expense of the Third World's poor.

Third World States therefore become increasingly impoverished in both relative and absolute terms. The significant 'surpluses' of large private corporations contrast with the 'negative surplus' of public enterprises: public enterprises in Latin America experienced, after depreciation, a negative surplus of at least 22 per cent (Griffin 1971: 17); in Colombia, both State and private savings are in chronic decline (52 per cent in 1950; 24 per cent in 1966) at the expense of increases in corporate savings and foreign trading (11.8 per cent in 1950; 46.5 per cent in 1966) (Bird 1970:19; Colombia Cuentas Nacionales 1950-61, 1960-6).[20] The same phenomenon is found in Africa, where it seriously handicaps the State's capacity to make social investment.[21]

At the same time as medium- and small-scale enterprises are disappearing or experiencing a reduction in their share of total production, profits and growth potential, the population is also becoming more impoverished.

The State, through its tax system, chooses from among the various sectors of production and different social classes, those who will pay for and those who will benefit from the process of economic growth. Indirect taxes are favoured in most underdeveloped countries and ensure that the mass of the population pays the price of technological modernization and concomitant monopolization.[22] This form of taxation is oppressive enough in developed countries, but is even more so in underdeveloped countries.[23]

The tax system constitutes a double protection of the upper circuit, particularly manufacturing industry: first, the State transfers via indirect taxation the burden which should realistically be carried by multinational and large corporations, to the lower-income strata;[24] indirect taxation also represents a type of forced saving whereby the government further facilitates the establishment and expansion of large firms; finally, the progressive monopolization of strategic markets often induces changes in the form of taxation, particularly an increase in indirect taxes.[25] Once again, the policy of the large corporations, with its focus on private interests, conflicts with the options that would serve the interests of both people and nation.

The protection of the upper circuit of the economy does not end there: the State is also induced to share part of its power with the monopolies (Kaplan 1970:170, 179). State collusion is manifested in the power of such firms to administer prices, thereby directly attacking the public interest and delaying national economic expansion. As Furtado points out (1970a:185): 'While the monopolist can set his own level of revenue within certain limits to the detriment of public interests, the source of this legitimate power is exclusively the government.'[26] Consequently, in sharing with the State the right to tax citizens, the large firms are, in fact, performing functions of public law (Furtado 1968: 16).

The ideal situation would be for the State to correct distortions in the price system, thereby increasing the dynamic efficiency of the economy and promoting economic development. However, monopolistic mechanisms have been established throughout the capitalist periphery, so such a goal is at present impossible. Consequently, the large enterprises play an increasingly significant and powerful role in national decision-making.

Escape from this dependence seems beyond the means of most governments. It seems that Griffin's contention that, in Latin America, the State offers a poor medium for the mobilization of surplus (1971: 19) could be applied throughout the capitalist periphery.

In reality the State's role in national development should not be limited to mere manipulations of the budget, but should extend to the elaboration of major options, which will be dependent upon the decisions made on such issues as tax, monetary and agrarian policy, the future role of multinational firms and monopolies, and the distribution of the surplus available to the State among the different strata of the population.[27] Yet due to a collusion between the State and large corporations, incorrectly assumed to be the only path to development, such decisions are largely predetermined.

Consequently, the accuracy of Myrdal's term 'the soft State' (1969) in describing underdeveloped countries, is open to question. If only one could ignore the formidable power these States wield against their political opponents and concentrate upon their impotence in the face of multinational corporations! In so far as they collaborate with the monopolies, they are weakened and intimidated by external influences whose interest is to maintain such pliable governments in power.

As Quijano (1972) accurately observed, the State is weakened in three ways: first, it becomes incapable of independent decision-making because of foreign dependence and collusion with the monopolies; second, it becomes handicapped by increased debts and the reduction in its investment capacity, forcing it to limit investment in certain sectors; finally, the State in its role as an investor finds itself less and less able to orient the country towards maximum growth and authentic national development. It is hardly surprising that, in these circumstances, the State is allowed to take increasingly authoritarian steps for the establishment of a strong, even military, government without fear of outside intervention from the supporters of monopolies and multinationals.

PART III

6

Third World poverty and the lower circuit

Conditions of poverty in the Third World are largely the result of the combined operation of monopolistic structures and the State; indeed, all monopolies have undesirable repercussions on the standard of living of the population. As we have seen, the State aggravates this through its economic and fiscal policy. The present pattern of economic growth is responsible for an increasingly unequal income distribution and hinders both employment expansion and the development of a domestic market for modern products. One of the principal results of this is the existence of the lower circuit of the urban economy. The main distortion created by the monopolistic structures affects the type of goods produced. Dynamic industry produces for export markets and the rich rather than the less-favoured domestic classes (Barros de Castro 1971: Volume II, 113-14), a tendency which may appear in an extreme form: Kaldor (1965:261) has observed that the proportion of national resources invested in goods and services destined for upper-class consumption was at least three or four times higher in Chile than in Great Britain.

The development of this trend means greater capital accumulation, reduction in the propensity to consume of the masses and increasing monopolization of national income by a privileged few.[1] A vicious circle is established; as income continues to concentrate, the consumption of the high-income groups increasingly diversifies and the expansion of demand becomes even more socially inadequate, resulting in the underutilization of factors of production. The poor are doubly disadvantaged for they only have access to the products that entrepreneurs find it profitable to produce, whilst the production of consumption goods decreases. This places a ceiling on employment and makes available only a restricted choice of collaborators in the modernization process.

Income inequalities are therefore maintained by a structure of production that is oriented toward these sectors of the economy which are most susceptible to technological modernization and consequently the most profitable. Since the capitalist sector is not in a position to transfer sufficient capital to the domestic sector (Watters 1967:19) persons engaged in this sector suffer a cumulative decrease in income.

The adoption of an imported growth model has other consequences for the level of employment. Each new activity established in an underdeveloped country facilitates the creation abroad of a significant number of jobs. Factory construction, raw material supplies, commercial services, transports, and educational and research activities benefit directly. A recent survey conducted by the Harvard Business School suggests that 600,000 American jobs directly depend on the foreign activities of American-based multinational corporations (Rattner 1972a:23).

Employment for foreigners also becomes available in the underdeveloped countries, especially in the most backward countries. In Gabon, 'less than ten years after independence there are two and a half times as many whites in the capital as in 1960' (Lasserre 1972).

Unequal wages and the creation of a middle class

Dasgupta believes (1964:161, 183-8) that the low wages paid in the 'domestic sector' of the economy have no effect on modern-sector wages. He suggests that wages always tend to rise rapidly in the capitalist sector, even when labour is in abundant supply.

In most underdeveloped countries, the prices of capital and labour are not left unaffected by technical progress. There are many unskilled jobs in the upper circuit, for which labour from the lower circuit can be recruited, the price of which is in fixed proportion to modern sector wages though they are determined by supply and demand factors in the lower circuit. Since demand for this type of employment continuously increases, there is a tendency for wage levels to fall (Frankenhoff 1971:130-1), so the potential advantages accruing to wage-earners in capital-intensive activities are not realized.

Theoretically, reductions in the costs of production obtained through the introduction of advanced techniques should, as Sylos Labini (1969:108) has pointed out, result in lower prices, higher profits and an increase in the number of wage-earners. In reality, for prices to decrease, an as yet unheard of degree of agreement among producers would have to be established. Thus profits continue to rise while wages increase only in certain branches, and for certain categories of workers.

In technology-intensive activities, highly skilled workers are paid relatively high wages. These workers are not easily sub-stituted, and this may give them considerable bargaining power.

Among unskilled workers wages often vary according to the branch of activity. Nevertheless, wages of skilled workers may be twice those of unskilled workers, as in the South Korean city of Taegu (H.-S. Lee 1971:203). Industrial development has seen the number of skilled workers increase faster than that of unskilled workers, the latter being progressively replaced by machines. The minority of workers with relatively high wages consequently tends to increase, while conditions impeding the integration of the majority of workers are generated.

Economic growth is thus oligarchic and inegalitarian (Ramos 1970:231). The improvement experienced by some is not socially significant, for the *per capita* income of active persons increases only in the upper-income groups. Thus employees in strategic sectors gain preferential access to a larger part of the value of capitalist production in exchange for their prior entrenchment in a consumption-oriented society.[2]

Under these conditions, a limited expansion of the middle classes and their propensity to consume can be seen as a manifes-tation of the strength and assertiveness of the modern, capitalist sector (Niemeyer Pinheiro 1971:36-7). However, expansion has decelerated recently. Upward social mobility is selective and dis-criminatory, putting a more acute pressure on the wage-levels of the lower classes (Sunkel 1970: 46-7). Growth of the middle class does not make income distribution *more* equal, but on the contr-ary, makes it *less* equal (McGee 1971a:26).

Non-employment, underemployment and tertiarization

The modernization of the economy is accompanied, as Eckaus (1955:548) has pointed out, by a technological rigidity which, by severely limiting the scope of input-substitutability, inevitably inhibits the growth of upper-circuit employment. The most efficient techniques for industrial expansion seem to have been conceived as if labour were a scarce commodity. Such a formulation is inappropriate even in the context of developed countries, and completely untenable in respect of the underdeveloped countries; 'modernization of this sort produces industrial growth accompanied by increased employment problems, such that the creation of jobs leads to the increase in non-employment' (Singer 1970:70-1).

Under monopolistic or oligopolistic market conditions the successful absorption of surplus labour is at its most difficult. The problem of non-employment is dynamic and not static, since monopolistic organization has such a limited ability to provide jobs and thus drives prospective workers into other sectors of the economy, which are, for the most part, unable to offer either regular wages or permanent employment. Technical factors are also important: larger firms, especially multinational corporations, are not interested in using labour-intensive techniques, because the larger labour force thus constituted would represent both an economic and a political threat. Meyer (1964:71) believes that the source of the problem lies in the slow growth of the modern sector relative to population increases in the 'traditional' sector; thus employment opportunities do not expand and *per capita* income remains low and may even decrease. But in reality, there are not *two* employment problems in the Third World, as he clearly intends us to believe. On the contrary, the labour market is *unified*, though it is characterized by an extremely differentiated structure (Quijano 1974:324).

As Durroux points out (1970:9), what we call a relative surplus population 'is created at certain points by the trend in accumulation in each of the spheres of capitalist production'. This idea goes back to Marx, for whom 'the "relative surplus population" was made up of the labour-power rendered superfluous in the very process of capital accumulation itself.'

The creation of indirect employment largely depends on the technological level of the new industry in question. The wider is the gap between the industry and its new economic and social environment, the more the concomitant employment ignores the very regions that would most benefit; it is the large cities of the host country, or the countries exporting the technology which benefit. Consequently, as the host country industrializes, urbanization becomes more and more tertiary in character.

Modernization, poverty, and the lower circuit

'Poverty is even consistent with rapid growth, if the growth is of recent origin' (E.A. Johnson 1970). Currently, poverty is worsening everywhere, in underdeveloped countries recently having embarked on 'the path to material progress' as well as in those which began the process at an earlier date. The reason for this poverty is that technological modernization produces growing social and economic disparities. In the name of progress, a large part of the nation's resources is allocated to those who are already rich.

The poor carry the heaviest burden of Third World modernization because the unemployed and other groups at the bottom of the wage scale 'bear proportionally more than others the social cost of various development projects' (Rattner 1964:129), such an industrial reserve army being a general condition of capitalist production (Durroux 1970:2).

Impoverishment is universal, but in the rural areas it takes on the most flagrant forms of social inequality. Amsdem (1971:145) in analysing the case of Kenya, showed that the relative improvement of urban wages had taken place partly to the detriment of earnings in rural areas. This phenomenon continues to characterize the underdeveloped countries, and is caused to some degree by the inability of the small farmer to pay the price of even realtively inexpensive technological improvements. In Mexico, an industrial worker in 1950 earned 393 per cent more than an agricultural worker; ten years later, the former's wages were 454 per cent that of his rural counterpart. This situation has only changed in areas influenced by Third World economic metropolises where the countryside has been penetrated by industrial forms of production. The rural-urban difference in wage levels exacerbates the exodus from the country to the towns, to the extent that one can justifiably speak of a transfer of poverty from rural areas to the city (Ardant 1963).

The time has long since passed when Hoselitz's question concerning Asian ubanization (1957:48) might still legitimately be asked; the expansion of Third World cities can no longer go hand-in-hand with the massive abolition of poverty. He believed that, in the long run, the process of industrialization would be accompanied by income redistribution in the cities as well as in the rural areas. However, under the present conditions, urbanization facilitates the capitalist process and aggravates inequalities. As Rattner points out, 'economic and spatial concentration is correlated with the parallel phenomenon of cumulative poverty (. . .) within economic growth centres themselves' (1972b:35). It has even been observed that in preceding periods, the assimilation of migrants into urban activities took place relatively quickly, as did that of established urban residents (Munoz Garcia *et al.* 1971: 104).

The proliferation of Third World shanty towns coincides with the growth of urban poverty and the acceptance of imported consumption models. Money is scarce, and various consumption needs must therefore compete; new tastes are acquired through intensive advertising campaigns, and are satisfied by the expenditure of either cash or credit, even at the risk of reducing essential expenditure on food (Frankman 1970:7).

At Porto Alegre, in Brazil, the percentage of shanty town residents has increased rapidly in recent years (1 per cent in 1940, 5 per cent in 1950, 13 per cent in 1960). Even in São Paulo, the economic metropolis of the country, the 'favela' population has increased from 2 per cent of the city's population in 1960 to 4 per cent in 1966 and to 20 per cent in 1974 (Valenzuela 1970:207; K. Schaefer 1976); in Manilla, the squatter population has increased from 360,000 in 1962 to 767,000 in 1968. This tendency coincides with economic growth; Taiwan, a 'fast-growing' economy, according to the conventional definition, can boast that one-third of its population lives in hovels (Simon 1971).

It is not enough merely to construct accommodation with rents which are theoretically within the reach of the lowest wage-earners or day labourers. Often people will abandon new housing to return to the shanty towns closer to their places of employment, as recently happened in Rio (Valladares 1972).

It can be easily seen why South American sociologists have used the term *marginal* to describe the disinherited masses, the victims of the evolution of capitalist production: they wished to juxtapose the problem of poverty with so-called modernity. Thus the theory of 'marginality' was elaborated (Quijano 1974; Cardoso 1971;

Nun 1969; Cardona 1968); yet it is a relatively old term used to define a new situation. Park (1928: 892) was one of the first to use it to refer to cultural hybrids, to those living 'on the margin of two cultures and two societies'. Cuber (1940: 28) also spoke of those occupying a peripheral position between two unrelated cultural structures, complexes or units.

Yet, concerning the impoverishment of the mass of the population by the modern Third World economy, one may no longer speak of marginality in the above sense of the word. While Joan Nelson (1969:5) has accepted the utility of the concept, she rightly wonders whether the urban poor recognize themselves as marginal. This population (or overpopulation, as certain people wish to call it) is not surplus in rural areas, and is not superfluous from an economic viewpoint (Bettelheim 1950:74; Niemeyer Pinheiro 1971:14): rather, there has been a distortion of the development process through technological modernization which has prevented the economic participation of that part of the population which McGee (1972b) calls the 'proto-proletariat'. These poor, as Gunder Frank has vehemently stated, 'are not socially marginal but rejected, not economically marginal but exploited, and not politically marginal but repressed.'

This situation is responsible for the creation and perpetuation of the lower circuit of the urban economy in underdeveloped countries. The poor do not have access to many modern products, and the poorest among them are only able to obtain current consumer goods through a specific distributive system which is often parallelled by non-modern production activities. Poverty and the lower circuit are locked together in an indisputable relationship of cause and effect.

7

The nature of lower circuit employment

The conditions under which the modern economy develops and the existence of a massive and predominantly poor urban population, continually expanding as more and more rural migrants arrive, results in the maintenance alongside the modern circuit, of a non-modern economic circuit consisting of small-scale manufacturing and crafts, small-scale trade, and many varied services. Small-scale production and trade are based on the buying, selling and/or transformation of small quantities; Lasserre (1958) described the small-scale trade in the African districts of Libreville, capital of Gabon, as 'unkempt little shops where cigarettes and sugar cubes are often sold individually'. Family enterprises and self-employed individuals are the rule. The amount of capital invested is limited, technology generally either out of date or traditional and the level of organization primitive. Profit margins, however, are high and many jobs are available. Since the system is based on non-institutional credit, cash is constantly in demand. Advertising expenditure is almost nil and few merchants bother to arrange their store windows.

This is an apparently unconventional economy in which debts are much more common than bank deposits, and where 'classical' unemployment is unknown. How can these activities, often considered to constitute underemployment, be identified and differentiated? The organization of the lower circuit has been ignored by many Western observers, deterred by its apparently irrational and illogical management: control of operating costs and precise knowledge of profits is uncommon and book-keeping practically non-existent; Lisa Peattie (1968:36) noted that in a shanty-town of Ciudad Guyana 'none of the businessmen kept accounts, none of them are capable of doing so, and none of them are able to tell me with precision what the sales were. This does not necessarily mean, however, that they do not understand the general outlines of their economic situation.' While good management facilitates larger profits, it is not essential for a business' survival (Orlove 1969:59).

The transport system of this lower circuit is often obsolete; the truck, of course, is the primary means of transport, although its use may be limited by road conditions, cost, and lack of merchandise requiring shipment. Also, animals and man himself are often used for transport.

The equipment used in the lower circuit is generally of poor quality due to the scarcity of capital. The sewing machine represents the capital investment of the tailor, but its relatively high price often forces him to rent one until one can be purchased second-hand; a new model can be bought only when the business becomes more successful (Bettignies 1965).

Craft-production, the skills of which are often passed on from generation to generation, generally employs obsolete methods. For example, in Colombia, 47 per cent of the leather-workers of Medellin had been trained in and continued to use traditional techniques. Each production unit has limited product-diversification and produces in small quantities. Fifty-three per cent of the artisans made only one article and 56 per cent worked only when they had firm orders (Uribe *et al.* 1965). Selling directly to the consumer is current practice and little standardization is normally to be found. Table 7.1 illustrates the situation in Medellin.

In the lower circuit, most commodities are recycled and little is wasted, and we could very well use Lavoisier's famous formula about matter: 'nothing is lost, nothing is created, everything is transformed'. For example, old newspapers are used for packing, scrap pieces of wood are made into chairs, metal boxes become flower pots. Clothing is handed down from father to son or from older to younger brother, whether or not the article was originally bought second-hand. In Lima, it has been observed that even the clothes of dead people are sold and re-used, and that exploitation of the city garbage is a source of income for 5,000 people. The construction industry uses all sorts of cheap and/or recycled

Table 7.1   Number of craftsmen

	Direct sale	Sale through intermediaries	Both
Ceramics	23	1	–
Wood	101	5	17
Iron	37	2	2
Cloth	100	4	4
Candles	10	1	4

Source: Lopez *et al*. (1968).

materials. Many commercial and domestic articles are salvaged, ingenuity often extending the lives of many electrical and mechanical devices. The disproportionate number of old cars in underdeveloped countries is perhaps the most striking example of the miraculous capacity for salvaging and recycling to be found in the Third World, compared to the waste which characterizes developed countries.

A tertiary sector?

The lower circuit is commonly called the 'tertiary sector' in literature on Third World urbanization. 'Tertiarization' is the term now used to define activities and employment situations resulting from urbanization without concomitant industrialization. Certain writers have criticized these terms. Myron Frankman (1969: 2) points out that 'the definition of services greatly varies' whilst Castells (1972:78) considers the terms 'services' misleading. Despite this criticism the expressions 'tertiarization', 'tertiary', and 'services' remain in general use.

The concept of tertiary activity stems directly from Colin Clark's (1957) tripartite division of the economy in which he formally delimited the primary, secondary, and tertiary sectors. This approach has since been given the official stamp of approval. The collection of international and national statistics has thus been based on a classification which takes little account of country-specific or, indeed, dynamic phenomena. Courtheoux (1966) and Kusnetz (1966), among others, have criticized the use of this classification for *developed* countries, whilst Bauer and Yamey (1957:42) have observed that the economics of underdeveloped countries could not be satisfactorily studied on the basis of this tripartite division.

Indeed, it is unreasonable to ignore the proliferating activities existing at the interface between the so-called secondary and tertiary sectors, but because statistical norms perpetuate the use of a questionable model even the most skilful and well-meaning researchers find themselves prisoners of formal classifications, the use of which distorts the results of their research. An accurate analysis of Third World realities is thus made practically impossible, and this is especially true in the field of urbanization.

The expression 'lower circuit' appears to embrace much more of reality than the term 'tertiary sector'. The lower circuit is more concept than name, for it describes the result of a dynamic process and includes services (e.g. transports and domestic activities) as well as craft forms of manufacturing. All these activities have both common traits and a common origin.

The 'marginal pole of the economy' (Quijano 1974:318), called the 'primitive tertiary sector' by Beaujeu-Garnier (1965), and the 'refuge tertiary' by Lambert, (1965) is a fundamental element of Third World urban life. Its importance lies in its role as both a pole of attraction and 'sponge' for migrant and established residents both of whom are seldom able to find employment in the modern circuit.

The lower circuit and small industry

The term small industry, as most often used, takes the number of employees as its basic criterion. Fryer (1963), for example, proposes that small industries in Malaysia be considered as having less than 50 employees, or less than 20 if machines are used. In Brazil, the National Development Bank classifies small industries as having up to 99 employees (B.N.D.E. 1966). Kus'min (1969:11) suggests that 50 employees be the upper limit while Dwyer and Lay Chuen Xan (1967) place small industry between 20 and 50 employees.

The problem of a statistical definition stems from the difficulty of defining the criterion of smallness (Fisher 1967:341). Staley (1962:199-233) prefers a definition which stresses functional characteristics and attempts to avoid any confusion between small-scale industry and enterprises having a local market. For Staley and Morse (1965:2) small industry includes all small-scale manufacturing, such as small factory and non-factory producers of manufactured goods, modern and traditional enterprises, hand and machine types of production, as well as urban and rural establishments. They recommend that establishments with 1 to 9 employees be called 'very small industry' and that this class of producers be included in statistics. This position is close to that taken by Beguin (1971: 147-8) in his study of Morocco, and opposed to that of Harris and Rowe (1971:15) who excluded firms with less than 10 employees from their survey of Nigerian entrepreneurs.

However, the classification proposed by Staley and Morse must not be automatically identified with lower circuit manufacturing activities, since in underdeveloped countries, small industrial establishments may well belong to the modern circuit. The definition of lower circuit manufacturing must also not be confused with that of 'cottage industry', which, while being a traditional activity, often has a large capital turnover and sometimes contributes significantly to exports (Herman 1956).

The definition of lower circuit manufacturing must be arrived at through an examination of the technical and other conditions under which the enterprise operates and how it is integrated into both the modern and non-modern economy.

Employment in the lower circuit

The lower circuit absorbs recent migrants and long-term urban residents who lack either capital or skills. These people are able to obtain employment quickly although the jobs they find are generally marginal and insecure. The upper and middle classes tend to use more services when manpower is cheap, which together with the fractionalization of both jobs and enterprises, multiplies certain employment possibilities and accommodates a large number of employment seekers such as shoe-makers, tailors, small grocers and street vendors, rickshaw and taxi drivers, construction workers, shoe shiners, drawers of water, night watchmen, errand boys, and household servants. The situation in Tunis where 60 per cent of the active population subsists on a day-to-day basis, substantiates this hypothesis (Eckert 1970:35).

The ramifications of the lower circuit's distributive system are extreme; Gertz amusingly illustrates this for Java: 'perhaps the best, if slightly caricatured image of a highly labour-intensive trade is that of a long line of men passing bricks from hand to hand over some greatly extended distance to build slowly and brick by brick a large wall' (Geertz 1963:31).

A lower circuit division of labour exists, though different from that of the upper circuit: in the lower circuit, this entails a fractionalization of activity and its corollary the multiplication of jobs. In the upper circuit, it means specialization (the separation of tasks via the specialization of operatives, with a hierarchization and reduction of employment). The specialization and hierarchization required by modern production increases with the level of industrialization. The two circuits thus represent opposite forms of division of labour. In the upper circuit, it is imposed by the necessity of capital accumulation; in the lower circuit, by the need for the survival of a numerous labour force. In the latter case, circulation of capital ranks above accumulation, labour being the essential element.

Petty employment has often been considered to 'conceal a social parasitism' (George 1969:195), but in reality it is the frantic effort to subsist through economic activities in no matter which level of the economic system, rather than parasitism which exists.

Lower circuit employment in underdeveloped economies includes both poorly paid, temporary and unstable employment,[1] so according to which criteria should the definitional distinctions between employment and underemployment on the one hand and, on the other, between underemployment and unemployment be based?

The notion of unemployment as understood in the industrial countries is irrelevant to the Third World, yet one is immediately struck by the unemployment rates observed in Third World cities.[2] For example, an unemployment rate of 40 per cent was recorded in Bucaramanga, Colombia (Mangin 1967). Yet, how can the number of unemployed be enumerated when employment is not permanent? Certain situations cannot be represented in the statistics, such as that of the small shopkeeper who leaves his shop during certain periods of the year. Are urban workers who return to the countryside at harvest-time unemployed? Whenever demand slackens, craft workers take on odd activities or work on a part-time basis. Can 'awaiting or looking for work be considered unemployment, or is the person already employed? Can a person be considered employed when he travels a great distance to take an inconsequential job, even if the job requires four or five times less time than that of this journey?' (Lacoste 1968).

A systematic study of the Third World urban economy would clearly show that externally imposed forms of modernization have created socio-economic structures in which employment cannot be defined in accordance with Western norms. Knapp (1969) used the term 'employment' to designate all persons engaged in any economic activity, 'unemployment' for persons without a present job but available for work under present conditions, 'non-employment' for those without employment but unable to work under present conditions. Therefore, in the lower circuit there are both employed and unemployed but never non-employed persons. Since today's *employed* might be tomorrow's *unemployed*, the use of statistics supposes both a knowledge of the structural elements of the economy and the rules by which the system operates.

Lower circuit: entry requirements

Entry into the lower circuit is relatively easy since it is labour, not capital, which is the key factor. Since labour is cheap it is not difficult to start up a business; a sufficient number of employees can easily be found, as news of job opportunities travels quickly.

The lower circuit entrepreneur does not necessarily need an education (see Table 7.2) and business is often done without the proper papers. Illiterates sometimes have even less trouble in finding a job than those having some education (Tagri 1971: 216). In an Indian sample, though 50 per cent of unemployed illiterates had not worked for at least one year, 75 per cent of those with primary school education were in the same situation. Often illiterates or semi-illiterates earn more than those who have completed some form of education (Carnoy and Katz 1971:25; Munoz Garcia *et al*. 1971:107).

It has been observed that new arrivals in the city almost always find employment quickly (Table 7.3). Curiously, lower non-employment rates are more often found among migrants than among long-time urban residents.[3] Joan Nelson (1969:16) suggests that this may be because the former are more willing to accept poorly paid and insecure jobs; this is certainly one factor, but not the full explanation. For example, this phenomenon may well be explained by the desire of employers to skirt labour legislation.

In a simplified manner, lower circuit activities can be characterized by three types of entry requirement: activities requiring small quantities of personal or borrowed capital; those requiring

Table 7.2 Illiterates in the labour force (%)

	Total labour force	Trade	Services	Small-scale crafts	Government employees
Kinshasa [1]	23.7				
Calcutta [2]	25				
Accra [3]		34			
Ciudad Guyana Venezuela [4]	11.5				
Belo-Horizonte, Brazil [5]					10
Recife, Brazil [5]					11
Fortaleza, Brazil [5]					20
Saida, Algeria [6]					27.9
Barquisimeto, Venezuela [7]	30.7			66.3	
Fort Jameson Copperbelt [8]		40			
Nigeria [9]		48			
Taegu, S. Korea [10]		35.5	22		
Shalapur, India [11]		69			
Algiers [12]	34.4				
Iseyin, Nigeria [13]			66.6		
Liberia [14]		88			
Dakar [15]	57*				
Urban Tanzania [16]	48**				

* of casual workers
** self-employed

Sources: (1) Thomas 1972:121; (2) Sen 1960:70–5); (3) Garlick 1971:33; (4) Ciudad Guayana 1968:37; (5) Carnoy and Katz 1971:32; (6) Champseix *et al.* 1972:565; (7) Garcia 1970; (8) Rotberg 1962; (9) Geiger and Armstrong 1964:130; (10) Chang 1971:71; (11) Gadgil 1965:186–207, 307–14; (12) Menauge (1969: 63–4; (13) Bray 1969:545; (14) Hardwerker 1974:234; (15) Gerry 1974:96; (16) Bienefeld 1974: table 6.

neither capital, nor skills; and finally, those requiring both skills and capital. The first type includes domestic activities, most 'primitive' services and certain transport activities; the second, commercial as well as other tertiary activities, and the third group consists essentially of artisans.

Table 7.3 Brazil: Waiting-period between migration to the city and first paid employment

City	Less than one month Male	Female	More than six months Male	Female
	%	%	%	%
Rio de Janeiro	84.3	75.8	3.4	13.2
Sao Paulo	86.0	74.1	3.8	5.4
Belo Horizonte	75.2	70.8	12.1	13.8
Volta Redonda	90.3	76.2	3.8	9.5
Juiz de Fora	87.4	80.0	5.8	10.0
Americana	87.1	71.2	3.4	8.5

Source: Hutchinson (1963).

Ghana: Unemployment before current employment
Length of unemployment

Location	Under 1 week	1 week to 1 month	1½–3 months	4–6 months	Over 6 months
Accra	38	25	17	10	10
Tema	17	28	19	18	18
Kumasi	37	30	18	9	6
Takoradi	33	24	16	8	19
Rural	48	15	14	10	13
Occupation					
Unskilled	18	36	24	11	11
Semiskilled	22	25	20	13	20
Skilled	44	23	14	9	10
Lower clerical	19	29	18	20	14
Higher clerical	50	14	15	3	9
Foremen	52	24	7	5	12

Source: Peil (1972:68).

A *Services*

Due to an inequitable income distribution, it is via services that the mass of the population to some extent participate in urban accumulation. Consumption of personal services is one of the most important components of the standard of living, and in this

Morocco: Length of job-search among Casablanca shantytown residents

	No job offered before migration	Job offered before migration
	%	%
Less than 1 month	42	75
Less than 3 months	54	85

Source: Bulletin Economique et Social du Maroc (1966).

respect the behaviour of the middle class is almost identical with that of the upper classes. Services provide a livelihood for a large number of people: it is easier for new arrivals or those without education, skills or financial resources to find such employment. A survey conducted at Taegu, South Korea, showed that 35.3 per cent of those questioned had been employed in the service sector at the time of their arrival in the city (Barringer 1971: 308).

The following table shows the different levels at which services are consumed by the component parts of the Latin American social class structure:

Table 7.4 Latin America: Consumption ratios by class and commodity

	Food	Non-food products	Services
Upper class Lower class	2.90	48.0	56
Upper class Middle class	1.44	8.5	10
Middle class Lower class	1.90	6.6	6

Source: E.C.L.A. (1965).

In Latin America, combined middle- and upper-class expenditure on services is greater than the value of *all* lower class consumption. Of the $9 billion (1960) spent on services by the upper class and the $9.4 billion by the middle class – $18.4 billion altogether – a large part financed the $13 billion of aggregate consumption (services, manufactured products, food) made by the lower class. The proportion spent on services increases with income, as the following Venezuelan example shows:

Table 7.5 San Cristobal, Venezuela: Proportion of income spent on services

Income (in bolivars)	Average monthly expenditure	Average monthly expenditure on services
0 – 500	549	2
501 – 1000	944	6
1001 – 1500	1336	17
1501 – 2000	1659	26
2001 – 3000	2236	62
3001 – 4000	2355	72
4001 – 5000	3626	134
Over 5000	4352	184

Source: Banco Central de Venezuela y Universidad de los Andes (1969).

In Kinshasa, Zaire, 31.7 per cent of the labour force was engaged in services; yet in Ngombe, the rich quarter, 45 per cent were engaged in services, while in Tshangu, the poor area of the city, the proportion was only 17 per cent (M'Buy 1970:61).

B *Domestic activities*

Domestic wage-labour constitutes one of the most important types of services and provides much employment. More than other services, it absorbs large numbers of migrants. A survey undertaken in Calcutta showed that domestic activities (12 per cent) constituted the single most common initial occupation in the sample, whilst the other occupations mentioned were trade, some other services, and crafts. Also in Calcutta, the small shop-owners made up 11.8 per cent of established city residents and 8 per cent of migrants; by contrast the percentages were 8.3 per cent and 12 per cent for domestic activities (Sen 1960:187). Similarly, in a district of Rio de Janeiro, 31 per cent of the migrants were found to have been first employed in domestic activity, as compared to 1 per cent as merchants and shopkeepers (Perlman 1971:212).

The relative importance of domestic activity as an occupation tends to diminish as a country modernizes and industrializes; this is due both to the introduction of electric household appliances and to increases in wages. Certain specific factors, such as the presence of Europeans in Africa, may modify this trend. Moreover, domestic wage-work like any other service, may experience periodic 'booms' and 'slumps'.[5] In certain areas, such as West Africa or the Arab World, men serve as household employees, while in other regions, in Latin America for example, women generally furnish these services. In Medellin, Colombia, 98.4 per cent of domestics are women, while in Algiers approximately 70 per cent of such employees are men.

C Trade

Commerce is another large employer; this can be partially explained by the small amount of capital required for this activity. Moreover, capital can be obtained easily through personal credit in either cash or kind. Experience is not necessary and taxes can easily be evaded.

For example, in Sierra Leone, whilst a large-scale shopkeeper needs several thousand leones (1 leone = $1.20) to set up business and where a licence to operate a service station requires capital of 1 million leones, a small-scale shopkeeper needs only from 5 to 10, a hawker from 5 to 20, and a market vendor from 1 to 20 leones (Isaac 1971:289).

Among the market vendors questioned in Fort Jameson, Rhodesia, 46 per cent had less than a week's experience (Rotberg 1962:594). In the Copperbelt 42 per cent of the shopkeepers had never had another profession and 29 per cent had less than one year's experience (Miracle 1962:715-16). In Morocco, 26,000 urban shopkeepers had not bought the necessary licence (Beguin 1970:294). In Accra, Ghana, in 1966, only 5,000 out of over 15,000 market vendors paid the full tax for their stall (Lawson 1967a:179; 1971: 387). In Peru, for example, many municipal authorities do not collect licence permits and taxes are only paid after a certain turnover is reached (Brisseau-Loaiza 1972:36); thus the smaller the business, the easier it is to avoid taxes. Market trade is particularly undertaken by women, this being true of Latin America, Asia and especially Black Africa. The high percentage of women in the Laotian secondary sector (Lejars 1971) can be explained by the law which prevents foreign men from owning factories: the women merely operate as a front for their Chinese or Thai husbands.

Table 7.6 Female labour force

Place	Number of working women	Number of female traders	% of female traders in total female labour force
Accra [1]	18,500	16,500	89
Saigon [2]	–	–	41
Lagos [3]	–	–	77
Freetown [4]	28,000*	7,000	25
Towns on the River Senegal [5]	–	–	25**
Kumasi, Ghana [19]	–	–	61

Place	Total	Women	% Women
All Traders			
Saigon [6]	101,760	51,660	50
Ibadan [7]	39,000	–	80
Ghana [8]	323,900	–	83
Accra [9]	25,000	20,000	80
Mexico City [10]	316,000	91,500	30
Market Traders			
Porto Norvo, Dahomey [11]	2,000	1,800	90
Accra [12]	5,890	5,500	93
Haiti [13]	65,000	50,000	77
Dakar [14]	5,000	3,000	60
Sholapur, India [15]	–	–	47

Merchants (% of total employment)	Men	Women
Saigon 1962 retailers [16]	19·1	40·9
Luanda [17]	15·9	23·7
Lagos (central) [18]	26·0	87·0

* number of adult women
** merchants and artisans

D *Artisans*

The advent of mass-consumption society and increases in industrial production have diminished craft activity throughout the Third World. This type of activity is much more vulnerable to the influx of modern products into the countryside and small towns (Sari 1968). In an urban milieu, and especially in large cities, craft activities are better paid and also play an important role among modern (including manufacturing) activities. Since self-employment or family activities are often carried out in the home, taxes can easily be either partially or totally avoided. Moreover, these activities require little equipment and what is used does not need to be constantly updated. Though artisans are sustained by local demand they are also capable of adapting to demand fluctuations.

Certain craft professions have a large number of members: tailors and dressmakers are found in great numbers, especially where industry is limited and the price of imported ready-made clothing is high. In a sample of 755 working individuals in Bangui, 146 tailors were enumerated (Lebeuf 1951), 416 out of 3,256 self-employed merchants and artisans in the native quarter of Leopoldville (Kinshasa) (Capelle 1947), approximately 300 tailors out of 1400 working in various craft activities in the small southern Indian city of Tindivanam (Charleux 1970). At Ouagadougou, Upper Volta, there were 400 tailors out of a total of 16,000 workers (Pallier 1972).

Small-scale activities

The 'bana-bana' of Saint Louis, Senegal, the 'lolo' in Pointe-à-Pitre, Guadeloupe, like all small shopkeepers in Third World cities, are characterized by a small scale of operations. This is also true for all other lower circuit activities – small manufacturing, crafts, or services. Both capital and turnover are low; stocks are limited and the number of persons per establishment is small. These small-scale activities require little space and can even be set up in the home of the owner.

Sources: (1) Santos 1965; (2) Saigon 1962; (3) Marris 1962:67; (4) Saylor 1967:98; (5) Seck 1965; (6) Saigon 1962; (7) Mabogunje 1964; Hodder 1969:50; (8) Lawson 1971:380; (9) Lawson 1967a:179; (10) Beaujeu-Garnier 1967 (11) Brasseur and Brasseur 1953; (12) Santos 1965; (13) Belshaw 1965:55; (14) Seck 1970:76; (15) Gadgil 1965:169; (16) Saigon 1962; (17) Amaral 1968, 76; (18) Marris 1962:67.

Table 7.7 Activities with few employees

Place	Less than 4 employees (%)
Taegu, South Korea [1]	99.0
Cairo (industries) [2]	87.5
Barquisimeto (industry) [3]	40.8
Saida, Algeria (vehicle repair) [4]	100.0
Saida, Algeria (artisans) [4]	92.3
Paisandru, Uruguay [5]	92.0
Lagos [6]	69.0
Mexico City (trade) [7]	31.0

Sources: M.-G. Lea (1971:361); (2) Abu Lughod (1971:162); (3) Directorio MOP-FUDECO (1969); (4) Champseix *et al* (1972); (5) Collin-Delavaud (1972:84); (6) Mabogunje (1968:256); (7) Bataillon (1971:191).

Tables 7.8 and 7.9 permit a comparison between the modern trade of the upper circuit and the small retail trade of the lower circuit. There is a clear difference, for example, between the number of enterprises and employees on the one hand and the amount of stock and turnover on the other.

Lower circuit activities occupy little space; for example, in Saigon (1962), commercial activities occupied only 0.5 per cent of total urban floor space. To the innumerable small shops must be added the market stalls, corner stands, the goods carried by the pedlar, and the few sticks of chewing gum hawked by children in the streets. Artisans are usually found in crowded workshops, parts of which are often used for other activities; this was found to be the case among 23 per cent of the artisans surveyed in Medellin, Colombia (Lopez *et al.* 1968).

A Fractionalization of activities

Lower circuit activities, and particularly commerce, are carried out in a very large number of small-sized enterprises. One research worker, on seeing the number of barbers in a Latin American shantytown, could not understand how these 200 persons could possibly earn enough to survive (Orlove 1969:61).

Similarly, the density of commercial activity is striking. 'One sometimes has the impression that everyone is trying to sell something' says Vennetier (1969) of West Africa. Barlow (1953:27) observed that in Mexico City 'a visitor gets the impression that

Table 7.8 Comparison of large and small commercial establishments in Pointe-à-Pitre (Guadeloupe)[1] and Bouaké (Ivory Coast)[2]

	Large	*Small*
Surface area (ratio)	34.5	1.0
Permanent wage workers (average no.)	62.0	Almost none
% of total commercial employees	10.6	89.4
% of commercial firms	3.5	96.5
% of stocks held	89.2	10.8
Daily turnover (ratio)	42.0	1.0
% of total commercial turnover	70.0	30.0
Customers/day (ratio)	126.0	1.0
% of profit margins	44.2	55.8

Sources: (1) Menauge (1969:94, table 15)
(2) Etude Régional de Bouaké 1962-4 Volume II (1966).

everyone is engaged in selling. . .'. This generalized commercial activity, especially in the case of African women, has been interpreted as a type of leisure activity or habit which cannot be considered as employment (Bauer 1954:11; Saylor 1967:98) – at least no more so than household work. Such a micro-scale proliferation of commercial activities has geographical and socio-economic explanations: on the one hand, the residents of poor urban districts buy locally since the high cost of transportation precludes their access to the modern trade sector which is often located in the city centre; the density and distribution of small shops is closely related to the degree to which the shops are within walking distance of their customers. On the other hand, the small scale of commercial activities is an adaptation to a limited and irregular consumption pattern. Sale on the micro-retail level permits the poor customer having only a small and uncertain income to obtain small quantities of goods. Credit, however, more generalized in residential districts than in the centre, is the mainstay of the small trade sector. This point will be discussed in greater detail below. The poorer the population, the smaller the scale of commercial activities. At Pointe-à-Pitre, for example, in the rich residential districts the average daily turnover was 311 francs while in the poorer quarters it never went over 85 francs (Menauge 1969). These findings confirm those of Seck (1970:77) for Dakar, where 'the more the quarter is provided with modern urban infrastructure the smaller is the number of shantytype shops.'

Table 7.9 Saida, Algeria: Surface area occupied by commercial enterprises (% of sample)

Type of commerce	10m²	11-15m²	16-20m²	21-30m²	31-75m²	76-100m²	100-150m²	150m²	Total
Food wholesalers	–	3.2	9.7	16.1	29.0	–	22.6	19.3	99.9
Furniture	–	–	14.3	28.6	28.6	14.3	14.3	–	100.1
Household goods	–	10.0	10.0	25.0	10.0	20.0	7.5	17.5	100
Cloth and leather	–	8.7	20.4	33.0	15.5	20.4	1.0	1.0	100
Food retailers	5.2	29.7	43.5	13.4	7.3	0.4	0.4	–	99.9
Beauty and hygiene	10.8	24.3	29.7	10.8	2.7	–	2.7	18.9	99.9
Services	21.4	14.3	21.4	7.1	21.4	–	–	14.3	99.9
Tobacco and stationery	25.0	37.5	12.5	12.5	–	–	–	12.5	100

Source: Adapted from Champseix, et al. (1972).

Table 7.10 The fractionalization of commercial activities

Place	Traders as % of urban population	Urban inhabitants per retail establishment
Saigon 1969 (food traders) [1]	5.09	–
Pnhom-Penh [1]	6.12	16
Pointe-à-Pitre[2]	2.00	50
La Laja (Ciudad Guyana) [3]	–	81
Haiti [4]	1.86	–
Asilah, Morocco [5]	8.80	–
Lareche, Morocco [5]	7.30	–
Ksar-el-Kebir [5]	11.22	–
Porto Novo, Dahomey [6]	5.97	16.7
St. Louis, Senegal [7]	3.30	–
Brazzaville [8]	3.77	–

Sources: (1) Ngoc-Du 1968; (2) Menauge 1969:32; (3) Peattie 1968:35-6; (4) Belshaw 1965:55; (5) Troin 1968; (6) Brasseur and Brasseur 1953; (7) Lottin 1972:10; (8) Auger 1970.

B *Work in the home*

Often both artisans and merchants work at home, even if some also have a stall in the market or elsewhere in the city. Use of the home as place of work represents a saving in time and money which is often indispensable for the entrepreneur's survival. Artisans also can sometimes avoid taxes, whilst tradeswomen are able at the same time to engage in other activities, such as dressmaking, laundering, and clearly also motherhood.

Use of the home as a work-place fosters neighbourhood linkages: local customers are sure of being looked after at any hour, Sundays and holidays included.

Work in the home also makes it possible to work the long hours characterizing the lower circuit. Sometimes the workday is 15 hours, as Gadgil (1965) observed in Sholapur, India; such long hours may be required by the seasonal nature of the activity, or complementary activities, or the need to maximize incomes, especially when profits are low.

C *Family employment*

Family employment is common in the small enterprises of the lower circuit and permits increased output without advancing more variable capital. If small enterprises were to pay wages, they would be less competitive and would have to pay employees' social benefits and taxes. In certain cases, especially when demand is uncertain, the transformation of a family enterprise into a capitalist enterprise would lead to bankruptcy.

Table 7.11 Family labour

	% of total employment
Sto Amaro, Bahia, Brazil [1]	
food trade	48.2
non-food trade	43.2
Saigon (trade) [2]	14.7
Saida, Algeria	
lower circuit [3]	40.0
craftsmen [4]	17.2
Bogota (trade) [5]	40.8
Kermanshah, Iran[6]	
tailoring etc.	11.0
textiles	24.7
metallic, mechanical and	
electrical equipment	10.0
Latin America [7]	
small craft enterprises	30.0
Hong Kong [8]	88.0
Ciudad Guyana, Venezuela (trade) [9]	11.0
Taegu, South Korea [10]	8.3
Pointe-à-Pitre, Guadaloupe [5]	
turnover – 50F	46.3
50-100	27.1
100-300	8.5

Sources: (1) Motti 1970; (2) Saigon 1965; (3) and (4) Chamseix, *et al.* 1972; (5) Santos 1974; (6) Clarke and Clark 1969:56; (7) Lambert 1965; (8) McGee 1970; (9) Ciudad Guyana 1968:20; (10) Chang 1971:64.

Not surprisingly family employment is most in evidence when turnover is small (Menauge 1969: 77-8).

D *Limited stocks*

The small quantity of stocks held by the lower circuit entrepreneurs and their day-to-day renewal is a phenomenon which astonishes the Western observer. 'Opening a small business simply involves obtaining a store of goods on credit which is to be paid at the end of a period varying from 30 to 90 days' (Brisseau-Loaiza 1972:36). Stapleton (1967) wonders why eight men bother to sell 100 tomatoes each in a Nigerian city market when a single barrow-boy in the East End of London can sell 800 tomatoes. Wouldn't it be better, he goes on to say, if some of these men were to grow tomatoes and other vegetables, and others to engage in transporting the production, while others would be free to build highways or fill the many vacant teaching posts? The logic of this reasoning, however, is not that of the poor who must eke out a living in Third World cities.

The causes of this situation must be sought in the consumption patterns of the lower circuit, where day-to-day micro-purchasing corresponds closely to the hand-to-mouth commerce so characteristic of the poor districts of tropical cities.

Limited purchases are made daily in small quantities; the trader, for his part, does so in order to have the most varied stock possible in the small space available. Moreover, he often is not equipped to keep perishable foodstuffs. This manner of restocking is also related to the trader's limited financial ability which makes him dependent on credit from wholesalers, retail-wholesalers, or sometimes even other retailers.

The trader stocks only the amount he can sell or safely keep in stock. As a general rule, the rate of stock renewal increases as the capital investment decreases. For example, at Toumodi, Ivory Coast, traders with fixed stalls renewed their stock on average 26 times annually, and over 30 times for certain products such as cigarettes, cola nuts, or bread (Bettignies 1965:80). Stock turnover is normally faster for foodstuffs, averaging ten times *per annum* reaching 13.5 times for certain perishable goods, and dropping to 5 times for clothing.

E *Hawkers*

Hawkers constitute the lowest level in the fractionalization of commercial activities – the last link in the chain of middlemen between importers, manufacturers, or wholesalers, and final consumers. The number of hawkers in Singapore in 1967 was estimated to be between 40,000 and 50,000, or 2-3 per cent of the total or 8-10 per cent of the active population (Buchanan 1972: 161-2).[7] Hawkers should not be confused with push-cart operators found in the streets of large Western cities. These pedlars have their own capital, while the hawkers are supplied by traders with merchandise on credit. As Buchanan points out in his study on Singapore (1972:156), 'hawking is both a response to poverty and a product of it'. The hawker is less dependent on customers than other traders for he goes out to meet and attract them. He also knows how best to profit from an opportunity; on rainy days, the streets are full of hawkers selling raincoats and umbrellas. Though his itinerant mode of operation usually allows him to avoid taxes, the minimal capital-requirement, however, is his most important characteristic (McGee 1969:9; 1970a). All he needs for his business is several crates, a board, a basket, or even just a strong arm..

Hawking may be a response to the needs of the commercial and manufacturing activities of the upper circuit. Merchants and even small manufacturers use hawkers in order to avoid taxes, to employ minors or old persons, to reach customers not having the time or inclination to frequent large stores, or to get rid of unsold or unsaleable merchandise, such as clothing no longer in fashion. Often hawkers are not self-employed, but employees with 'invisible' bosses who control micro-chains of commercial outlets often operated by cripples or children. Three general classes of hawkers can be identified: the more-or-less sedentary who have a fixed stall on the pavement, those moving their goods throughout the city centre, and those who go from quarter to quarter in search of customers.

F *The self-employed in trade and industry*

In the cities of the underdeveloped countries, particularly those countries experiencing a large rural exodus, income largely comes from non-wage-earning activities. In Yaoundé (Cameroons), 67 per cent of the labour force were wage-earners (S.E.D.E.S. 1966) whilst in Algiers, in 1967, the percentage was barely two thirds. The 31.5 per cent of the labour force who are non-wage-earners in Algiers can be compared to the Mexican figures of 22-32 per cent.

While some of these non-wage-earners are landowners and other persons living on rent, the majority are the very self-employed workers often erroneously termed 'underemployed' in international statistics. In Saigon 68.8 per cent of the traders and 54 per cent of the transporters, but only 15 per cent of the artisans, were self-employed (Saigon 1962). In Saida, Algeria, the largest number of self-employed was found among transporters and certain categories of trader.

Table 7.12 The proportion of self-employed in Saida, Algeria

	a *Total*	*b* *Self-employed*	*c* % *b/a*
Trade			
Food	334	289	86.5
Hawkers	55	45	81.8
Cloth, leather	103	89	86.4
Services			
Beauty shops, hygiene	39	31	79.4
Miscellaneous	17	14	82.4
Transportation			
Carts	12	12	100
Other	11	11	100

Source: Champseix *et al.* (1972).

Modernization has resulted in the emergence of two trends: the economy is becoming more concentrated and at the same time, the rural exodus is accelerating. Since wage-employment is declining relatively, self-employment in small-scale activities appears to be the solution, self-employment being sometimes more profitable than salaried activities. According to statistics published for Egypt by Hassan Ryad (1964), the income of a self-employed artisan was between three and four times the wages of the average worker in the same profession. In Colombia, only 225,000 self-employed individuals had income below 10,000 pesos, while four-and-a-half million other people were below this income level (Bird 1970: 14-15). In Lagos, Nigeria, many cases were found where the self-employed made more money than wage-earners (V.R. Harris 1967: 69).

The self-employed sometimes work alone, providing the management, capital, and labour themselves. In Saida, Algeria, 43 per cent of all artisans had no employees (Champseix *et al.* 1972). In the urban markets of the Zambian Copperbelt, the percentage of traders working alone varied between 72 per cent and 100 per cent depending on the product (Miracle 1962: 738). Even if the business grows, it can often do so without recourse to salaried employees due to the availability of family-labour.

Table 7.13 Self-employed (% of labour force)

Accra (crafts) [1]	
Kinshasa [2]	
Ciudad, Guyana, Venezuela [3]	
Djakarta [4]	
Dakar [5]	
Bouaké, Ivory Coast [6]	
Cuzco, Peru [7]	
Pointe-à-Pitre, Guadeloupe [8]	
Medellin, Columbia [8]	
Bogota [8]	
Nairobi (non-squatters) [9]	10% – 20%
Calcutta (crafts) [10]	
Abidjan [6]	
Algerian towns [11]	
Tlemcen	
Sidi Bel Abbes	
Oran	
Constantine	
Annaba	
Blida	
Kermanshah, Iran [12]	
Saigon [13]	
Vientiane [14]	
Taegu, South Korea [15]	20% – 30%
Madagascar (cities) [16]	
Elizabethville, Zaire [17]	
Aroquipa, Peru [8]	
Chiclayo, Peru [8]	
Cali, Columbia [8]	
Braz do Pina (favela de Rio) [8]	
Taiwan [18]	
Banako [19]	
Santiago de Chile (shanty towns) [8]	30% – 40%
Nairobi (shanty towns) [9]	
West Malaysia (urban) [20]	
Madagascar (urban) [21]	
Mexico City [8]	
(small trade)	
(women trade)	40% – 50%
Peru (cities) [22]	

Accra [23]
Toumodi, Ivory Coast [24]
Lima (trade) [25]
Saida, Algeria (crafts) [26]   50% and over
Kumasi, Ghana (trade) [27]
Lima (street vendors) [28]

Sources: (1) Planungsruppe 1974:49; (2) M'Buy 1970:33; (3) C.V.G. 1969; (4) Sethuraman 1974; (5) A. Hauser 1972:361; (6) Santos 1965; (7) Santos 1971:83; (8) Santos 1974; (9) ILO 1973; (10) Lubell 1974; (11) Recensement Général d'Algerie 1966; (12) Clarke and Clark 1969; (13) Saigon 1962; (14) Lejars 1971:96-7; (15) Chang 1971:64-5; (16) Gendreau 1972:601; (17) Chapelier 1957; (18) Hoselitz 1957:46-7; (19) Meillassoux 1968:25; (20) Lin Lin Lean n.d.:33; (21) Lecaillon & Germidis 1974; (22) Dollfus 1966; (23) Hallett 1966:112; (24) Bettignies 1965:32; (25) CONAPS, 1967:23; (26) Champseix *et al*. 1972; (27) Hanna and Hanna 1971:78; (28) Santos 1974.

8

The financial mechanism of the lower circuit

The fundamental factors in the operation of the lower circuit are credit, financial middlemen, and ready cash. From these three factors one can attempt to analyse the corresponding financial mechanisms. *Credit* is essential both to entrepreneurs for whom it is often the only possibility for entry into, or maintenance of an activity, and to consumers, for whom it represents the possibility of access to consumption even for those without fixed income.

Middlemen furnish credit, most often in the form of merchandise but also in cash, to traders and artisans; moreover, they mediate between urban or rural producers and urban traders. The wholesaler is the most representative of these middlemen providing at the same time one of the principal links with the upper circuit.

Ready cash fulfils several functions within the lower circuit. It represents the money required by the final consumer as well as the entrepreneur to pay off part of their debts so as to obtain new credit. It is also essential for the wholesaler either to buy directly from producers or to pay interest and bank charges. The expansion of modern consumption combined with progressive monetarization of the economy intensifies the need for cash and consequently accelerates its circulation.

Credit, though essential to the survival of many families and businesses, nevertheless leads to an increased indebtedness at all levels. In an economy where cash is both indispensable and scarce, the practice of *usury* becomes generalized. At the same time, those lacking sufficient funds are often able to devise ingenious solutions to their problems of dependence on middlemen. *Prices are both an aspect of the functioning of the lower circuit and a form of adaptation to the continually changing situation therein.*

Dependence on middlemen
(wholesalers and transporters)

The proliferation of middlemen is a phenomenon common to the economies of both developed and underdeveloped countries, yet the causes are not the same. In developed countries, the specialization of activities both by sector and by region is intended to increase productivity and create a market for services. By contrast, in the Third World, middlemen provide the fundamental condition for the functioning of the economy, income distribution being so unequal. The poorer the individual, the more he depends on middlemen for his purchases. Moreover, this dependence increases with the size of the city; for example, in small cities, it is often possible to avoid a certain number of middlemen in the food sector.

The role of the middleman has been modified by economic modernization. He first served as a distributor of imported products and as buyer of export goods, but as urbanization progressed he took on the new role of bulking food products. His importance is due to the fact that most traders are unable to get supplies directly from rural producers, importers, or wholesalers.[1]

When the consumption level of imported products, as well as the level of exports, is low, trade is limited and the number and function of middlemen diminishes. Is this also the situation described by Brookfield in Melanesia (1969: 2), where even the large markets appear to function almost without middlemen?

The chain of middlemen may assume different forms with either the bypassing of one or more levels or the presence and articulation of all. Direct relations between rural food producers and urban consumers tend to disappear with urbanization and as a function of city size. Transport modernization strengthens this tendency, for small producers cannot afford to buy the necessary large trucks.

The middleman, either the wholesaler or the transporter, acts as the link between a supply and demand which is never in equilibrium either in quantitative or qualitative terms. This situation gives the middleman a privileged and strategic role in supply, a situation which may make speculation widespread. This role is all the more dominant, because of the middleman's privileged access to bank credit and the concomitant ability to purchase in bulk either directly or indirectly. Compared with him, small traders in the market and poor districts seldom have access to the financial resources necessary to acquire agricultural products in this way. Moreover, the number of farmers who take their produce to the city is never high. For example, in the markets of Puerto la Cruz and Barcelona, in Venezuela, producer-sellers represented only 3.6 per cent and 3.9 per cent respectively of the total number of traders, all other merchants buying their produce from middlemen (Erdens 1969). Similarly, at Santo Amaro, near Salvador, in Brazil, only 15 per cent of the foodstuffs sold on the market had been brought there directly by farmers (Motti 1970). In Melanesia, however, producers rarely need to make use of intermediaries as is often the case elsewhere in the Third World (Brookfield 1969:2).

The position of wholesalers is strengthened by their ability to store merchandise whereas, as we have seen, lower circuit traders only store limited quantities of stock because their customers buy in an irregular and small-scale manner. Similarly, once a certain level of urbanization has been reached, perishable food products require a modern system of wholesale trade. The wholesaler, due to his ability to stock goods, becomes an essential middleman between farmer and retailer. Even in general food trade, the wholesaler plays an important role in supplying local merchants, despite competition from transporters.

As previously pointed out, transporters can play either or both of two roles – exclusively serving the wholesaler, and/or the trader. Moreover, he may either own his vehicle or be an employee of a larger operation. Sometimes large firms in the agricultural export trade help drivers purchase their vehicles on condition that they remain available during the busy season. Outside this period he is free to engage in other activities. This is one reason why food prices on the urban markets tend to increase during the period of peak agricultural activity.

The role of the lorry-owner as a retail-wholesaler, transporter, and seller is becoming more widespread for various reasons, such as regional specialization and complementarity in agricultural production, the rapid transport of perishable produce to different markets, the increased distance of cities from areas of production and the inefficient organization of the urban food market.

Table 8.1 Sources of lower circuit food retailers' stocks in two Venezuelan cities (%)

	Coro[1]			Calabazo[2]		
	Producer	Wholesale store	Trade	Producer	Wholesale store	Trade
Rice	37.5	12.5	–	2.6	76.9	20.5
Beans	–	80.0	10.0	–	73.1	26.9
Sugar	4.2	25.0	24.2	4.0	76.0	20.0
Potatoes	11.1	5.6	55.6	–	100.0	–
Non-prepared cereals	2.9	37.1	60.0	–	66.7	33.3
Prepared cereals	81.8	18.9	–	–	80.0	–
Canned goods	13.4	51.2	22.0	3.2	67.7	29.0
Eggs	23.1	37.2	19.2	33.3	26.7	33.3
Pâté	–	71.4	21.4	2.9	51.4	40.0
Oils	–	–	–	33.3	50.0	33.3
Corn	–	–	–	–	55.6	22.2

Sources: (1) Chollet et al. (1969); (2) Albertini et al. 1969.

Transporters often act as middlemen between farmers, from whom they buy, and market traders, whom they supply. A survey conducted at Punto Fijo, Venezuela, showed the purchases by market-traders from transporters to vary from 25 to 100 per cent of the total, according to the product; at Coro they fluctuated between 20 and 100 per cent (Chollet et al. 1969). At Barcelona, 61 per cent of the products were normally supplied by vehicle operators (Erdens 1969). Transporters have more than one source of supply, however: at Coro, which is in a poor agricultural region, 67 per cent of their purchases are made directly from producers and 33 per cent from warehouses. At Punto Fijo, they purchased around 80 per cent of their goods directly from local producers (Chollet et al. 1969). Transporters sometimes supply each other: for example, 20 per cent of the vehicles covered in the El Tigre market survey had obtained their merchandise from other vehicles (Valladares 1969). This can be explained by the existence of many poor roads which will not allow the passage of heavy vehicles. It would be unprofitable for small quantities to be taken to the city so many sell their goods to the owners of larger vehicles.

The importance of liquidity in the lower circuit

Certain writers such as Bognar (1968:165) believe that a large
part of the population in underdeveloped countries lives in a
subsistence economy outside the normal flow of goods and
money. However, this view stems from confusion between the
wage-earning class and the monetary economy (see, for example,
Kay 1970:69 on Rhodesia). Though a country may have only a
small number of permanent wage-earners, which is the case for
many Third World countries, the population may still participate
in a monetary economy. Moreover, it has been affirmed that the
use of cash is becoming more widespread. Even if transactions
take place on credit and on a very small scale, they are still made in
money terms. The development of unorganized trade and the
introduction of new models of consumption has contributed to
the spread of monetarization.

Non-monetary urban consumption is disappearing as
urbanization progresses and city size increases. Orlove (1969:53)
on Rio de Janeiro, Mangin (1967:76) on Lima, and Lisa Peattie
(1968:31-4) on a Ciudad Guyana shantytown (where she found
that production for use was limited and marginal), all agree that
the cash economy is now the general rule in poor urban districts.
Urbanization in effect requires the use of cash as the medium of
exchange, i.e. the introduction of the *cash nexus* (Hay and Smith
1970:121). Moreover, while exchanges generally take place on
paper in the upper circuit, in the lower circuit transactions are
carried out in cash. For example, at Saida, Algeria, in a survey of
801 businesses, only 6 per cent admitted to using cheques in their
day-to-day operations. Of these 50, 19 were food wholesalers,
and 15 sold household goods. Only one of the 334 small food
traders used cheques (Champseix *et al.* 1972).

A *Monetary circulation*

The increasing ratio of money-in-circulation to the money-
supply[2] arises out of a rate of monetarization of the underdeveloped economy which has far outstripped the expansion of its
banking system (Engberg 1967:52-3). Consequently, transactions
should be effected in cash; this assertion is not in contradiction
with Short's thesis (1973) in which he states that the expansion of
the banking network and subsequent changes in consumer-
behaviour (e.g. the tendency to open medium and long-term

bank accounts) intensifies the demand for the remaining money supply, thereby increasing the velocity of monetary circulation. The monetarization of agriculture also accelerates circulation, since its products are almost invariably sold for cash. Moreover, a dynamic modern economy tends to absorb capital, thereby aggravating its scarcity in the lower circuit where monetary demands are usually met by a more rapid circulation of money.

There is a great disparity between the money supply available to the lower circuit and the number of users. This has two results: first, credit becomes essential and second, the velocity of monetary circulation accelerates to compensate for the scarcity of capital; these results are always inextricably linked and their relative importance depends on the local economic structure and its cyclical variations. Le Chau (1966) has shown for the Ivory Coast that during periods of heavy trading and concomitant accelerated monetary circulation, urban market-women make larger unit profits. In Latin America, the practice of paying an extra month's wages at Christmas helps increase the amount of money in circulation a well as the number of temporary businesses.

The effects of inflation on the lower circuit must be examined within the context of this rapid monetary circulation. Deflation does not benefit workers, for their real wages tend to fall (Maneschi 1971; Ianni 1971; Rattner 1967); inflation, however, is no better, for it acts as a mechanism to exploit the poor, increasing prices faster than wages. Those who benefit from inflation are those able to invest in sectors where value expands along with the inflationary spiral. This is perhaps why certain governments prefer inflation to taxation as a means of financing the budget (Griffin 1971:16).

Within the lower circuit, inflationary cycles help to increase employment, since it is at such times that upper-circuit money-supply expands and the velocity of circulation accelerates. It would, however, be wrong to examine the consequences of inflation on either the poor or the lower circuit without placing them firmly within the context of urban society as a whole. It can be shown that inflation benefits the *favela* inhabitants who own their homes (Orlove 1969:60), and, moreover, that inflation may benefit the indigenous elements of the distributive system. However, the essential question lies in the distribution of benefits among all sections of society. Whilst inflation affects all levels of tertiary activity, landowning classes are the major beneficiaries

(Lambert 1968), for inflation acts as a form of regressive taxation (Frankenhoff 1971:133-4). Once again, there is no inconsistency between the absolute expansion of the lower circuit taken as an isolated entity, and the fact that one of its functions is the enrichment of the upper circuit.

The lower circuit is clearly 'hungry' for cash, though this does not alter the fact that the poor urban economy can only function through credit. Capital-scarcity means that credit must often be used to establish or maintain a small business; yet to maintain credit some liquidity is necessary, at least to pay the initial part of the debt. Cash primes the credit-pump and then keeps the mechanism 'lubricated' (Geertz 1963:39) through its function as a means of payment.

However, whilst the total money in circulation throughout the lower circuit is considerable, each individual transaction involves only a very small sum. Small denominations of currency are therefore essential to these commercial activities. Brisseau-Loaiza (1972:36) cites the case of 'a small Sunday market at Puno, near the Peruvian city of Cuzco, where it was impossible to change a 50 *sol* ($1) note'. Often there is such a shortage of small change that traders are forced to actually buy it, the rate of exchange between small change and banknotes varying with the scarcity of the latter; bus conductors often benefit from this particular form of trade. In certain Indian cities the shortage of small change is so severe that merchants accept postage stamps as payment and give change in the form of merchandise (Johnson 1970). This practice is also widespread in Latin America and has been observed in Indonesia (Boeke 1953).

Rapid circulation of money is facilitated by the large number of middlemen and entrepreneurs in the lower circuit. Moreover, a high rate of circulation permits more subsistence employment and consumption as Bray (1969:544) points out; yet as the capital is in current circulation, little of it can be accumulated. This is one of the reasons why people remain poor.

B *Lack of liquidity and the demand for credit*

The scarcity of capital affects all small enterprises; the lack of liquidity being even more serious than that of fixed capital. This problem is often attributed to formal banking procedures but, in reality, the causes must be sought in the functioning of the entire economic system. Capital is only invested in operations where profitability is assured. If each lower circuit enterprise were taken individually, many would probably show a high rate of return on invested capital; this is especially true given the rapid circulation of capital.

The major obstacle to the acquisition of capital, however, remains the need to pay accounts on fixed dates. The rules of the upper circuit banking sector are incompatible with those controlling the lower circuit. Because of this conflict between the banks and the lower circuit, people turn to more flexible wholesalers and moneylenders. This is as true for the rural population, as Myint (1965:71) has shown, as it is for the urban poor. The banks (given their scale of operations) are well behind the moneylenders in extending credit to the lower circuit population. Compromises are often found, as in Thailand (Rozenthal 1968:40) where the banks entrust sums to local moneylenders who in turn lend it out according to the market. However, this practice is declining. Myint (1970:140-1) believes that the existence of even a large number of financial middlemen represents a less costly solution for the economy than the bank's extension of credit to lower circuit activities.

Credit is sometimes granted by customers. For example, an artisan may receive credit in the form of cash or raw materials as an advance payment from customers or from the trader who sells his production. The artisan is thus doubly disadvantaged since he is forced to accept an imposed price for his product and often must pay usurious rates of interest.

The scarcity of investment-capital in lower circuit activities is not always due to poverty or insolvency. Those who manage to accumulate capital in lower circuit commerce often do not reinvest the profits in their primary activity, but in sectors such as transport, housing construction, or agriculture.[3] This lateral investment can be explained by the fact that successful traders attempt to diversify their investment mainly to reduce risk or avoid market fluctuations. Yet by tying up capital elsewhere they often have recourse to external financial sources for the maintenance of their primary activity.

C *Financial ingenuity and mutual aid associations*

The availability of cash means financial middlemen can be avoided and larger profits realized. Therefore, it is not surprising that traders sometimes find ingenious methods of protecting themselves against liquidity crises. One example is selling at a loss, which constitutes a form of self-financing from debt. A trader may obtain credit in merchandise from his regular intermediary, reselling for cash but at a loss; with this cash he then buys goods which have an assured and lucrative market. This 'gold coasting', found in Uganda (A. Martin 1963:16-17), Nigeria and several other African countries is just one of many forms of cash sale at a loss. The practice results directly from the need for capital, and according to Katzin (1964:188), it is an excellent example of trading ingenuity.

A common way of increasing profits lies in the practice of a type of 'trade triangle'. Traders with cash reserves visit different places where they know in advance it is possible to buy cheaply and to sell with a good margin of profit. This technique, however, requires constant travel and an excellent knowledge of regional conditions. A simpler mechanism used by certain traders is to supply themselves directly from the producers. For example, manioc bread is sold in this way in Brazzaville (Auger 1972:295) bringing to those who bring the raw materials from the manioc-producing areas a weekly profit of 31 per cent.[4] Traders in the same commodity also often meet to decide a single price to be offered to the producer or middleman. Such groups as these in Kumasi, Ghana have been called commodity associations by Polly Hill (1962:12-13).

Alongside these particular commercial practices are to be found the real mutual aid associations, in which various ingenious ways of improving financial conditions through group action have been devised, such as the *tontine* of the Cotonou market-women of Dahomey. Every day a group of market-women collect a sum of money from each of their members, the total being made available to just one member of the group on a rotating basis. This cash allows each woman in turn to buy a larger quantity of goods at a cheaper unit price, thereby avoiding usurious interest rates, enabling a larger profit to be made and thereby temporarily strengthening her market-position. The same method is to be found in Dakar under the name of *nath*[5] and similar arrangements can be observed in many other African cities, such as Brazzaville (Balandier 1955), the Yoruba and Ibo towns of Nigeria (Katzin 1959; Geiger and Armstrong 1964:56; Katzin 1964: 185) and among the Bantu, Kikuyu and Bakanda (Hoyt, 1952:170). In Singapore, the same groups are to be found (Buchanan 1972:237); in Korea, they are known as *kye*,[6] with many traders often belonging to more than one at a time (Bar-ringer 1971:310; M.-G. Lee 1971:368-9).

Lastly, financial associations are often formed. One of them, observed at Onitsha, Nigeria (Onyemelukwe 1970) is the 'bank of the poor' described as follows by Katzin (1964:192): 'collector calls daily at the place of business of each customer and records his contribution in a book retained by the saver. At the end of each month the total contributed during the month is returned, less one day's retained by the 'bank' in payment for its service. It is probable that the money is put out on short-term loans by the bank during the month it has these funds.'

These methods, often called improvement associations (Has-king 1964; Katzin 1964) are indicative of a great creative ability on the part of the poor. As Kotter (1964:24) has pointed out, this is a relatively recent development and does not exist in the coun-tryside. It should be noted, however, that these are not imported, but rather local innovations satisfying to some extent the same pressing demand for liquidity and providing a temporary relief from usury.

These mechanisms therefore permit a greater degree of capital accumulation than would be possible through the modern bank-ing system. Could this informal, non-institutionalized, fragile system be replaced by an institution which remained nevertheless well-adapted to the unique conditions of the lower circuit and able to guarantee the permanence of these small-scale activities? Would this not maintain the level of employment, and contribute to the growth of the economy? Yet co-operatives such as those found by Choldin (1968) in Comilla, Bangladesh (where 60 per cent of the farmers belong to co-operatives) and which brought together small traders, artisans and rural producers, are all too infrequent.

From credit to indebtedness

A *Consumer credit*

Credit is a necessity for the consumer who is more often than not both poor and without a permanent job. Without credit, it is impossible for him to provide for his family, since temporary or occasional work only gives a correspondingly insecure income.

The urban poor are not able to obtain credit from the modern trade sector, which is generally located far from their residential districts and reserves such a service only for the creditworthy. Products sold in modern commerce (e.g. in supermarkets) are standardized and indivisible; moreover, relations between employee and customers are impersonal. Only lower circuit small-scale commerce is adapted to the conditions prevalent among the urban poor; it provides credit and breaks up merchandise into smaller quantities. (Lasserre 1958:184-5). As Vennetier (1960) has pointed out, the retail trade 'responds to economic necessity – the buyer may have 10 francs a day to buy sugar, but he will never have spare the 80 francs necessary to buy a kilogram'. The poor are not indifferent to prices as some writers have maintained; it is a mistake to interpret their behaviour from a purely cultural standpoint. In reality there is only one type of economic relationship possible in the conditions obtaining in the poor urban economy.

Modernization of consumption has increased the need for credit not only among the most deprived but also among the middle classes. Demand profiles have become distorted and the number of wants has increased without a parallel rise in income. Consequently, the individual finds that he must simultaneously budget at two levels: (i) expenditure on goods and services requiring immediate payment or installments, and (ii) goods that can be obtained through delayed payment are bought in the lower circuit through personal credit. The relative importance of each form of payment in aggregate expenditure primarily depends on an individual's income position. Thus the lower circuit allows everyone to participate (though to varying degrees) in modern consumption whilst continuing to assure daily and essential current consumption to both by the poor and middle classes.

Since lower circuit food traders appear to have customers in different social classes,[7] it is hardly surprising that such commercial activities are so numerous in Third World cities, as Table 8.2 shows.

Whilst a small number of people become indebted in order to eventually increase their wealth, most of the Third World urban population run up debts in order to consume. Both conspicuous consumption (induced by modernization) and essential consumption maintain the growth of the lower circuit. Credit is supplied through a downward chain of middlemen generally starting with the wholesaler, since he is the one with access to bank credit. The raison d'être of such credit, however, is found by

Table 8.2 Food-marketing as a proportion of all commercial activities (%)

	City	Market
Tindivanam, India [1]	42.5	
Port-au-Prince [2]	63	
Kinshasa (a quarter) [3]	49.2	
Point-à-Pitre [4]	58	
Merida, Venezuela [6]	70	
Grand Delphi [6]	23.5	
Haut Sanaga, Cameroon [7]	41	
El Tigre, Venezuela [8]	72.5	
Abidjan [9]	77.7	
Toulepleu, Ivory Coast [10]		89
Lima [11] (wholesalers)	75	77 (average)
(street vendors)	62	
Accra [12]		54.5 – 84.5
Santo Amaro, Brazil [13]		60
Hong Kong [14]	68-74	
Anyama, Ivory Coast [15]	66	85
Sholapur, India [16]	47.1	72
Bouaké, Ivory Coast [17]	80	

Sources: (1) Charleux 1971:389; (2) Casimir 1965; (3) Denis 1954; (4) Menauge 1970:33; (5) Valbuena 1966; (6) Rao and Desai 1965:392; (7) Tissandier 1970:11; (8) Valladares 1969; (9) S.E.T.A.P.1959; (10) Schwartz 1969:63; (11) Santos 1973; (12) Lawson 1967a:169; (13) Motti 1970; (14) McGee 1970b; (15) Verrière 1969; (16) Gadgil 1965:169-70; (17) Joshi, *et al.* 1976.

examining the upward process which begins with the consumer. While credit is made available by the upper circuit to stimulate production, consumption forms the basis of credit in the lower circuit.

Since credit is personal and usually extended among friends, acquaintances, and neighbours,[8] many small businessmen are reluctant to give credit to civil servants whose high inter-city mobility increases the risk of non-repayment. Normally those with small and irregular incomes do not default on their debts.[9] A debt (both in terms of gratitude and money) assures a given size of clientele; a personal relationship between debtor and creditor is established at all levels of the lower circuit.[10]

The conditions under which credit is furnished to both entrepreneur and consumer make many usurious practices possible: upper circuit money is expensive, and when coupled with a lack of security, results in a high interest rate on loans.[11] Mintz (1956: 19) tells of a street vendor who every three days paid a shilling on

every pound he had borrowed; this was equivalent to an annual
interest rate of 600 per cent! As it is practically impossible to
penalize bad debtors, the money-lender becomes dependent on
his debtors to a certain extent.

The lower classes go into debt primarily for current expenditure while the middle classes go into debt for non-essential expenditure; a survey conducted at Pointe-à-Pitre, Guadeloupe shows
the variation according to the degree of poverty among (i) shantytown residents, (ii) residents who have been relocated, and (iii)
public housing tenants:

Table 8.3 Use of credit

	Shantytown %	No. of house-holds	Relocated %	No. of house-holds	Public housing %	No. of house-holds
Current expenditure	34.9	44	57.7	65	12.7	15
Non-essential expenditure	20.6	26	9.4	12	42.3	50
Current and non-essential expenditure	42.8	54	39.3	50	26.2	31
No use	1.5	2	0	0	18.6	22
Total households	100.0	126	100.0	127	100.0	118

Source: Goudet (1969).

Going into debt permits the poor to survive and the majority of
the population to respond in some way to the demonstration
effect; this constitutes a mechanism for the appropriation of
popular savings. The profit margins which protect traders from
risk and maintain them until credit is repaid, are part of the same
exploitative mechanism in which the profits which apparently
maintain the lower circuit *return* to the upper circuit through
various channels, such as the bank, for example.

B *Entrepreneurial credit*

The wholesaler serves as the link between the modern circuit and
the lower circuit because of his position at the head of a long chain
of dependent retailers; he is the only operator in the circuit with
sufficient guarantees to obtain bank credit. One could possibly
even speak of collusion between the banks and wholesalers (Engberg 1967:64).

The following examples from Saida, Algeria (Champseix *et al.* 1972) show the differential use of banks according to the size and type of enterprise: 68 per cent of the wholesalers had a bank account in Saida or Mascara. All wholesalers dealing in food, beverages, and gas had an account and 33 per cent could obtain bank credit. All middlemen kept a bank account and 71 per cent were able to obtain credit. In contrast, 85 per cent of the artisans questioned in Saida, said that they did not have a bank account; for them, bank credit was even less possible than possession of an account. Of the 803 businesses interviewed in Saida, only 19 had been established through bank credit. The following table shows the situation for commercial and service activities:

Table 8.4

	Total no. of establishments	Establishments obtaining bank credit	
		No.	%
Transport	11	3	27.3
Food wholesalers	31	18	58.1
Cloth/leather	103	5	4.9
Food	334	1	0.3
Beauty and hygiene	39	0	–
Street vendors	55	0	–
Hotels, restaurants	45	0	–

Source: Champseix, *et al.* (1972).

As can be seen, bank credit is not readily available except for the wholesalers. The small-scale activities of the lower circuit cannot offer sufficient guarantees to obtain this type of credit and the very nature of their operations prohibits payment of bills on a fixed date. In any case, the small scale of the operations would not be profitable for the bank. Moreover, lower circuit traders, as well as small farmers, are aware of the dangers of taking bank credit which would ruin them were they unable to honour their debts.

Since most wholesalers impose conditions for the supply of goods, both new arrivals in the profession and small-scale traders are forced to seek credit from small wholesalers, retailers and large market traders, whose terms of credit are very different from those of the major wholesaler and are adapted to the particular functioning of the lower circuit. The further one goes down the scale of middlemen, the smaller the size of operations, the shorter the duration of the loan and the higher the risks and interest rates. The major and minor wholesalers' permanent fear of default restricts his loans to relatively small amounts made available to the most creditworthy clients.[12]

Credit generally takes the form of an advance in merchandise, the amount varying according to the ability of the borrower and the turnover of his stock. Fast-moving lines receive smaller and shorter credit than slow-moving lines. The term for which credit is extended is generally short, ranging from a morning to a week, or more infrequently to a month. The time-limit may also be adapted to seasonal fluctuations – shorter, for instance, during active economic periods when there is more money in circulation. In Guadeloupe, for example, the small trader must pay his debts in 30 days during the sugar-cane harvest and in 45 to 60 days between harvests (Menauge 1969).

It is not in the interests of the wholesaler to tie up his capital for long periods since frequent loans make more profits for him. Moreover, the terms of commercial banking credit are much shorter than those of industrial or agricultural credit. Finally, a reduction in repayment-time may be observed throughout the Third World. The expansion of the modern sector, which has greater access to banks, has reduced the direct sources of wholesalers' finance. His chances of obtaining bank credit reduced, the wholesaler is forced to circulate his capital even more rapidly.[13]

A loan is seldom repaid in a lump sum.[14] The borrower will often wish to remain in debt in order to obtain more credit, while the creditor on the other hand limits the new supply of credit in such a way that default would not endanger his future operations, a situation which involves a delicate balance. The wholesaler would survive with difficulty if he did not continually supply traders lower down the scale, even if he sometimes sells at a loss. Neale, Singh and Singh (1965:137) note that, in India, the Arthiyas 'to avoid losing money on sales, held stocks and consequently became illiquid'. The middleman looks for permanent stock-replacement, whilst the lender needs regular and sizeable clientele, assuring him of potentially larger accumulation.

Profit margins

The division of goods into small quantities leads to an increase in retail prices for the final, usually poor, consumer.[15] Under such circumstances, the small stock of the retailer is the result of his merchandise having passed through many middlemen's hands. The small trader sells only very small quantities to each customer; Table 8.5 from Bouaké, Ivory Coast illustrates both the phenomenon of multiple middlemen and that of micro-retailing.

The result of these parallel tendencies is a rise in prices because of the large number of middlemen and the high profit margin per unit required by the small trader. This high margin is due to the small, uncertain nature of his sales as well as the fact that the small trader sells on credit; total profit on the other hand remains relatively limited.

Whilst in principle the profit-incentive exists among commercial activities in the lowest levels of the lower circuit, in reality the prime preoccupation is survival. 'Few traders can think in terms of selling at cost plus $x\%$ (Hawkins 1965:108). It has even been observed that traders do not wish to make large profits: one of Fox's informants said, 'I get my daily bread from the shop and that's all I need. Why should I think of more when I meet my expenses from it?' Another declared, 'Whatever I have, I am satisfied with and whatever the future will bring will be alright too. When I earn little I spend little' (Fox 1967:303).

It is difficult to determine accurately the profits made by small-scale commerce; nevertheless, enough studies have been conducted, particularly in Africa, to conclude that profit margins are sizeable, which contradicts Belshaw's (1965:57) remarks on the subject.

Profit margins depend upon the type and origin of the product, the size of the establishment and the rate of stock turnover. For example, it is commonly found throughout the Third World that profit margins vary from 100 to 2000 per cent for local commodities while ranging only from 50 to 350 per cent for imported products. This situation is explained by the fact that variations in local production do not have a marked influence on consumer prices. When the harvest is poor, the law of supply and demand operates freely, but when the harvest is better, middlemen intervene to maintain high prices for their own profit. Profit margins are generally higher for perishable foodstuffs.[16]

Moreover, profit margins are highest in small-scale commerce. For example, in the Ivory Coast, they are estimated at 5 per cent for import-export trade, 10 per cent for wholesale trade and 18 per cent for retail trade (Amin 1967). Foodstuffs in particular often have even higher profit margins. At Toumedi, Ivory Coast they may reach 27 per cent for beverages and spices (Bettignies 1965:70). Street vendors seem to have even higher profit margins than small merchants. Could one infer from this that profit margins increase as the level of commercial activity decreases?[17]

It seems that the smaller the amount of capital invested, the higher the profit margin, as Marris has observed in central Lagos (1962:76). In Anyama, Ivory Coast, profit margins average 10 per cent in the bazaars, and somewhat higher among the Syrian and Lebanese traders whose stock sells more rapidly. In the African shops profit margins rise to 15 to 18 per cent yet the static hawkers have the highest profit margins of all, generally fluctuating around 30 per cent but varying on each product: sugar, 66 per cent; flashlights, 60 per cent; cigarettes, 68 per cent; chewing gum, 43 per cent; underwear, 33 per cent; candles, 25 per cent; sandals, 43 per cent (Verriere 1969). The low-income consumer is penalized because he must buy at the extreme end of a long chain of middlemen; having little money, he must pay relatively more for his subsistence.

Total profit must not, however, be confused with profit per unit. While total profit increases with the size of an establishment, the smallest commercial units are the ones having the largest profit margins. The street vendor limits his wares to several products with both attractive cost and selling prices, whilst small, local merchants must offer a wider range of products. Hawking is more risky, however, for sales are less sure and some days may amount to nothing. Consequently, while the profit per unit is very high, total profit may be very small or even nonexistent.

Price mechanisms

Prices in the lower circuit depend on the supply conditions facing the trader and his existing customer-relations. For instance, there is considerable fluctuation in the quantity of foodstuffs offered on the market; prices tend to rise when supply is limited, especially when wholesalers are able to speculate. Seasonal variation in transport costs also causes price fluctuations. Finally, prices may increase during periods when more money is circulating in the lower circuit. Yet the relations established between seller and buyer result in short-run price variations. It should be noted, however, that haggling originates as much in seasonal conditions as in a gradual process of agreement between buyer and seller.

Supply, like demand, according to Marshall (1927:182) should

Table 8.5 Division of major consumer goods, Bouaké, Ivory Coast

Commodity	As received by wholesaler	Sold by wholesaler	Sale by retail-wholesaler	Retail in city to high income consumer	Retail in shops and by vendors
Kerosene	5,000–30,000 litre tank	200 litre barrel (28 francs per litre)	10 & 20 litre barrel (30 francs per litre)	35 francs per litre	45 francs per litre (sold in 5 franc measures)
Sugar	25 kg carton	25 kg carton	5 kg carton	1 kg package	5 F heap
Salt	25, 18 and 9 kg bags	25, 18 and 9 kg bags	18 and 9 kg bags	25, 18, 9 and 1 kg bags	5 F heap
Wine	Case of 10 or 15 litre bottles	Case of 10 or 15 litre bottles	Case of 10 or 15 litre bottles	1 litre bottle	1 litre bottle or 20cl glass in bars and restaurants
Cloth	bales of 50 12-yard pieces	bales of 50 pieces	12-yard pieces	6-yard pieces	6- or 2-yard pieces
Dry batteries	Box of 300 batteries	Box of 300 batteries	Pack of 50 or 12	Individually	Individually
Cigarettes	1200-box carton in 40-carton case	1200-box carton	10 or 100 box carton 25-package box	1 or 10 box carton package	5 F for 2 cigarettes, or individually

Source: Republique de Côte d'Ivoire (1966).

not be considered as stock but as a flow over time. Therefore, entrepreneurial behaviour and decisions should be examined in terms of a given time-horizon (Adelman 1966:37). Is Marshallian theory applicable to the lower circuit, where the time scale is clearly not the same as in the upper circuit? This difference explains the different prices charged for the same product by two neighbouring traders, or the spectacular variations in prices charged by a hawker from one day or hour to the next. This situation may appear to the observer to be economically irrational, and one might well wonder how trade survives under such anarchic price conditions. However, the anarchy and irrationality are only apparent; in fact, the system's internal logic is based on, among other factors, the time scale characterizing lower circuit commerce. To hold stocks for a few hours or days may be more detrimental than selling it at such a low price that a loss is apparently made. In reality, 'lost opportunities' are compensated for by the return to liquidity necessary for new purchases to be made and thus permit the trader to reinvest and return to active business.

According to Scitovsky (1971:40), there is generally a relationship between changes in consumer demand and price fluctuations.[18] In underdeveloped countries, however, the essential consumption of the poor is independent of price fluctuations mainly because it is usually obtained on credit.

Prices depend in part on the perishability of a product and the seller's ability to affect this. The latter tries to sell the most perishable goods as fast as possible, and if they cannot be sold at the regular price they are offered at what could be called a bargain price. An example of this flexible opportunity cost is the vegetable seller without a refrigerator who sells at a loss when it becomes clear that stock will be left over; another is the taxi driver who cuts his rates when the number of customers decreases during certain periods of the day. Such products are perishable and must be sold at a loss rather than be wasted. The ability of a customer to postpone purchase also affects prices; these tend to be relatively higher for essential daily consumer goods than for non-essential products, whose purchase can be postponed. Moreover, merchants are often forced to sell at a loss in order to honour at least a part of a debt.

A trader's profit depends on total sales, a situation which could be compared to the *cultura promiscua* in which many crops are grown to ensure that at least one will provide sufficient returns.

This 'lottery' is the only solution open to farmers who are subject to both the vagaries of the climate and scarce financial resources. Bargaining is one of the most characteristic aspects of price formation in the lower circuit. As Scitovsky (1971:19) points out, bargaining is only possible within the framework of small-scale economic activity. Dewey (1962) defines it as an operation of adjustment between interested parties due to the fact that quality and quantity of goods supplied are both variable. Thus there would be three possible outcomes – more goods for the same price, a fall in price, or a combination of both. Dewey's explanation, like that of Hagen (1968:65) who sees haggling as a form of pleasure, has a purely psychological perspective.

In addition to these cultural explanations, economics has also been used to explain bargaining. Price is subjected to the fluctuations of supply and demand, so market-operations need a self-regulating mechanism (Belshaw 1965:8); Uchendu (1967) adds that bargaining thus becomes an economically rational act.

It must be remembered that the phenomenon of seasonal price structure has become much more marked with the tendency toward geographical specialization of production. In regions where transport is poorly developed, such as Melanesia, relatively uniform price structures can still be found; traders prefer to retain their goods or to destroy them rather than sell at a price judged too low (Brookfield 1969:19).

Bargaining does not have equal importance for all products; rather it depends on whether the product is perishable, seasonal, indispensable, necessary, or simply useful. The pressure on the seller (due to the nature of the product to be sold) and that exerted on the individual wishing to purchase, are both crucial; most foreigners are unable to participate in such transactions because of these two factors (Hodder 1969: 88; Loupy 1971:9; Dewey 1962:74). Hagen (1968:61-2) thinks this 'sliding system' is reserved for non-standardized goods and occasions when bargaining-time is disproportional to the range of possible financial outcomes. However, today's lower circuit trade includes both standardized and non-standardized products while the concept and value of time varies from society to society.

9

Adaptability and rationality
in the lower circuit

The hypertrophic nature of the lower circuit

Dasgupta (1964:188) has asked how the labour surplus to the requirements of the modern circuit can continue to be absorbed by the non-modern circuit: one reply (McGee 1971a:74) is that the bazaar system has something of a self-inflationary quality, the more people entering the system, the greater the market. Hodder (1969:68) also observed this phenomenon in the Yoruba markets of Nigeria, suggesting that the bigger the city, the more frequently are markets held, and the more important they become. The size of the lower circuit thus appears to be directly proportional to the number of people concerned.[1]

The extreme division of labour within the lower circuit is another factor explaining its self-inflationary nature. First, it stimulates the productive use of capital, the frequency of trade increasing the speed of transactions and consequently raising profits, irrespective of their volume. Moreover, the increased number of transactions accelerates the velocity of monetary circulation.

The 'micro-specialization' of lower circuit activities creates numerous intermediary and mediating services as well as a chain of other activities. The modern tertiary sector often creates its own system of lower circuit services.

The fractionalization of activities favours the creation of other occupations. The large number of tailors allows complementary retailers (such as haberdashers) to flourish, just as the increase in the small construction enterprises gives work to a host of carpenters, blacksmiths, etc. Any pretext serves as a new source of income. Supplying the city's daily needs is a pretext for all sorts of activities connected with small-scale buying, selling and transport. The mere presence of civil servants or students, even in the smallest town, has a multiplier effect on small commercial, service and craft activities. Masons and carpenters find employment in the construction of houses requiring modernization; hotels, small restaurants, pharmacies and transport businesses emerge; bakers and photographers widen their markets; all types of repairmen (radio, television, bicycle) also manage to make a living.

Lower circuit adaptability to a changing economic climate

The upper circuit tends to generate the economic climate rather than adapt to it; adaptation can only be achieved with varying success, since some discrepancy always exists between the decision of large firms and existing market conditions. By contrast, the lower circuit can only function through a rigid adaptation to cyclical conditions. As it is favoured by the divisibility and mobility of both labour and capital, entrepreneurs can adapt to quantitative and qualitative variations in demand and thus improve the marginal returns of the enterprise.

The small quantity of invested capital permits the artisan or trader to switch activities easily if business cycles necessitate a change of tactics. Though such a changeover often involves uncertainty, it does not constitute a real problem. The same premises may be used for a new activity or else the entrepreneur can move with the tide of fellow sufferers to some other part of the city. Changes in the type of goods sold may take place due to seasonal changes in demand. One can even speak of a flexible adaptation in employment since extra help is hired during busy periods and is later dismissed.

While upper circuit entrepreneurs fear unsold stocks and always attempt to avoid this through accurate forecasting, lower circuit traders remain in and rely totally on the local market. Their behaviour responds directly to demand, for petty manufacturing tends to be either intermittent or seasonal.

When viewed in this way, the emergence and disappearance of firms within the lower circuit is only to be expected and is the direct result of structural factors and a rigid adaptation to highly

variable market conditions. In the lower circuit, bankruptcy is not
the end but the beginning of a career (Isaac 1971:292-3), at least,
much more so than in the upper circuit.

The smallest activities are generally the most insecure: a
change in consumption patterns may even put them out of business. Failure also stems from an over-extension of credit either to
customers or suppliers. In the first case, lack of liquidity makes
stock-replacement impossible, whilst in the second, the enterprise
suffers from over-stocking, making for delays in the settling of
bills and therefore an increasinly usurious rate of interest.

A *Labour market mobility*

Lower circuit occupational mobility is impressive: clearly
specialization is counterproductive in many activities, since what
is often required is the relatively easy movement from one
occupation to another. This flexibility is the saving grace for
many of the inhabitants of Third World cities. Bauer and Yamey
(1957:37) in suggesting that when the economy develops
occupational specialization, the mobility of labour between
occupations diminishes, cannot be referring to the lower circuit.
The expansion of industrial activity imposes specialization and at
the same time leads to a relative and even absolute reduction in
the number of jobs. The lower circuit through its expansive
capacity then intervenes to absorb the excess labour.

People working in the lower circuit tend to change activities so
frequently, not because it is exciting to do so (Hagen 1968:63) but
because they are forced to adapt rapidly to a highly fluctuating
life-situation; the search for short-term benefits is clearly characteristic of the system. Long-term preoccupations are more important in the upper circuit.

B *Adaptability and modernization*

Modernization, which is accompanied by a change in the consumption structure, directly affects the structure of the lower
circuit. The lower circuit increases the demand for modern products, even though those it manufactures or markets are the
results of less modern technology.

The increased consumption of modern products by the poor
gives rise to new lower circuit activities, a good example of which
is the automobile repair shop. The automobile, coveted by every-

Table 9.1 Repair activities

	% of total employment	% turnover of local craft activity	% of total employment in small industry and crafts
Sierra Leone [1]	24.3		
Toumodi, Ivory Coast [2]		30	
Martinique [3]			23.0
Eastern Nigeria [4]			10.4
Kermanshah, Iran [5]			21.0
Saida, Algeria [6]			18.1
Small towns of Northern Morocco [7]			23.0
Puerto-la-Cruz, Venezuela [8]		22.7	
Barcelona, Venezuela [8]		29.0	
Freetown, Sierra Leone [9]			25.0
Abidjan (employment) [10]	8.0		
Bamako, Mali (employment) [11]	6.5		
Port Gentil, Gabon [12]	22.0		
Sabon Gari, Nigeria [13]	26.2		
Zaria, Nigeria [13]	24.0		
Santo Domingo [14]		44	25

Sources: (1) Saylor 1967:146; (2) Étude Régionale de Bouaké 1966:51; (3) Cazes 1970:415; (4) Lewis 1967:34; (5) Clarke and Clark 1969; (6) Champseix *et al.* 1972; (7) Troin 1971:523; (8) Erdens 1969; (9) Saylor 1967:146; (10) Santos 1965:87; (11) Meillassoux 1968:25; (12) Roumegous 1966:334; (13) Remy and Weeks 1973: table 15.1; (14) Dominican Republic 1970.

one, and the truck, an essential means of transport, are two such modern products. Often bought second-hand, they require frequent repair in small garages using only locally available resources supplemented by the innovative ability of the self-educated mechanic. Outisde large cities it is impossible to import and stock vehicle-spares. Even in the large centres, vehicle-owners do not always have enough money to patronize modern garages. Auto repairs are linked to metallurgic, mechanical and electric trades which, though created via an adaptation to modern consumption, belong to the lower circuit principally because of their size and characteristics, and, as such, are responsible for the creation of a large number of jobs.

Many of these activities are 'between' secondary and tertiary activity. Repairs contain an element of manufacture yet closely resemble services destined for final consumption. When the city reaches a more advanced stage of industrialization, repair activities may offer external economies: auto repair workshops can be transformed into metallurgic workshops serving a wider market, possibly even supplying modern industry, and thereby facilitating the latter's access to spare parts.

Here, as in all petty occupations, production levels out at a particular scale because of a lack of bank credit and integration into the commercial circuit. Paradoxically, when integration does take place, the enterprise is helplessly exposed to the risks of market fluctuations and problems worsen since the techniques it uses are often out-of-date and the forms of production and commercialization used are those of the lower circuit.

Productivity, dynamism and rationality

A *Lower circuit productivity*

Anderson (1964:57) states that productivity is an exclusive attribute of the modern industrial sector. On this basis it may be suggested that the lower circuit is by definition non-productive. But first, however, the term productivity must be adequately defined: Lean (1969:172) points out that a comparison between output per worker and capital invested is not sufficient. Consideration must be given to the time lag between investment and its effect on output, which tends to vary between industries. This refers to the modern economy, yet also seems applicable to lower circuit activities.

The lower circuit as well as tertiary activities is often considered unproductive because, as Frankman points out (1969:1) 'economists have generally neglected the role of services. Analyses of this sector have largely been limited to an evaluation of its function in the industrially advanced economies. Economic literature on the problems of developing countries continues to manifest a strong anti-service bias.' Elsewhere, he suggests that the productivity of services is never measured, only its value is appraised (Frankman 1970:6). Wage levels cannot be taken alone as a measure of productivity; in order to explain income disparities, entry barriers should be considered. Wages are low in tertiary activities because there are few barriers to entry; income disparities do not, however, necessarily denote differences in productivity.

In any case, the concept of productivity has been elaborated on the basis of the economic reality of the developed world, and therefore must be adjusted before being applied to underdeveloped countries. Notwithstanding the popular opinion that productivity is a rigidly quantifiable concept, Buron's definition (1964) seems probable: he considers productivity to be 'the relation between the number of units of a determined quality produced or sold and the cost of all technical, financial, and human inputs used in their production or sale'.

B *Lower circuit 'dynamism'*

Maunder (1960) belongs to the school that considers the traditional sector of the urban economy to be 'static' as opposed to the modern sector which is judged 'dynamic'. Leloup (1970:199) goes even further when referring to the cities of the Brazilian state of Minas-Gerais; he says that 'the marginal class is a reserve of cheap labour but also an enormous mill-stone on the city'. Such reasoning is based on the naive assumption that service activities, i.e. the lower circuit, block the process of development. However, the tertiary sector is *not* parasitic (Peillon 1970: Volume 1, 75); indeed the poor economy has some elements of dynamism, as suggested, *inter alia*, by Beaujeu-Garnier (1965b, 1970) and George (1969).

Moreover, the extensive literature on shantytowns often shows them to be characterized by considerable upward social mobility (Mangin 1967; Turner 1969; Laquian 1971). One would therefore criticize those who restrict their research to the upper circuit in order to prove at any price Schumpeter's (1961) classical formulation on the creative role of entrepreneurs, viewed as men capable not only of seizing opportunities for change and growth (Berry and Rao 1969:21) but also of creating opportunities (Hagen 1968). This concept of entrepreneurship can be applied to those in the lower circuit, if the 'operational' definition of Katzin is used, whereby an entrepreneur is 'an independent self-employed manager who carries the risk and claims the gain of an enterprise conducted with the object of obtaining money profits' (1964:182).

It would be wrong, however, to confuse the individual with the group or to generalize from a particular case. In reality, while the lower circuit has its own internal dynamism and power to create and foster economic activities, its fundamental function is to perpetuate poverty. The urban elite absorbs a disproportionate share of urban income; the dynamism of the lower circuit is therefore absolute when this economic subsystem is considered to be closed (Reiber and Eckert 1971). Yet when its dependence on the upper circuit is examined, this dynamism turns out to be at best relative, and at worst illusory.

The rationality of the lower circuit

The lower circuit constitutes a permanent integrative mechanism, involving for the most part the mass of insolvent and unskilled migrants to be found in all Third World cities. It supplies maximum employment for a minimum capital-outlay, responds both to changes in consumption patterns and to the general conditions of employment and capital.

The functioning of the lower circuit has therefore a perfect inner rationality. The preoccupation with comparisons between the realities of the developed and underdeveloped worlds has often led to ethnocentric interpretations, as in the case of Anderson (1964:57) who believes that industrial urbanism is the only rational framework for thought and labour. Gutkind (1968) likewise linked rationality to modernization, and modernization to all things scientific, thus reviving Weber's dichotomy between the 'traditional' and the 'rational'. Such simplistic formulations have been described by Gusfield (1971:16) as 'a great distortion of the realities of many concrete situations'. Geertz (1963:43), Saylor (1967:99) and Polly Hill (1970:4) among others have shed light upon the rationality of the poor economy of Third World cities. The best example of this rationality is the 'equilibrium in scarcity' characterizing much of the lower circuit. If irrationality is closely linked with impulsiveness in so far as action is elicited by blind psychological forces rather than deliberate calculation, then there is no irrationality in the behaviour of the inhabitants of Latin American shantytowns.

For McGee (1970b:40) who carried out detailed studies in several cities of the Far East, the activities of the 'informal sector' (in this case street-hawking) were totally efficient within their own context.

To be entitled to label a human action as irrational, one should be in a position to prove that it neither leads to a permanent goal nor behaviour stable enough to give rise to actual rules. In the lower circuit, as shown elsewhere (Santos 1975), there exist certain relationships, universal in time and geographical space, between businessmen, between buyers and sellers, which are central to the very execution of productive activity. For example, operational costs are considerably lessened in the lower circuit; but on the other hand, what of the role of middlemen, personal credit, price formation, and the fractionalization of lower circuit activities? Even the relations of dependence with the upper circuit are governed by logic. Rationality, which each civilization or ruling class seeks to attribute only to its own actions, also characterizes the activity of the poor economy. Its functioning is governed by laws, that is, by an evenness of behaviour based on regularly recurring causal factors.

The characteristics of the 'informal sector', put forward by Keith Hart (1973:5) (namely a hand-to-mouth existence characterized by an unevenness of expenditure over time, flexibility of consumption and proliferation of credit for all commodities) constitute a manifestation of the very rationality this economic circuit is deemed to lack. The principles governing its activities are those of capitalism at large, whose logic remains the same even when appearing in different forms in each subsystem. In fact, the lower constitutes a subsystem within a larger urban system, itself nothing more than a component of the national economy.

In a given society, the 'informality' or irrationality of one of the two circuits would imply that society does not operate in an aggregate manner. This view supports the dualistic conceptualization wherein the two circuits function in parallel; this notion conveniently eliminates the possibility of one sector being dependent on and/or subordinate to the other.

The functioning of the lower circuit is determined by different factors linked together by a logic which is at the same time economic, social and political. Here, it is more a question of necessity than choice, a universal result of the general laws governing the capitalist system in its present stage. And, as Avineri (1970:15) puts it, 'only the universal can be rational'.

As for Max Weber's notion of rationality, it constitutes, according to Lukacs an attack on reason. This rationality or rational reckoning is based on the conformity of action with the logic of a system of values. This system of values can only be that of capitalism in which the Weberian rationality is a prerequisite for expansion. For a production system based on exchange value and surplus value to be successful, a total rationalization in the utilization of factors becomes necessary, rationality here meaning a move from quality to quantity, from the pre-eminence of concrete systems to that of abstract ones, in other words of alienation. Lukacs thinks that there is a parallel between the Weberian category of rationality and the Marxist category of reification, which is itself a part of the total concept we call alienation. Bringing them together, he shows how capitalist expansion is accompanied by a reified objectivity (Riu 1968:24), coupled with the progressive elimination of the worker's human and individual qualitative attributes. The workers of the lower circuit escape much of this alienation, so characteristic of human labour in the advanced economics of the 'First' and 'Second' Worlds.

10

Inter-circuit relations and the parameters of growth

The two circuits of the Third World economy do not function as isolated systems but permanently interact with each other. On the one hand, the existence of a middle class precludes *closed* circuits, for the middle class consumes with a varying frequency in both circuits.[1] On the other hand, the functioning of each circuit requires an internal and horizontal articulation, characterized by different degrees of integration, as well as a vertical articulation which takes place through interaction between the activities of the two circuits.

The first condition, which constitutes the internal logic of a circuit, is always locally more fully developed in the lower circuit than in the upper circuit, except in the exceptional case of a city having a complex domestically oriented industrialization.

The second condition, in which relations may be either continuous or irregular, simple or hierarchical relations of both complementarity and competition. Complementarity means that the activities of one circuit require inputs from the other circuit or that certain activities of one circuit constitute external economies for the other. However, the functional relations *between* the two circuits may be completely different: there may be hierarchical relations of dependence and domination, exerted downward in the case of decision-making, but also upward inasmuch as the dominated and dependent elements unwittingly help maintain and strengthen the position of those higher up in the hierarchy. The wholesaler who acts as 'banker' for other lower circuit activities (but who could not survive without them) is an example of this dialectic of domination-subordination.

Relations of complementarity and competition epitomize all aspects of the urban system. The two subsystems are in a permanent state of unstable equilibrium; their complementarity, whether regular or not, does not necessarily prevent competition: it represents only one aspect of the development of the dialectic between the two circuits.

The mode of development and operation of each circuit is linked to variables unique to each circuit. These variables (such as the continuous rural-urban migration of the poor and the consequent expansion of the lower circuit, or the existence of State-provided infrastructural and financial assistance in order to encourage the development of upper circuit activities) are constantly changing the size and relative significance of each circuit. Variables common to both circuits, such as the production and consumption structure (income distribution, the role of credit, and consumption patterns) modify the control-relations between the two circuits to the advantage of one or the other. However, since the domination of the upper circuit over the lower circuit prevails in the long run, competitive relations also only represent one aspect of the development of this dialectic.

Therefore, in a less developed economy, the lower circuit itself creates most of the external economies it needs. As an economy becomes more modern, and as different intermediate and final consumer goods are demanded, the lower circuit must increasingly turn to inputs from the upper circuit. Equally, upper circuit demand for lower circuit outputs decreases as the economy becomes more complex.

Variables specific to each circuit

New migrants to urban centres tend to lack both skills (except for certain artisanal and other occupations) and capital. Their main attribute is an ability to provide labour. Since the upper circuit is unable to absorb no more than just a small proportion of this labour, the majority of migrants are absorbed by and therefore maintain lower circuit activities. However, in order to explain the continued existence of the lower circuit, it is essential to take into account certain factors which are not directly concerned with inter-circuit relations, such as the dispersion of the population, the seasonal nature of regional and urban economic activities, etc.

Three essential factors facilitate the expansion of the activities of the modern sector: the city's size, its functional level, and the external economies available to it. Equally, the establishment of modern circuit activity may depend either on decisions made by public bodies, or on those made by large firms. In the latter case, the initiative is often taken by decision-makers outside the city; such macro-decisions only affect the city's modern sector because of its location.

Variables common to both circuits

A city's production and marketing structure is important in determining in which circuit consumption will take place. Nevertheless, since supply and demand are interdependent within each circuit, additional variables are required to explain the relative size and significance of each circuit at a given moment. These other factors will include income distribution and the accessibility of credit, the degree of the popular exposure to modern consumer goods, the extent of government employment and regional migration, the rhythm and nature of regional activities, and the urban transport system. These variables will either facilitate or impede consumption in either or both circuits.

Urban transport organization and the use of private vehicles are important in explaining the forms taken by both complementarity and competition in the commercial activities of both circuits. Transport facilities are sometimes so limited that certain individuals, even if they have money available, do not have access to products sold by the commercial upper circuit.

Cultural considerations are also significant. The speed and depth of penetration of modern activities and the continuation of non-modern activities, both depend on the resistance or acceptance of modern consumption patterns by the poor and/or recently urbanized population. The increasing numbers of the urban poor also ensures the continued consumption of traditional goods manufactured by non-modern methods. The production of modern goods and services through non-modern or outdated techniques must also be added. This co-existence and competition with modern techniques is possible given the overall socio-economic context in which the lower circuit operates. The explanation is to be found in the propensity of the urban poor to consume new products even though they have only limited financial resources, eventually resulting in a decline in the quality of the product and its specific forms of production and marketing.

Modernization may hinder certain lower circuit activities when these activities compete with similar lower-priced products from the upper circuit. However, it is not clear whether this competition results in the disappearance of non-modern activities; these latter are generally able to survive because of the unique conditions in which the lower circuit operates.[2]

Credit acts as a key variable in determining the circuit in which consumption will take place. The extension of institutional credit benefits the upper circuit and is one of the tools it uses to modify consumer behaviour. Since modern industry requires a large market, a downward chain of credit is created. On the other hand, the lower circuit's chain of credit, linked to essential current consumptions, develops upward. Indeed, as we have seen, upper circuit mechanisms are based on production, while lower circuit mechanisms are based on consumption; that is, on the current needs of the population. As Herkommer (1966) points out 'we must differentiate between demand created by the structure of Engels curves, benefiting producers with a high elasticity of demand for inputs, *and* demand generated by population growth which favours the production of low quality goods.'

An understanding of the mechanisms of the commercial circuits therefore requires an examination to be made of the credit-system. Various forms of credit are used by different social classes; the poor population uses credit at usurious rates of interest to purchase food, whilst the rich population uses bank credit for durable consumer and luxury goods.

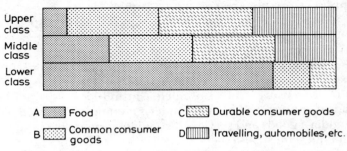

Figure 3 Availability of consumer credit by social class

An examination of Figure 3 indicates that the upper and middle classes have access to bank credit to purchase current, durable and other commodities, and, especially in the case of the middle class, for purchasing foodstuffs. The lower class has wide access to personal credit for its expenditure on food but less for the purchase of mass consumption goods, which results in credit only being available at usurious rates of interest. The poor also have at their disposal a narrow margin of personal credit for other expenditures, channelled into the banks through merchants thus serving local and/or externally controlled modern industry.

In this respect, the situation of the small and medium wage-earners merits attention. Since they have steady employment, they are able to use the upper commercial circuit for many purchases. This change in the method of payment means that other purchases, previously made in cash, must now be made through direct, personal credit (the *fiado* system as it is called in Spanish and Portuguese). This helps to expand or regenerate the lower circuit. It can generally be said that under conditions where consumption-patterns have not been modified, the amount of income remaining after this new type of consumption has occurred will determine whether wage-earners will have a greater or lesser propensity to buy consumer goods on credit in the lower circuit; thus the rate of diffusion of modern consumption patterns, as well as the rate at which the market for each consumer good is saturated, appear to be decisive factors. Account must also be taken of the effect of the enormous number of public and private sector office-workers and administrators working on a contractual basis, whose salaries (sometimes large, but generally uncertain and seasonal) will depend on the volume of investment, a situation which also helps to sustain the lower circuit.

None of the variables mentioned above has an independent effect on one or the other circuits, but constitutes part of a complex of factors, whose individual and aggregate influence varies over time and space. For example, within one city a given factor may contribute at a particular moment to the growth of one circuit and then later to the growth of the other circuit, according to the historical conjuncture and the corresponding modes of organization. Similarly, such combinations of variables will have a differential impact according to their spatial location or focus.

PART IV

11

Monopoly, the State and macrospatial organization

The two circuits and geographical analysis: A macrospatial perspective

The analysis of the spatial implications of the two circuits of the Third World urban economy represents one of the more fruitful approaches currently being undertaken; State and circuit activities (particularly those of monopolies and multinational firms) form the essential elements of macrospatial organization,[1] whilst lower circuit activities are limited to a more restricted area. Far too few studies have been made of the nature of monopoly in underdeveloped countries; those available tend to deal more with stability than growth (Merhav 1969:7) and often neglect problems of economic development (Mason 1967:79). While some interest has been shown in the relations between monopolistic structures and urban space (e.g. Greenhut 1963), their area of concern has generally been limited to the 'topological space' occupied by the firm as Perroux (1950) has termed it, though Claval (1968) has introduced the concept of space into geographical analysis in a systematic fashion.

Systematic and extensive studies of the relations between the State and the different organizational forms taken by production are equally lacking for underdeveloped countries. Such studies would nevertheless be crucial to our understanding of the intimate relationship between wealth and poverty, as well as their spatial repercussions.

The role of monopoly is crucial to spatial theory, but its integration into the analysis is no easy task due to the large quantity of unknowns and the difficulty of correctly interpreting the available data. However, an examination of the spatial impact of monopolies in underdeveloped countries will supply data from concrete examples, essential to an understanding of their geographical role.

The analysis of monopolistic influence on spatial organization obviously cannot be made without consideration of other factors, such as transport organization, the level of industrialization, international dependence and geopolitics. Spatial analysis has not yet really considered these factors in relation to underdeveloped countries.

Monopolistic behaviour has different spatial implications for developed and underdeveloped countries. In the former, large national and multinational firms operate within the framework of an international division of labour which is based upon and caters to the needs of the developed metropolitan economies. Complementarity is essential. Such is not the case in underdeveloped countries since they have little or no control over their own or others' markets.

From the spatial viewpoint, and regarding the establishment of such firms, we may speak of a *vertical specialization* in developed countries. Spatial proximity is relatively unimportant and the well-developed transport system assures functional complementarity between different centres of complementary production. In underdeveloped countries, we can speak only of a *horizontal specialization* with spatial selectivity for different levels of industrial production, because so few zones have significant locational advantages. There is therefore a cumulative tendency toward concentrations.

The role of the State is felt at all levels, spatial and otherwise, but is unique at national level since, for reasons of efficiency, all other elements must adapt, unless they themselves are in a position to control the State. The nation state is itself a spatial system which embraces all the economic systems operating within its territory.

State power stems essentially from the new requirements of the international economy (Navarro de Brito 1972, 1973), which force the State to modernize and exert its influence throughout the country. Participation in technological modernization places constraints on the State machinery either in terms of external relations, or in response to new needs of its own population. In the first case, the need to create certain mechanisms of international exchange requires that the State assumes control of currency, tax, foreign trade and banking. Modernization both produces and exacerbates the quality of opportunity in a given population, whilst monopoly gives rise to unequal income distribution (Claval 1968:160; Jalée 1969:129; Preiser 1971:189; Sylos Labini 1962). The level of technology crystallized in the instruments of labour has exceeded the individual's competence whilst becoming essential to collective life. Only the State can solve such a problem, and has attempted to do so by increasingly intervening in formerly private spheres.

In these various fields, such as education, health, communications, transport, and electricity, progress and diffusion are essentially due to the intervention of public authorities.

Hirschman (1958:216-17) wrongly attributes what he calls the 'fragmentation' of investment projects to either a lack of talent, technical direction and planning or to electoral considerations. In reality, this 'fragmentation' is due largely to the impact of technological modernization on poor countries. Governments are forced to respond as much to real needs perceived by the population, as to the 'needs' created by the demonstration effect and structural changes in production.

The widespread provision of certain services by the State leads both to new (usually upper circuit) forward and backward linkages (the latter activities belong to both circuits). The resultant increased employment fosters the development of modern commercial and manufacturing activities. On the other hand, however, infrastructural modernization, such as that of transport, benefits large firms that are located in the largest centres, by widening and unifying their potential markets. The role of the State as a modernizing agent therefore seems an essential condition for the creation and strengthening of modern, monopolistic activities.

The tendency toward concentration of financial resources in the hands of the central government is widespread. The central government takes the lion's share of taxes and leaves the other administrative levels a relatively small part of total State income. Moreover, since municipalities are generally numerous, their own resources tend to be fragmented. In Colombia, for example, between 1949 and 1959, the percentage of taxes going to the central government rose from 53.8 per cent to 59.6 per cent while the portion going to the regions declined from 25.3 per cent to

18.8 per cent and that going to the municipalities remained relatively constant.[2]

Do federal systems play a lesser role than a centralized State? Perhaps this was true in the past, but contemporary technological modernization requires the existence of centralized decision-making power: the largest portion of taxes therefore goes to the federal State which then controls most of the decision-making and investment-planning.

On the other hand, since the complete modernization of State machinery is impossible, control over the country's modernization is increasingly ceded to a parallel administration, formed by more or less autonomous organizations, dependent upon the central government which thereby increases the scope of its decision-making. Yet, since a portion of aggregate savings is absorbed by monopolies, the resources left to the State are in any case decreased.

Such a distribution has implications for spatial organization. Space is organized according to the dialectical interaction of forces of both concentration and dispersion. Monopolistic structures make up the former, whilst the diffusion of both information and consumption-patterns constitute the latter, the State playing a dual role. When the State supports monopoly through a programme of infrastructural concentration, it encourages economic and demographic concentration; when it builds social infrastructure (such as hospitals and schools) throughout the country or, for example, gives incentives to farmers, it plays a dispersion role. Whenever capital-formation policy favours the activities of large corporations and monopolies, resources become scarcer as the forces of spatial dispersion make their presence felt.

Since modernization and rapidly changing technology are synonymous under present conditions, concentration is encouraged by strong and often disturbing technical arguments. Nevertheless, reality is somewhat different: poverty is not only concentrated at growth-points, but also dispersed widely throughout society. This is one of the most serious consequences of the State's partnership with the monopolies.

Complete and partial metropolises

The modernization of the State has made possible the existence of metropolises even in the smallest and poorest countries. The general conditions of technological modernization require that even the smallest capital city acquires its own first-order services, essential to the modern State's operation, though the level of such services need not be commensurate with the level of economic activity.

Metropolises are the product of the recent modernization experienced by underdeveloped countries, initiated by industrialization at both the national and global level. Such urban areas did not exist before (Roweiss 1970:2-6); the large Latin American cities of the mid-nineteenth century cannot be considered to be metropolises if we are using the term to describe a large city at the centre of a large catchment area, and disposing of a sufficiently wide range of economic and commercial activities to be able to satisfy the basic daily needs of the dependent population. Although eighteenth- and early nineteenth-century Salvador and Lima dominated vast hinterlands, neither was capable of catering even to the basic needs of their privileged classes: much of these had to be satisfied by imports. Few, if any, of the basic necessities of the poor were furnished by these cities.

The metropolitan, large city, and modern capital-city phenomena are all closely connected. With the world-wide revolution in consumption patterns, many large cities became metropolises. However, new consumer demand (manifested at the level of international relations rather than that of individual needs) not only increased the size of urban areas, but also encouraged the proliferation and diversification of economic activities. The phenomena of the metropolis and the large capital city in fact are linked together in a reciprocal chain of cause and effect. This explains why contemporary Third World cities are usually overgrown, macrocephalous, hypertrophied. Those countries previously unable to boast large towns have none the less entered the era of urbanization with a vengeance.

The new forms of production which developed out of the technological revolution could only operate in an urbanized milieu. Also, the spread of new consumption patterns to the most distant and backward corners of the Third World released a wave of migrations to the cities and this added considerably to the population of the more developed urban centres.

Agreement must first be reached on the term *metropolis*, however. One of the greatest sources of ambiguity in the study of Third World cities has stemmed from a taxonomic problem: the most common classifications are: (i) those differentiating cities according to their population (i.e. small, medium, large and very large cities; (ii) those using a functional classification where the urban area is often analysed with scant regard for its own *spatial* organization (for example, industrial, commercial, administrative, holy and university cities). I would propose a different classification, based on the proposition that a city's ability to organize space depends on its own place in a functional hierarchy of urban areas. Therefore I would advocate the terms local city, intermediate city, partial metropolis and complete metropolis (Santos 1971).

The metropolis represents a form of concentration, and the local city a form of dispersion; the intermediate cities represent a compromise between the two. Often only the metropolis is capable of combining modern forms of economic, social and political life, the dynamic interaction of which causes a cumulative concentration of resources. Local cities develop in response to new (usually consumption) demands; they constitute the first urban tier able to satisfy the minimum basic demands of a given population. Intermediate cities are a response to more sophisticated demands, and are characterized by increased production and/or distribution capacity. The appearance of these intermediate cities will depend on the amount of space to be served, the intensity and density of economic activity and its transport organization, the latter acting to modify the other two variables.

The terms *primate*, *intermediate* and *small* city can only be used if a country is considered in isolation; however, they lose all comparative value if a definition is sought relating the urban agglomeration to its international context. Therefore the terms metropolis, intermediate, and local city are preferred, being much more qualitative than quantitative.

At each level (metropolis, intermediate city, and local city) the agglomeration fulfils functions particular to its level as well as lower-level functions. Thus the metropolis is simultaneously metropolis, intermediate city and local city. The local city, however, has only its unique function as a local city, even if periodic market activity may expand its importance significantly, although temporarily. This distinction is not unwarranted since the lower circuit, as will later be explained, has only a local range.

What is true for the surrounding area (umland) is equally true within the city. The major operative factor is still the accessibility of different goods and services. Some people may have permanent access to all goods while others must spread out their purchases over time; some, although living in a multifunctional city, are unable to make use of its manifold possibilities. The idea of a 'city-region' is useful, for physical distance is replaced by social distance, which is a function of the different social classes' standards of living (Santos 1971:158-61).

The metropolis is responsible for macrospatial organization, but a distinction must be drawn between complete and partial metropolises. 'Metropolises' are too frequently spoken of as if they were homogeneous.

In underdeveloped countries, the metropolitan function operates at two levels. A complete metropolis is capable of responding autonomously to most of its social and economic needs, such as the production of capital goods and/or the adaption of foreign technology to the requirements of the national economy (Santos 1971:32). Partial metropolises, on the other hand, whilst also serving a wide area, cannot fulfil these functions without external assistance, mainly from the complete metropolises.

The complete metropolises constitute the major economic poles of the already industrialized, underdeveloped countries (Brazil, Argentina, Egypt, Mexico, India and, according to one's definition of underdevelopment, possibly also China and South Africa). Most contemporary industrialized, underdeveloped countries began their industrialization process before other underdeveloped countries, and thus were able to supply themselves with many of the necessary manufactured and some of their capital goods, and contribute to the creation of a national infrastructure (Santos 1971).

Partial metropolises result from delayed industrialization (whether within a national or international framework) and the form this process eventually takes.

A partial metropolis is usually able to fulfil its macrospatial organizational functions only with help either from a national metropolis (as in the cases of São Paulo for Salvador, Buenos Aires for Rosario, Mexico City for Guadalajara, and Cairo for Alexandria) or from abroad (Paris for Abidjan, London for Accra, etc.). In the first case the partial metropolises are regional and in the second national.

In developed countries (except in a few exceptional cases such as France) complete metropolises do not control a network of partial metropolises. All metropolises have regional or national functionality, but at an international level may simultaneously be

Upper level (complete metropolis)

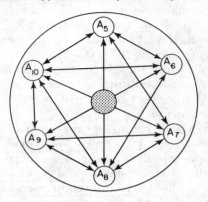

Lower level

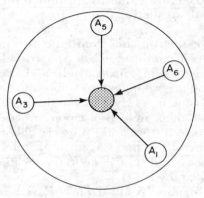

◯ Population

↑→ Integration

A_1, A_2 Economic activities

Figure 4 Levels of urban economic complexity in
underdeveloped countries

  both complete and partial metropolises, due to the fact that
'developed space' is both highly flexible and integrated, which
facilitates a marked degree of specialization and complementarity within the international process of production and distribution.

Integration and spatial reorganization

The importance of the State's contemporary role partly explains
the hegemony of capital cities. Political co-ordination of a nation's
economic and social life necessitates an improvement in the
transport and communications infrastructure, or in the case of
many new African states, its very construction. There is often a
relationship between such infrastructural developments and the
location of capital and major cities. During the colonial period,
communications infrastructure was established by European
governments, principally to facilitate the flow of raw materials
toward the colonizer's economy. Neither the terms 'network' nor
'local economic integration' describes this situation, since the slow
development of national transport networks eventually created a
system in which inter-urban relations were minimal. One of the
most important roles played by the modern State has been the
construction of a unified transport network. Labasse, for example, feels that 'the transport system is the fundamental geographical expression of the State' (1968:57).

An extensive highway network, irrespective of its quality, is
necessary for State authority to be felt throughout the country.
However, a road or rail network is not synonymous with authentic economic or spatial integration, which requires that not only
the effects of State decision-making reach the most remote corners of the country, but also that the economic activities of one
region are linked with those of other regions, and vice versa (for
example, the provision and distribution of manufactured products made or procured in the more developed regions, combined with the provision of foodstuffs, raw materials, capital and
labour which move principally in the opposite direction).

Without attempting a more thorough definition, some degree
of inter-regional complementarity can be observed despite the
existence of the unequal exchange so characteristic of relations of
domination and dependence. Previously, regions created to meet
external demands maintained direct economic relations with
foreign countries, despite the fact that they formed part of a
national political and administrative unit and often despite the
existence of a national road network, a situation particularly
manifest during the colonial period in Asia and Africa. Prior to
industrialization, many such countries had a road and rail network linking strategic points in the interior to the port instal-
lations; only industrialization permits a more comprehensive
network to be established.

Even though privileged external relations may still exist or may yet be established, those relations which determine both the urban hierarchy and the degree of national spatial integration stem from internally oriented industrialization. Thus, once a level of industrialization has been reached which permits or requires continuous exchange between the highest-level city and the others, the aggregate urban complex tends to be controlled by the former, which is generally, though not necessarily, the capital city.

The higher a country's level of industrialization, the more developed is the industrial integration in the 'core' and consequently, the more rapid the integration of national space. Yet the latter must be regarded as relative, since true integration is only found in the developed countries.

Among those underdeveloped countries with a relatively developed transport network (generally to be found in the most dynamic regions), a distinction can be made between those who managed to achieve this relative integration before their industrialization began, and those whose national integration resulted from industrialization.

Developed transport networks may also be found in non-industrialized countries such as Algeria, which suffered European colonization and the establishment of export-based commercial agriculture. Yet this type of integration was both partial and peripheral[3] and, while it enriched certain regions, it did not spread the benefits throughout the rest of the country. In reality, a pocket of simultaneously 'integrated' yet marginal space existed within a non-integrated country, simply because no real industrialization had taken place.

In certain countries, such as Brazil, different regions have long satisfied European demands by adopting export crops and creating ports. These historical conditions encouraged the formation of discrete spatial systems directly linked to foreign countries through the region's export-import centre(s). Modernization and industrialization, as well as the progress of national integration through infrastructural development, helped the new metropolises to gain ground whilst the historical centres stagnated. The new metropolises unquestionably became national economic poles, for the old centres could no longer satisfy the population's increased demand for consumer goods. The regional cities of the interior also increased in importance and began to compete with the old centres, a trend which was reinforced by the establishment of certain public services in these regional cities. Historical centres develop at different rates, but in general do not have the power to maintain bilateral relations among themselves.[4] The new agglomerations favoured by the concentration of activities become the major disseminators of regulations, orders, and innovations from an economic, social, cultural, and often political perspective, and form the nucleus of the national economy and society.

This polarization leads to two results common to all Third World countries. First, a hierarchical urban network is created, and secondly, except for the industrial metropoles, practically no relations exist between cities of the same 'level'. All agglomerations rely on higher-level cities for the commodities they are unable to produce themselves.

As a country industrializes and improves its internal transport system,[5] a short-circuiting within the urban system takes place: lower-level agglomerations no longer need to interact with cities immediately above them in the hierarchy, but can deal directly with the most important cities (see Fig. 5).

Even market traders, under certain conditions, escape the control of local suppliers and can bypass them by supplying themselves either partially or completely from the major cities. Distance, in terms of time and price, is as important a factor as the type of merchandise to be sold.

The phenomena termed 'urban basin' by Kayser (1966) and 'isolated regional economy' by Friedmann (1966) are becoming progressively more exceptional: 'horizontal' sharing of space among cities is now almost non-existent and has been replaced by a 'vertical' sharing with a growing interaction between cities of different functional levels. Several differentiated functions compete in the same spatial framework, making the attempt to delimit a city's 'dependent space' superfluous (Santos 1971). The disintegration of the 'traditional' urban network, and the development of local activities cannot conceal the inequalities which exist between the more prosperous, dominant regions and the less developed, dominated regions. In any case, regional and local urban areas are relegated to the socio-economic periphery and consequently pay higher prices, which results in a cumulative and relative impoverishment of their inhabitants. Isolation from access to basic goods and services is sufficient cause to consider an individual or an enterprise as occupying a peripheral situation.

Consequently, our major focus should be the location of pro-

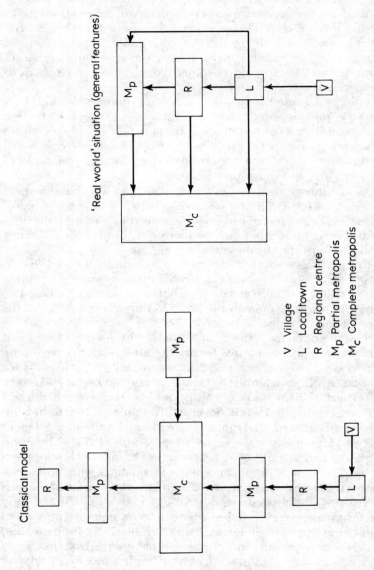

V   Village
L   Local town
R   Regional centre
M_p   Partial metropolis
M_c   Complete metropolis

Figure 5 The urban system: relations between agglomerations

duction, the organization of transport, and the physical and
financial accessibility of individuals to desired goods and services.
Using these factors as a starting point, we can attempt to define a
peripheral situation or a state of 'geographical marginalization' as
Kayser (1972a:521) prefers to call it.

In general, access becomes more restricted as one moves from
the largest city to the countryside. However, an asymmetric
spatial distribution of agglomerations and levels of agricultural
income complicates the picture. In underdeveloped countries, a
spatial coincidence of different modes of transport is to be found:
modern buses use the same highway as horse-drawn carts or
rickshaws; modern means of locomotion are constantly competing with traditional animal and human methods.[6] This coincidence and juxtaposition of old and new is most evident in
peripheral areas, where the quality of roads causes an extreme
specialization of means of transport to be established. Since even
in developed countries, those people living outside large urban
centres have much less access to the means of transport, it is not
surprising that this problem is all the more serious in underdeveloped countries,[7] whose limited resources and externally
oriented economies prevent the necessary level of communications investment from being made. Consequently even
fewer resources remain for the construction of a secondary road
network,[8] and this reduces even further rural inhabitants' access
to market, commercial and service centres, and is instrumental in
their further impoverishment.

An agglomeration's isolation and distance from the industrial
'core' gives merchants, if few in number, the possibility of establishing a monopoly (Mason 1967:101), giving them complete
freedom in setting prices. Consequently, this decreases the
number of consumers and has repercussions for the rest of the
economy, though the merchant himself is not affected. The construction of a new highway makes available previously difficult-
to-obtain and expensive commodities, and consequently local
prices often fall sharply.

Individuals are in general handicapped by being far away from
the economic centre(s) of the country. In underdeveloped countries, such isolation dooms much of the population to poverty.
The concept of 'distance' must be seen in a socio-economic context characterized by the geographical situation of peripheral
areas; this is not a question of physical distance *per se*, but rather of
access. Also there is an increased difficulty of access to private and

public services. These conditions imply a 'devaluation' of the individual as a function of his spatial location.[9]

The rural producer is generally handicapped both as a seller and as a buyer. The producer's weak bargaining position *vis-à-vis* the buyer depends on several factors – the success of the harvest, the type of product sold, whether the product is perishable or not, the ability to substitute imported products, and finally, whether the product will be sold in local or distant markets. The number of middlemen also plays a significant role. Only one thing is certain: the farmer almost always loses out.

Even credit, granted in a number of varied forms, is more limited in periphery. In Tanzania, Hawkins (1965:134) observed that in the major cities 85 per cent to 90 per cent of all merchandise was bought on credit, whereas in the small hinterland cities, the proportion dropped to 60 per cent, indicating both the availability of a more limited range of commercial products, and consequently much higher prices.

The impoverishment of the rural producer implies a reduction in the development-potential of the local city, as well as for the corresponding regional city. Since the benefits of production are appropriated by *compradors* or middlemen, or diminished through the peripheral manifestations of market forces, rural purchasing power is reduced. This means that many activities otherwise capable of developing in the local city cannot do so. As a result, the price of imported products rises and both rural and urban residents become more impoverished. The local city and its surrounding countryside are thus unable to stimulate each other's development, and production and commerce consequently become concentrated in the more important centres. The problem of 'geographical marginalization' constitutes an extreme aspect of regional inequalities.

Regional inequalities and internal colonialism

Regional inequalities may be defined as chronic, structurally-determined, locally interdependent and cumulative disparities between the component sub-spaces of national space, whose primary causes are to be found outside the region; this is why it is so difficult to remove the inequality. Myrdal (1971: Chapter 2) writes of circular accumulation, but one could also speak of circular 'disaccumulation' since regional growth has the capacity to bring about impoverishment (in either relative or absolute terms) in other regions. Favourable local alliances can resist the effects of inequality but even if they manage to prevent absolute impoverishment, either temporarily or permanently, none the less relative impoverishment remains. This tendency is unavoidable, unless imaginative and forceful measures are taken to counteract it.

Spatial inequalities are essentially of three types: regional disparities *per se*, urban-rural inequalities, and differential development between different city-types. Each category of inequality contains various sub-types, which are a function of historical and contemporary factors, usually manifested in the form of situations of dependency.

historical circumstances taken into account.

A *Internal colonialism*

Industrial concentration leads to what has been termed 'internal colonization'; the rest of the nation becomes dependent on these concentrations for the supply of manufactured products or even foodstuffs. As a corollary, the 'colonized' regions themselves finance the growth of the rich regions by sending capital and labour surpluses to the expanding area. However, the analogy often made between this form of domination and *international* domination is inappropriate. There is an essential difference between increased demand and production for domestic consumption, and increased demand resulting in the need to import. One must also, of course, consider the country's level of industrialization. If industry is well developed, the effects of diffusion are much greater, as will be seen later.

The profits accumulated by the dominant classes constitute an obstacle to the dominated classes, for they cannot increase their share of the benefits from collective labour. 'Internal colonialism' can be explained, however, by 'external colonialism', which became generalized in the Third World after the onset of technological modernization. External colonialism is responsible for the selection both of regions capable of polarizing growth as well as firms and individuals (not necessarily foreigners) capable of benefiting from this polarization.

There are many differences between a situation of external economic colonization and one of internal economic colonization. However, two of these differences are particularly significant; on the one hand, despite conditions of dependency, the effects of growth with internal colonialism can be cumulative, for there are fewer obstacles to their diffusion.[10] On the other hand, market forces are free from institutional restraints, especially when taxes and tariffs are absent.

One may also add that the State, in theory, has the power to rectify regional disparities and establish a new equilibrium. It would, however, be necessary to investigate the limits of such action in the present phase of economic history. In the present phase of technological change, unless there is a modification in the individual State's relations with the international economic system, any intervention is likely to come too late.

The State, through its transport, communications, investment, general economic and fiscal policies, can intensify present inequalities or create new ones. Regional disparities can also be aggravated by specific forms of State control of demand.[11]

The expression 'internal colonialism', when used to define a situation of regional or urban inequality, involving the transfer of value to richer regions and/or cities, is dangerous, to say the least, since it tries to draw a parallel with an *international* process. The analogy could lead to great confusion by placing within the same methodological and analytical framework two processes with wholly distinct characters and consequences. As Emmanuel has pointed out in similar fashion, the notion of 'unequal exchange', whilst wholly relevant to the sphere of international trade, has no meaning within a national framework. Hirschman (1958) for example defines 'internal colonialism' of 'north' over 'south' (or coast over interior) in a national context; this amounts to the abandonment of all attempts to industrialize or integrate at the national level. Hirschman appears to advocate the continuing dependence of the 'south' on imports, arguing that the manufactures thereby acquired are cheaper than those who could be locally provided.[12] Such a policy would lead to higher customs barriers *within* the country and lower ones for imports of an industrial nature. This would amount to the loss of any hope for industrialization in the 'south', and also considerably weaken the possibilities of growth in the 'north'.

B *Regional disparities*

Today, regional disparities and what is known as 'internal colonialism' are virtually synonymous. This has not always been true. While situations of regional inequality have become more marked since the arrival of European colonizers, they have always existed, although in other guises. Yet we may only really speak of internal colonialism when, in addition to selective modernization at a geographical level, there is also selective accumulation of capital within the country itself.

How does this mechanism function? Regions, as production areas and no matter how dynamic they may be, do not have the wherewithal to develop integrated production processes. The necessary resources are under the control of cities. One question raised by this is whether regional disparities create different levels of urban development or whether cities, through the diverse nature of their urban 'dynamic' themselves foster regional disparities. The impact of international and national variables upon regional structures generates specific and privileged urban growth. Regions themselves also develop through contact with external forces (national and/or international) and as a function of urban stimuli, whether emanating from specific cities or from the national urban system as a whole.

An historical approach must be used to pinpoint the moment when the city grows independently of the surrounding region. Only those countries colonized – politically and economically – after the second phase of the industrial revolution (when land-transport was revolutionized) were able to create a degree of spatial integration prior to industrialization and the modernization of the State. In such cases, the development of the system was, at least at the beginning, externally dependent within a colonial framework, and hence it was difficult for the city to develop a marked degree of autonomy.

In other countries, only isolated urban systems evolved. Before the 'transport revolution', no real urban network could develop: it was only when links were established between major urban centres that the urban network first became a political, then an economic reality. The latter process could not commence without at least an embryonic industrialization of the country.

Industrialization alters urban-rural relations, or more precisely, the relations between the entire urban system and its corresponding regions. The growth of these two spatial categories is then interdependent with, parallel to or even outside the influence of externally imposed factors.

Resource accumulation eventually becomes more complex and is accompanied by a concentration of economic facilities in certain cities or regions. The most powerful cities, from the point of view of industrial production, are in a position to attract, utilize and even export a substantial part of the value generated in other cities and regions. This ability is coterminous with the ability to nationally integrate the urban network, but one can only talk of the economic control of one city over the rest of national space when the stage of 'subsistence' industrialization and primary production is over. Diversified industrialization clearly requires a wider market and a more developed infrastructure.

While we may consider regional and income inequalities to be the result of the system of national decision-making (Robirosa *et al*. 1971: 52), that very system is both national and international. In Brazil, this situation is the result of a long evolution. During the period when industrial growth was primarily linked to the existence of an urban market and local infrastructure, Rio de Janeiro carried out most of Brazil's industrial production once a regional transport infrastructure had developed, São Paulo began to surpass Rio de Janeiro as an industrial centre, even though Rio was still the federal capital. As São Paulo's production increased, diversified and became more integrated, the industrial significance of other areas suffered a relative decline.

Table 11.1   Value of industrial production (%)

Year	São Paulo	Guanabara (city of Rio de Janeiro)	Rio Grande do Sul	Minas Geraes
1907	16.5	33.0	14.9	–
1920	31.5	20.8	11.0	–
1938	43.2	14.2	10.7	11.3
1959	52.1	14.9	7.6	8.3

Source: Carrion Jr 1970:43, 57.

The economy of north-eastern Brazil is presently experiencing a form of industrial growth partially integrated to that of the southern-central region (Barros de Castro 1971:283). However, this integration is directly tied to foreign countries. Maza Zavala (1969a) calls this 'peripheral growth' because it does not produce multiplier effects within the region itself.

The growth sometimes observed in certain depressed regions does not indicate the reduction of regional disparities: when new activities develop privileged relations with established local activities or use regional inputs, the cumulative effects contribute to a reduction in such disparities. In the reverse case, only economic growth takes place, and *not* social growth. Absolute levels of production increase but neither the population's welfare nor income distribution improve. This is especially true for the establishment of industrial towns, more or less enclaves of foreign countries; this is also true of export industries located so as to benefit from local comparative advantages, such as cheap labour.

The power of the centre becomes more noticeable in the peripheries, when they are interlinked by modern transport. Poor communications systems decelerate and hamper competition from the more advanced centres, and permit cities far removed from the industrial heartland of the country to develop their industries to a level at which regional infrastructural requirements are minimal.

Inter-regional relations may develop through the incorporation of new areas into a growing spatial dynamic: supplies of food, raw material, intermediate goods, labour, etc., are examples of this. The process can evolve in two ways: (i) by the 'contagion effect', when the two areas are contiguous and (ii) over long distances, when strategic inputs are not available at the centre of the dynamic process.

In these two cases, regional inter-relations can be advantageous for both areas. However, examples of such inter-relationships leading to the impoverishment of one or more of the component areas are more frequent. This may happen in three ways: (i) if there is a transfer of cheap, raw products through middlemen and the purchase of expensive, imported manufactured products and foodstuffs, (ii) if the regions impoverished in this way finance, through the transfer of their income, the growth of the most developed regions, and (iii) when the two preceding phenomena produce a migration of trained professional persons to the more developed centres. The poor also migrate, because they become aware that they are underprivileged, and perceive better opportunities elsewhere.

Migration and spatial structure

One consequence of spatial inequality is inter-regional, rural-urban and inter-urban migration, phenomena which have attracted great interest, unfortunately without producing results of great significance.

Morrill's criticisms (1963:4) of geographers are valid for all disciplines. Most research goes astray because it attaches inordinate importance to the personal motivation of each individual,[13]

instead of considering migrations as a spatial manifestation of
processes of historical change. Directly linked to theories based
upon the analysis of subjective motivations, the 'push-pull'
approach treats the two inter-related factors as alternatives in a
dualistic fashion, neglecting the possibility that they could both be
parts of the same system.

The 'underdevelopment' of migration studies is perhaps most
noticeable when examining purely statistical interpretations. For
example, in a frequently quoted article, Harris and Todaro
(1968:35), after vaguely defining the urban population as the
sum 'of the already present and migrant populations', summarize
their theory of the causes of migration by saying 'individuals
migrate in response to expected income differences'. For these
two authors, the rural exodus arises from the inequality between
agricultural and urban incomes. Consequently, if agricultural
income were increased to the level of urban income the causes of
migration would disappear and demographic equilibrium would
be established. Such a view stems from an over-hasty
generalization applied to all Third World countries from
situations existent in only some countries. In reality, the underdeveloped, industrialized or industrializing countries simultaneously experience (a) modernization impact emanating from
the large cities and felt by part of the 'umland' where the mode of
production is becoming industrial (thus making relatively high
wages possible), and (b) a rural exodus impelling many people
toward the 'primitive' tertiary urban sectors. Urban wages may be
lower than those of numerous modern agricultural activities,
even in poor regions. In the north-eastern Brazilian states of
Maranhão and Piaui, 41 per cent of those engaged in agricultural activities earned over 100 cruzeiros, while only 26 per cent
of the individuals engaged in urban services surpassed this
amount (Costa 1971b:5).

New jobs are not only created in the cities. Agricultural expansion into unsettled areas and consequent infrastructural investments improve regional productivity and create employment in
the rural areas themselves. McKee and Leahy (1970b:487) state
that '*per capita* income tends to increase in rural areas, whereas in
urban areas it tends to decrease in such a way that the rate of
migration is higher than the rate of expansion of the labour
force'. One does not go to the city only to find work, nor is it the
level of wages that determines migratory flows. Any explanation
that stresses one factor is liable to over-simplify the situation.

Although the population explosion (Dayal:1959) has been employed to explain migration, concepts such as 'demographic pressure' have been over used. Job hunting, in the Western sense, is insufficient to explain migration; neither is underemployment alone a displacement factor. We can criticize Robirosa's view (*et al.* 1971:60-1) that migrations are attributable to situations of non-employment or underemployment, for it over-generalizes a complex situation. It has already been asserted that 'while the city does not offer the certainty of employment, rural areas offer certain poverty' (Peattie 1968:134).

Migrations not only include unskilled workers, but also those such as artisans, whose skills are required in the city. In a modernization process, though traditional urban activities experience ever-increasing competition from modern activities, craft-products are increasingly in demand. Artisan migration to urban centres is also encouraged by the hope of permanent employment, since in the countryside artisanal activity is often seasonal. Artisans who migrate to the town generally increase their productivity.

Step migration (that is migration in stages – the legacy of ideas developed by Ravenstein (1885) for late nineteenth-century England) has long been venerated by geographers. A theoretical approach to the problem of step migration has been elaborated in several studies. The fact that numerous other studies have given rise to completely opposite conclusions (Pearlman 1971:199; Nelson 1969:11; C.H.I.S.S. 1971:13; Havens and Flinn 1970:201-3) implies that the situation facing the rural underprivileged may have changed.

Nowadays, as a consequence of the 'era of high technology' and the consequent lack of employment expansion, people move from the countryside directly to the metropolis without stopping in the regional or local city. Transportation facilities steer potential migrants toward regional and capital cities where the tertiary sector is more elastic.

The large city is the starting point for *downward* and *outward* migrations of agents of the State and important economic interests, and the focus for *upward* migrations from rural areas and smaller cities. Downward migrations are in harmony with modernization and economic progress, because they involve the transfer of the technologically sophisticated to technologically and economically backward levels. Upward migrations, merely represent a response to extremes of rural poverty.

In industrial countries, where the agricultural population is limited and is decreasing even further, tremendous 'turbulence' in terms of human movement (George 1969) is primarily due to what Kayser calls *the urban exodus*, i.e. population growth of certain cities as compared to others through a process of reciprocal feeding. Studies of this type are not available for the underdeveloped countries. However, Bataillon (1964) points out that in Mexico, the state of Baja California received more people than it sent to Mexico City, and that demographic exchanges between the capital and Monterrey were also considerable.

Surveys conducted among officials in Recife in north-eastern Brazil, revealed that higher echelon employees often originated from southern or north-eastern states incapable of employing them (Correa de Andrade, 1968).

A revolution in consumption patterns has gone hand-in-hand with the technological revolution: while the former has increased the number of consumption units, the latter has necessitated larger, more economically and spatially concentrated production units. This implies the spatial dissociation of the processes of production and consumption: thus we should not be surprised by the scale of contemporary movements of both commodities and people.

Transport and communications have developed rapidly to meet the needs of the modern State.[14] Circulation is a primary condition for the success of economic and social activities. Nevertheless, all goods cannot reach all points in space; nor can all individuals spend valuable time searching for the goods that will satisfy their needs. Since barriers to diffusion are considerable in underdeveloped countries, circulation of goods may be hindered. A smaller area and fewer people are served than in most industrial countries. Consequently, migrations are sometimes irreversible and of considerable proportions.

The more powerful the impact of modernization, the greater is the tendency towards the concentration of production. This results in massive migrations, all the more significant when they are contemporaneous with rapid demographic growth. This brings about a population increase without the necessary social and economic structures to receive them, resulting in the expulsion of people from agricultural activities. Miles (1970:244) suggests that 'mobility is not itself an objective', an idea that can be applied not only to the city but to space in general.

Accelerated modernization generally leads to considerable

spatial inequalities in productivity; internal migration, further aggravating underemployment, is one of the most important consequences of the resulting disequilibrium. The relative importance of cities can also be altered, especially if the conditions for distributing goods are modified. This has the effect of reinforcing the hegemony of the centre (even its current goods production) as the modern sector expands and economic and social distortions become increasingly aggravated.

Given a dynamic perspective, migration appears closely linked to economic and spatial organization. Migration constitutes a response to situations of permanent disequilibrium and yet it worsens the very economic and spatial imbalances which have spawned it, thereby favouring the relative progress of the previously more developed areas. *vicious cycle*

Cumulative concentration and macrocephalous urbanization

Macrocephalous urbanization, as experienced in contemporary underdeveloped countries, is the result of technological progress and its ensuing tendencies towards concentration whereby the initially privileged cities benefit cumulatively and selectively as the major loci of innovation from outside the national framework (McKee and Leahy 1970a:82; Perroux 1955:307).

Norro (1972) points out that 'the nature of urban concentration favours, in a privileged manner, the multiplication of external economies'. The advantages not found in other regions of the country act as a permanent enticement to investors 'since externalities and economies of agglomeration are used essentially by the capitalist sectors of the respective urban centres, while diseconomies are absorbed by the State and the entire population' (Funes 1972: xxx).

Furthermore, metropolises benefit from their strategic position in the modern transport network. This facilitates communication with the rest of the territory, thereby increasing their competitive ability. Experience has shown entrepreneurs that investment in locations other than growth-points is hardly viable (E.A. Johnson 1970:150).

Once established, this domination continues to assert itself, even if other centres register significant growth. 'When unequal growth rates develop, they tend to perpetuate themselves and

growth rate disparities increase because trade and industry concentrate in a particular centre, giving this centre advantages
which attract new development' (Hicks 1969:163). We can
therefore speak of the cumulative growth of permanent
economies of agglomeration (Remy 1966:69). But whether this
octopus effect of large city polarization is permanent remains a
difficult question. The presence of an ever-increasing population
ensures that new economic activities have much of the necessary
overhead capital and infrastructure. Moreover, specific spatial
concentrations of public investment increase the quantum of
capital necessary for the establishment of a new activity. This
tendency toward capital deepening is an essential factor in the
explanation of macrocephalous urbanization.

   The State also promotes macrocephalous growth through the
allocation of priority investments to the cities. For example, between 1970 and 1973 the Brazilian government budgeted 7,494
million cruzeiros for urban projects. About two-thirds were to be
allocated for housing development, and about 15 per cent was
spent on transport and communications. In the South Korean
city of Taegu, public works expenditure rose from 50 per cent of
the total expenditure in 1960 to 70 per cent in 1969, necessitating
reductions in other investments (Whang 1971: Table V, 274).
Thus macrocephalous urbanization appears to have an internally
generated propensity to create the most favourable conditions
for its reproduction.

   Urban primacy has been studied in different ways, but the
definition and characteristics remain the same: the ability to
attract investment and labour; cultural domination; negative
effects on economic growth of other cities; high consumption
rates relative to production (Hoselitz 1957). According to Berry,
primate cities are characteristic of countries that have only recently obtained independence, small countries once having had
larger national territory, and countries where economies of scale
are such that intermediate cities are not created.

   These definitions, however, remain descriptive, and consequently debatable. It is not certain that the rate of consumption
in the primate city is higher than that of production; nor is the
recent acquisition of national independence a major cause of
macrocephalous growth. The cases of Argentina and Mexico
contradict this assertion.

   What matters is not the primate city *itself*, but the factors
responsible for its existence. The same degree of primacy can be

efficient or inefficient from a strictly economic viewpoint. It is a mistake to limit the definition to a simple equation between demographic data, as if primacy were chiefly demographically determined.

Urban primacy must be studied historically: what led to the choice of that particular location? This selectivity is at the root of innovation and accumulation (Wingo 1969:121). Under present conditions concentration is occurring in economic, social and political spheres. The growing concentration of economic activities produces its own problems: large primate cities become increasingly difficult to control, and more and more detached from the needs and opportunities characterizing the rest of the nation.

Primacy is proof of neither parasitism nor unbalanced growth, as Browning (1958:116) and Britton Harris (1959) point out; it is not, itself, an obstacle to development (Alonso 1968:4). National urban systems are primarily the result of historical capital accumulation and impact of conditions imposed by the international system. The emergence of primate cities has intensified the trend toward a monopolization of economic space: such cities have even earned the apt epithet 'monopolises' (Morrison 1972).

Is macrocephaly irreversible, as certain people believe?[15] Under present conditions in underdeveloped capitalist countries, a spontaneous change of situation would be primarily due to external causes. Nevertheless, coherent action by the State can also yield results. Selective and sectorial initiatives as suggested by Gauthier (1971:2) generally produce the opposite results to those intended.

Let us therefore re-examine the question raised by Harrison-Church (1972): 'Is it possible to think of an undesirable decentralization?' To answer this, all national and international causes of macrocephalous growth must be considered. This, however, implies the elaboration of a comprehensive and courageous programme by a State cognizant of the difficulty of attempting to modify the status quo. We must consider urbanization as a sub-system of the world and national system, and macrocephalous urbanization as just one of its manifestations.[16]

When powerful forces are present,[17] especially if they are exogenous and representative of multinational capital, governments find themselves planning in a totally defenceless and vulnerable environment, unless they decide to alter the nature of their relations with the international economic system, a change rarely envisaged by the State.

Metropolises and intermediate cities

The intermediate city and the national metropolis have the same origin, but only the latter benefits relatively from spatial concentration.[18] Situations in which dynamic and highly productive industries move from the centre of the country to the less developed periphery, such as Berry (1971:116) describes, are difficult to find in the underdeveloped countries, unless there is intervention through development programmes in the depressed regions.

Berry believes that, because of high wage-levels in the large cities, it is in the interest of industries to relocate in smaller cities. He does not seem to consider the monopolistic conditions generally accompanying the establishment of modern industries: wages do not increase faster than productivity, and profitability is largely dependent on conditions found only in the large cities. While some low-wage industries may find the conditions in middle-sized cities conducive, others will remain in the large cities because of their fundamental relations with most dynamic industries. In the middle-sized or smaller cities, oligopolistic conditions benefiting modern industries do not generally prevail.

The relationship between the intermediate city and the primate city is very often the same as that described by Myrdal (1971) for the relationship of cumulative causation between growth and backwardness. The lack of dynamism of the urban economy recoils on the region and vice versa. Prices are important: if a city does not produce a certain product, the product will be sold there at a higher price; consequently, the residents buy less and prices increase even more. As for mobile, well-off consumers, the intermediate city can be bypassed by purchasing in the more important cities. A negative feedback effect sets in to the detriment of the intermediate city and its region, and this may initiate the impoverishment of the region or a delay in regional and urban growth. The disparity with other regions widens and the tendency for economic and geographic development to be macrocephalous is further aggravated, at least in relative terms. A double polarization (E.A. Johnson 1970) takes place – the accumulation of possibilities and the worsening of deficiencies.

The marginal upper circuit

The relations existing between the industrial activity of the upper circuit proper and that of the marginal upper circuit (MUC) vary according to whether one is dealing with a complete metropolis, a partial metropolis, or an intermediate city.

In the complete metropolis, there is no spatial distinction between the two types of upper circuit. The market is unified despite cost differentials resulting from differences in technology and organization. Actually, these differences help establish a complicity within the market. The higher input costs in the MUC serve as a reference point to the upper circuit which adjusts its prices to those of the former, thereby increasing its profits.

In the partial metropolis, certain industrial branches cannot exist without the MUC. Because certain local external economies are absent in the upper level of manufacturing activity, two levels of the upper circuit crystallize. There is a distinction, however, between the partial metropolises of the underdeveloped, industrialized countries and those of the non-industrialized countries. In the former, partial metropolises display many characteristics of intermediate cities, while in the latter, they generally constitute the primate city of the country.

On the other hand, there is no question of an *alliance* between the upper ciruit of the metropolis and the MUC of the intermediate cities. The two types of activities, separated geographically, tend to be competitive. The MUC is capable of protecting itself partly because of spatial distance and partly due to its relations with the lower circuit (either directly or through wholesalers).

While large upper circuit industrial firms can easily create their own commercial outlets in the metropole, the same cannot be achieved in the intermediate city where the wholesaler is still an essential agent of distribution for the products of the metropolitan upper circuit as well as that of the upper circuit and the MUC of the intermediate city itself.

In the intermediate city, industries of the MUC must pay special attention to the prices they charge. Here, any upward price movement jeopardizes the MUC's activities by encouraging upper circuit competition.

The intermediate city's MUC, because of its inability to manipulate prices, is dependent on the level of consumption. There is consequently a basic difference between the behaviour of the MUC in the metropolis and in the intermediate cities. In the latter case, production increases as a function of demand, which plays the key role and not, as with monopolies, a subordinate role.

Does any factor in this situation constitute an element of strength for the MUC which could be used in competition with the monopolistic upper circuit in the country's heartland? Because it is adapted to regional life, the MUC is vulnerable only to strategies of integration emanating from the centre. Thus, whenever the metropolis has direct relations with local cities, the MUC of the intermediate cities becomes vulnerable.[19]

Accelerated urbanization might contribute to the disappearance of the MUC. Yet, accelerated urbanization follows accelerated modernization, and modernization does not take place without the relative impoverishment of the masses, especially in the periphery. Therefore, it is not so much a question of the disappearance of the MUC but rather of its co-existence, as much with the upper circuit as with the lower circuit.

Intermediate cities generally have industries whose markets are seldom wider than the region. Often, this market is confined to the city itself (Rochefort 1964; Norro 1972). Thus, as the economic heartland succeeds in comprehensively supplying more and more regions of the country (due to the expansion of the transport network) the peripheral cities see their urban sphere of influence shrinking, irrespective of the size of their population. Regional control is carried out through the highly specialized services of the government, or those directly springing from the needs of the mass of the population to be served. Every time a city is chosen for politico-administrative functions, these possibilities increase. The conclusion is clear: intermediate cities have little to offer to their urban or regional populations, or so we are led to believe by such studies as Resources for the Future (1966:40). But such cities are *not* the passive, stagnant and forgotten centres that they are often assumed to be; they are more than stepping-stones for migrants on the road to the metropolis. Intermediary cities offer at least a number of commodities which would otherwise not be made available. Most certainly they provide a most useful 'conveyor-belt' for government policy in the regions.

12

The shared space

Industrialization processes and urbanization tendencies

As outlined previously, there are two related industrialization trends in underdeveloped countries, one essentially linked to domestic consumption (which we shall call type 'A'), the other ('B'), based mainly on the external market. However, this generalization is far from perfect. On the one hand, firms created to serve an urban market can, at any given moment, increase in scale and export part of their output. On the other hand, firms whose output was originally earmarked for export can at the same time serve the domestic market. However, in this chapter, only the dominant tendencies will be considered: the term 'industrialization' refers more to process rather than form: certain forms such as the firm or city may be representative of *both* processes of industrialization.

Thus the present state of industrial activity in underdeveloped countries forces us to consider the whole urban system as being composed of two superimposed networks – one essentially linked to domestically oriented industrial activity ('A' industrialization) and the other to export-oriented industrial activity ('B' industrialization). These forms of industrialization should be defined in functional and not morphological terms. Each has its particular socio-economic and geographical implications, co-existing at the national, but not always at the local level. Certain urban agglomerations such as mining and specifically industrial towns have just one type of industrialization.

The probabilities of these two industrialization processes establishing themselves in the urban system are unequal (Fig. 6).

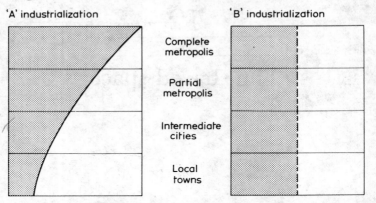

Figure 6 Industrialization trends and the urban system

Though the likelihood of 'A' industrialization is greater in the metropolis, especially if the latter is 'complete', the possibilities for type 'A' tend to diminish as urban complexity decreases. The feasibility of establishing industrialization process 'B' depends less on city-size or functional level: industries can be located anywhere in the system. 'A' industrialization requires external economies – external, that is, to the firm – and is supported by regional or national infrastructure, while type 'B' has no need of this infrastructure, and often creates its external economies *inside* the firm, or finds the necessary economies outside the country. Modern, externally oriented industry is therefore to a certain extent locationally mobile insofar as it is able to create easily and quickly its required environment.

'A' industrialization corresponds to Prebisch's concept of the *complex internal economy* (Amin 1971:251-2).

Until the Second World War, Third World industrialization was exclusively type 'A' (traditional colonial export industries excepted), but the present possibility of establishing re-exporting or less complex externally oriented industries has since changed the situation. The economy does not have to be completely extroverted for type 'B' industries to be present. The locational strategy of purely export-oriented industry has been considerably affected by the emergence and hegemony of the multinational corporation. Previous forms of industrial organization could satisfy all their requirements at one point, often the capital city and/or major port. The advantages were obvious: facilities for large-scale unloading of goods, the commercial, financial and communications infrastructure, and the machinery of the State. The transport network, initially based on the colonial railroad system, also favoured concentration. Difficult transport and communications conditions made it imperative that the services essential to commerce and industry were controlled *in situ*: thus a large administration and management group, often of foreign nationality, evolved in the developing countries, particularly in the mineral transformation and agricultural processing sectors. At present modern mining in less-developed economies, for example, requires only the appropriate infrastructure and a minimal usually foreign, tertiary sector.

The nature and objectives of many new export industries make them less dependent on regional conditions. Most of the raw materials are imported, regional infrastructure is no longer required and local infrastructure is relatively easily created by the State. This explains why many such industries are located irrespective of urban 'level'. It is hardly surprising that the large, developed country's enterprises locate parts of their production-processes in depressed regions, especially when the State, through regional development programmes and other incentives, creates such a favourable regional environment for foreign investment.

Modern externally oriented industries can be located without consideration of the potential or actual domestic market, simply because their market lies elsewhere. The position of a particular city within the urban hierarchy does not necessarily explain their presence: the reasons for their location there must be sought in the specific international conditions. Certain industries, particularly those using bulk raw materials, benefit from location in industrial towns solely created for them. The government often directly or indirectly intervenes in this process, believing such activities to be essential to achieve growth.

The urbanization process and its constituent subsystems

From the above analysis, we can posit an urbanization process comprising two subsystems of urbanization: 'Urbanization 1', the product of some combination of industrialization processes 'A' and 'B' and 'Urbanization 2' arising uniquely out of Industrialization 'B'. The evolution of 'Urbanization 2' into

'Urbanization 1' is always a possibility.

In the case of 'Urbanization 1', the more integrated a city's industrial activities the greater will be the multiplier effect on the surrounding region as well as on the rest of the country. Despite a certain dependence on foreign countries, the industrial activity of cities undergoing 'Urbanization 1' will be largely internally oriented. Thus 'Urbanization 1' could be defined as an *introverted* subsystem (nation-building) while 'Urbanization 2' is predominantly extroverted and exploitative.

To consider 'Urbanization 1' as introverted does not mean that profits remain within the country: a significant proportion goes abroad. Compared to the other urbanization subsystem, however, the introverted system has a certain generative capacity and domestic multiplier effects.

The existence of these two urbanization subsystems and their corresponding spatial organizations is a direct consequence of the new international division of labour. Not only are the two variants of industrialization coterminous, but so too are the activities of the urban economy's two circuits. The latter may overlap throughout the urban system, in metropolises and in industrial towns alike.

A *Introverted urbanization*

This variant of urbanization can be identified at metropolitan, regional/intermediate and local urban levels: however, precise content will depend upon the technical conditions and extent of spatial organization at all three levels, and the manner in which the three levels interact as a consequence.

The location of domestically oriented modern activity supposes the locational advantages of city size, degree of cosmopolitanism, externalities and the existence of a national and regional infrastructure serving the city. The concentration of activity in the metropolis is also explained by greater accessibility to general and specialized information.

Local cities have limited possibilities for generating and supporting modern activities because of the limited local market and the monopolistic nature of certain aspects of regional commerce, which have an effect on prices which further reduces the number of consumers. Such intermediate cities clearly cannot sustain modern activities commensurate with their potential market when such activities already exist in the metropolis under conditions which inhibit competition either partially or totally. Moreover modern communications-links between major production-centres and principal centres of consumption are an additional obstacle. Finally, the dominant role of the industrial metropolis enables it to bypass the intermediate city, leaving the latter without effective control. Stohr (1972) is possibly right in believing that the 'urban hierarchy' and the 'region' are more conceptual than factual.[1]

The many inter-urban flows (predominantly consisting of a migration of persons up and through the hierarchy, and the passage of goods in a downwards direction) and the absence of a rigid urban hierarchy are explained by this spatial distribution of modern activities. All cities within the system can have direct relations with the largest cities without regional city mediation (Fig 7). Gormsen (1972) demonstrates this for Mexico while Kayser (1972a, b) has constructed a more general theory for Latin America. I have myself tried to make a more general case for the whole Third World (Santos 1971).

This scheme is of course imperfect, for certain merchants can supply themselves from wholesalers in larger cities; moreover, the smallest urban centres, generally outside the principal road and rail networks, are incapable of direct communication with the

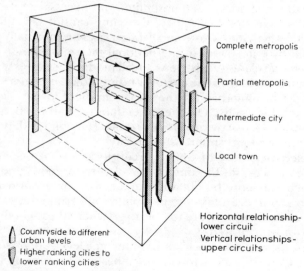

Complete metropolis

Partial metropolis

Intermediate city

Local town

Horizontal relationship-
lower circuit
Vertical relationships-
upper circuits

Countryside to different
urban levels
Higher ranking cities to
lower ranking cities

Figure 7 The macro-system of inter-urban relations

industrial metropolis, or even with the region's large cities, and thus remain dependent on the nearest agglomeration.

The degree of modernization of agricultural space should not be ignored: rural modernization takes place in response to foreign demand, as in the case of the introduction of commercial or industrial export crops, or as a result of domestic industrial demand. It may also be induced by governmental measures to encourage food production, or may simply be a 'spontaneous modernization' resulting from urban growth.

Rural modernization almost always involves a bypassing of the small cities, reinforced by the concentration of the upper circuit. Agricultural modernization requires commercial, administrative and banking facilities which small and intermediate cities cannot provide. Thus large cities monopolize most exchanges with the dynamic rural regions and leave the other agglomerations of the system only minimal responsibilities and benefits. The small city thus becomes increasingly distributive and decreasingly a combiner and transformer of regional inputs.

A complete integration between city and surrounding countryside can no longer be imagined, for relations tend to become asymmetric. The types of goods and services supplied by the city do not coincide with those demanded of it. Yet, while non-modern rural activities maintain limited but necessary relations with similar activities in the city, the same cannot be said for modern rural activities whose ancillary services are normally only carried out by enterprises in the national metropolis.[2]

Thus *vertical* relations exist between all modern activities within the urban network, with the corresponding flows of persons and commodities passing through the upper circuit of towns in other levels of the hierarchy. On the other hand, relations between urban non-modern activities are horizontal (Fig. 6); i.e. they take place within the local sphere of each city.

The selective nature of upper circuit location has essentially two consequences: (a) the immobility of certain goods and services which can only be obtained or used in or around their production-source, and (b) the immobility of certain individuals who, for various reasons, are unable to go where these goods and services can be acquired.

All persons, whatever their status or income level, are prisoners of their city with regard to certain types of consumption, for example, goods and services which by their nature or because of the frequency of demand, require mutual proximity in space and time. The ability to escape the restrictions of the local market for other goods and services depends on an individual's mobility, which is closely linked to income.

When demand is less dependent on an immediate spatial or temporal response, its satisfaction depends on other factors: for example, the consumption profile of each income group will determine whether the economies of scale necessary for the highly efficient production or marketing of certain goods can be achieved. Urban population distribution, the number of private vehicles and amount of public transport facilities similarly act to modify the situation. The position of a town within the urban system is another important factor: this will be a function of the 'rank' of the closest large city and its accessibility to the privileged classes of the lower-rank city and its catchment area. The greater this accessibility, the more difficult it will be for the lower city to promote its own modern production and commercial activities, even if a potentially viable local market exists.

Two other possibilities, however, should be noted: when the State creates certain local services, or when an 'export' firm, already established in the city, promotes new activities simultaneously serving both itself and other firms or the community, these new activities will be established without reference to the level of local demand. Therefore, the creation of modern activities in a city does not depend exclusively on the existence of a potential market, i.e. a certain pre-existing level of activity and income distribution. The establishment of local modern activity also depends on prices in the nearest higher rank cities, as well as on the feasibility and advantages of purchases being made in these cities by the rich. The nucleus of the potential market lies in the classes capable of frequent high-level consumption, but is nevertheless augmented by the periodic purchases of the less-favoured classes.

However, there is variability from product to product: factors, here, include the economies of scale particular to each product, the scale and the organizational level of production located elsewhere, the cost of transportation, the volume and turnover of local demand, and the poor's share in aggregate demand. The more complex and integrated the urban economy, the greater is the tendency for prices to be lower than in other cities of the system. Thus mobile consumers tend to seek certain goods in the upper-rank cities, to the extent that transportation costs are not an obstacle. This price differential, however, is irrelevant for immobile consumers, who remain prisoners of the relatively backward cities upon which they must depend for most if not all of their consumption needs. Figure 9 shows the typical situations facing cities with high and rudimentary levels of economic integration, though this is a simplification of the complete range of possibilities.

For each individual, according to his income, access to credit, mobility and the goods he buys, the role of the regional city can be played by the intermediate city as well as the metropolis. The privileged classes, having higher purchasing power and mobility will deal directly to the higher urban level. The local city, supplying goods and services for day-to-day consumption, exercises this role for all inhabitants. The local city is also called upon to fill higher level functions for those having only limited mobility (Fig. 8). Thus the urban network does not have the same repercussions on all socio-economic classes.

B *Extroverted urbanization*

Before the current high-technolgy era, extroverted industrial activity was confined to industrial or mining towns and to some ports. However, as we have seen, these activities can now be established in any city, provided it enjoys local comparative advantages such as a local infrastructure, externalities and cheap labour. Since this type of industry does not require a complicated and well-developed regional infrastructure, nor localized external economies, a certain decentralization is possible.

Export and re-export industries tend to distort the national economy at different levels, utilizing large quantities of public goods and taking advantage of export subsidies granted by the State. Their imports devour a significant portion of total foreign exchange and thereby worsen the balance of payments situation; they use a considerable part of the national budget whilst contributing little or nothing themselves. These serious drawbacks are further aggravated by non-national control of such activities: the mother company is dependent upon the production level in the host-country, and thus any relations existing between these industries and the rest of the economy are subordinated to foreign interests. Moreover, the facilities offered to these enterprises may encourage them to undertake an important role in the domestic market and even to attempt to eliminate any competing national industry, thus further reducing national control over strategic sectors of production.

Extroverted industries are often sited in industrial estates even if these were originally conceived with other objectives in mind. Nevertheless the principal industrial zones are the clearest evidence of the extroverted nature of many industrial activities in underdeveloped economies. Industrial towns specialize in a certain type of activity, and are therefore monofunctional. They serve largely foreign modern production, located specifically to profit from fixed external economies or other fixed advantages such a raw materials, energy and cheap labour. These agglomerations should be referred to as 'towns' to distinguish them from true cities: they enjoy no autonomous control over their basic activities, which are integrated to foreign production and distribution circuits.

In industrial countries, specialization usually results from the need to maximize productivity within a system based on national and/or international complementarity: local assets enter an integrated system of production, thereby contributing to the establishment of increased levels of national and *local* productivity, the latter precisely because local 'specialized' activities serve as external economies and provide multiplier effects for extra-local activities.

In underdeveloped countries, specialization usually does not stem from a regional or national productive network, but from externally imposed requirements. Specialization here is synonymous with a scale of production often greatly exceeding and/or completely indifferent to local consumption

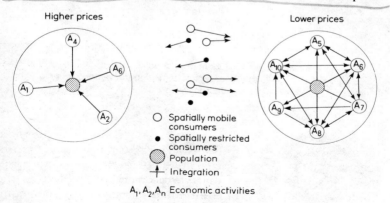

Figure 8 Consumer mobility and market access

requirements. The urban economy is subordinated to the principal production processes whose structure distorts the socio-economic life, not merely of the town but of the entire region, syphoning off much-needed public resources for its own sake.

Relations between dominant and subordinate activities depend both upon the nature of the former's input requirements and on the aggregate urban economic environment. Linkage or multiplier effects seldom exist because the high technology activity is usually externally oriented (Fig. 9) both in terms of its supply of factor-inputs and the demand for its output; moreover, when activity is seasonal, the creation of local complementary activities is difficult if not impossible.

Dependency upon a non-local market is a source of contradiction between relevant decision-making of the firm and the development of other urban activities. The relations between the zone of industrial concentration, the region in which it is located,

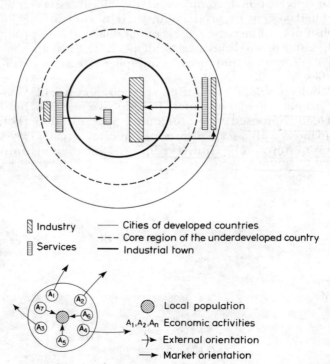

▨ Industry	——	Cities of developed countries
	‐‐‐	Core region of the underdeveloped country
▤ Services	——	Industrial town

Local population
A_1, A_2, A_n Economic activities
→ External orientation
→ Market orientation

Figure 9 Spatial non-articulation of activities at the national level

and the country as a whole depend on the type and scale of local, regional and national production. Access is also a strategic variable in determining these relations: the distance between dynamic urban centres and their hinterland inhibits the evolution of complementarities, positive linkages and a high degree of mutually beneficial exchange in precisely the same manner as it encourages and facilitates the integration of the dynamic centres into the international network of external relations. Thus the urban industrial concentration has the characteristics of an enclave, which necessarily militate against authentic national growth and development. Also contradictions evolve between the industrial centre and its surrounding socio-economic space, whereby the latter, unable to contribute to local industry's principal activities because of its low level of scale and technology, becomes incapable of imposing itself in any significant way at the regional level.[3]

From the point of view of national development, industrial towns may pose serious problems for underdeveloped countries: while contributing quantitatively to aggregate economic growth, their role in structural transformation is negative, particularly when industrialization is recent and when relative modernization has been rapidly achieved.

Little local dynamic influence is exerted by these industries, they are able to deeply modify national spatial organization in their favour, through the transport and communications system. The organization of national space responds almost exclusively to foreign interests, a process which is directly or indirectly subsidized by both national income in general and by public expenditure in particular.

Only the lower circuit is capable of maintaining relations with regional activities because the external orientation, high level of technology and consequent high cost of output in modern urban activities militates against any appreciable degree of exchange being established with the relatively more backward sectors in the regional economy.

Extroverted industry is often located in areas where the absence of industrial development has caused further deterioration in employment opportunities. Its presence, however, produces few multiplier effects: surrounding areas continue to depend upon central regions for many essential supplies. A wide gap between domestic industrial and agricultural growth may develop; linkages with local and national activities will be minimal, and, conse-

quently, other local activities will tend to develop into an expanding lower circuit the size of which will vary with the size of the
town in question and the intensity of migration (both at the
regional and national levels) affecting it.

The entire economy is dragged even further into the mire of
economic extroversion: employment expansion is minimal, the
distorted export sector comes under more pressure to generate
surpluses to pay for a growing level of imports. The rationale
behind the implanted industries is itself externally oriented; thus
little correspondence is to be expected between its own motivations and strategies and those relating to the development of the
national economy and the satisfaction of national aspirations.
Such industries operate with a short time-horizon: they can be
shut down at a moment's notice, or can cut back employment
and/or production at will. Should any favourable impact on the
regional or national economy be expected?

Yet 'depressed' regions are not the exclusive locational preference of extroverted industry: it often establishes itself in large
cities in order to take advantage of an already existing infrastructure. The creation of industrial zones and estates near ports
and major cities is a common infrastructural policy intended to
attract new industry, based on the belief that industrialization
should be achieved at any price. The benefits are often illusory,
for the policy neglects other locational factors, especially when
foreign industry has a high degree of monopoly. In many countries and regions the industrial estates have remained virtually
unused: in Venezuela, for example (Mendez 1970), practically all
medium-sized cities built an industrial estate, but many have
subsequently become local sports fields. In fact, industrial concentration in the major urban areas (Pericchi 1971) hampers the
diffusion of industry because of increasingly centralized
monopoly-power, relatively easy inter-centre transport, and
increasing population concentration in the regional centres. A
few successful estates provide good nationalist propaganda: consequently, more industrial estates are built without due consideration being given to the specific national economic structure
in question and the corresponding regional differentiation. Such
a policy merely enlarges the proportion of total resources
allocated to infrastructure to the detriment of other investments.
Industrial estate projects can only be efficient if integrated into a
general development strategy, which hardly seems likely in the
present conjuncture considering the nature of the industries

being established. Without authentic integration, industrial estates are totally inefficient in domestic terms, for their multiplier effects are transferred outside national boundaries (Perroux 1966) with minimal positive effects at the local level.⟩

The two circuits and the urban system

A *The upper circuit*

The various economic activities of the two circuits operate within specific types of city according to laws specific to the two circuits. Modern industry is attracted least to the lowest-rank urban areas of the system, and finds the available environment progressively more conducive to its activities as it ascends the urban hierarchy. There are, nevertheless, exceptions to this generalization, arising specifically out of the establishment of extroverted industry, which have already been discussed in this chapter.

The presence of modern trade seems to increase with the size and functional level of the city (Fig. 10). There are many reasons for this, a few of which will be cited here. The larger the city, the greater will be the size of its wage-labour force (including public servants and professionals) and consequently, the larger its market for modern consumer goods. The number of modern retail outlets increases, thereby reducing the number of petty middlemen which in turn permits a further increase in the number of modern establishments. The expansion of commerce

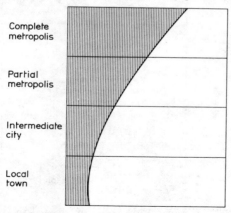

Figure 10 Modern commerce in the urban system

188 *The Shared Space*

is further encouraged by an increase in institutionally creditworthy persons, allowing a more liberal use of modern credit. The proximity of industry, whose qualitative and quantitative impact tends to increase with city size, contributes to the fall in consumer prices, thereby favouring access to the products provided by industry for the local market. Such factors contribute to increase the number of buyers (regular, occasional, urban or rural), thus reinforcing the scale requirements of establishing modern commercial enterprises.

The significance of export and import trade activities also varies with the city's functional level: the disparity is much more pronounced for the import trade, which is sensitive to fluctuations whilst the export trade, due to its direct link with foreign exchange earnings, is freely subsidized by the State. Less protected and more vulnerable, import firms have experienced a more marked economic and geographical concentration. Possibilities for expansion outside the national metropolitan area are more limited for import than for export firms (Fig. 11).

When industrial production is oriented toward the domestic market, it may require a wide range of services from its host city. Marginal industries (modern activities with limited levels of technology and management expertise and relatively high labour-intensity) and modern trade will be even more dependent on the local provision of services. On the other hand, extroverted indus-

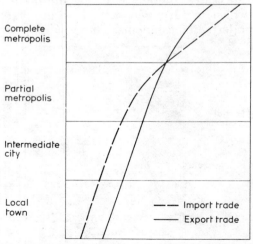

Figure 11 Imports and exports in the urban system

try requires relatively few local services, relying mainly on services provided externally, since their level of industrial activity is
generally well above that of other activities. Only major metropolises are able to provide the service-inputs required by
extroverted industry.

It is by no means certain whether tertiary industry is generally
more internationally foot-loose than secondary industries, as
Lean (1969:54) has suggested: minimal conditions for establishing many modern services are not usually found below particular threshold levels of general local economic activity. On the
other hand a larger proportion of industry in underdeveloped
countries is able to internalize external economies.

The complete metropolis has at its disposal a very large number
of modern services necessary for the proper functioning of its
economy and administration. This situation partly results from a
localized integration of the economy; the number and quality of
these services of course diminishes as one descends the urban
hierarchy. The State can introduce distortion into the service-
sector by creating services commensurate neither with the size of
the agglomeration nor the level of real demand, thereby disrup-
ting resource flows throughout the system. It is even possible, as
Richardson (1969:90) has shown, that certain public services can
be provided more efficiently in small cities.

Upper circuit activities of the local city (the lowest level on the
urban scale) generally serve the population and develop to a scale
commensurate with the size of the market. In the national metropolis, upper circuit activities are inter-related and interdependent: the more pronounced the country's industrialization,
the more local autonomy will be accorded metropolitan activities,
that is, they will be able to mutually support each other and create
their own markets, instead of being subject to the vagaries of the
market itself.

B *The lower circuit*

What is the significance of non-modern commerce in the various
types of urban area found in underdeveloped countries? What
determines its expansion in each city? The presence and impact
of lower circuit trade appears to vary inversely with the functional
rank of the city, and is positively encouraged by its proximity
(measured in distance, time or cost) from the most industrialized
city.

At the lower levels of the system, any obstacle to modern commodity production and/or marketing limits the total number of clients: many potential local consumers find it both more convenient and cheaper to purchase directly in larger cities. When this clientele becomes substantial, the conditions in these cities are ripe for an increase in scale for many activities, and for others to reach the minimum scale required. Thus the smallest cities lose the opportunity of having such activities of their own while the partial and complete metropolises reinforce their hegemony. It is evident that only the privileged classes can shop regularly and/or in bulk in the upper circuit; those who cannot afford to travel are consequently confined to the local market, and must therefore use the lower circuit's distribution system. Since the number able to travel decreases proportionally with the size and rank of the city, modern commerce will be less, and non-modern commerce relatively more significant, the lower we descend the urban hierarchy.

Employment in export-oriented industry in small cities can introduce an element of distortion into the commercial system by stimulating the creation of modern retail trade: however, this type of activity has minimal direct multiplier effects on other urban activities, especially if the retail outlets in question are for the exclusive use of company employees.

Service activities in the lower circuit are principally created to serve the mass of the population's economic activities with no regular access to upper circuit services; these services nevertheless function in aggregate as external economies for lower circuit activities.

The importance of lower circuit services increases with the size of the city. In the small city they fulfil the functions of an often non-existent modern service-sector, whereas in the large city, despite the large number of modern services, they respond to the needs of the impoverished urban masses. Also, in the large city, the specialization and diversity of lower sector services increases because of their collaboration with modern activities.

Above a certain level of urban population, two types of lower circuit can be distinguished according to their location: one is situated in the central areas, the other in the residential districts. There is not only locational specificity, but also clear distinctions in the mode of operation of the two variants of the lower circuit.

The 'central' lower circuit serves the mass of the population, but it is characterized by its privileged relations with the other central activities of the modern sector. Its customers, who often pay cash, may also be clients of the upper circuit. The residential lower circuit, on the other hand, is linked comprehensively to popular demand. Thus, in the city centre the connections between all the elements of the urban economy are more numerous and frequent. Since the centre constitutes the transport terminus, the bulk-breaking point and the place of interaction for different social strata, certain lower circuit activities can profit from these advantages and assume specific forms. In residential districts lower circuit activities can often be explained by the need to respond, often on credit, to the rudimentary needs of the urban poor. These two forms of lower circuit activity interact either through hawkers and street-sellers or through wholesalers generally located in the city centre.

The relative significance of lower circuit activities from one urban centre to another (Fig. 12) varies inversely with the size of the urban centre. However, the absolute number of lower circuit activities continues to increase as the size of cities increases. Even the populations of complete metropolises are experiencing a process of impoverishment, a phenomenon which has been accentuated by the fact that rural-urban migration has been primarily towards the large cities.

Population, through its role as generator of activities (Paix 1972) necessarily entails an expansion of the lower circuit, since, under conditions of technological change, the number of full-time jobs locally created tends to be considerably lower than the number of people requiring full-time employment.

Lower prices at the source of modern production exacerbate the demonstration effect, distorting the consumption-patterns of the urban poor. This distortion also represents an obligation to

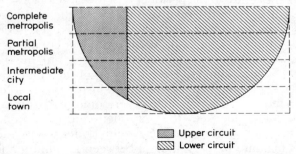

Figure 12 Relative significance of the two circuits in the urban system as a whole

pay either in cash or in instalments, which reduces or exhausts liquidity, and necessitates recourse to personal credit (and hence the lower circuit). There is clearly no paradox in the fact that the growth of the upper circuit stimulates a proliferation of lower circuit activities. Also, the phenomenon of 'friction of activities' (Haig 1926) helps to explain the multiplier effect found in small-scale activities; these enterprises serve and sustain each other, mainly due to the presence of a mass of people without permanent jobs, performing any petty activity in order to survive.

Two urban circuits and the problems of central place theory

Among others, J.H. Johnson (1966:99), Wheatley (1969:6), Marchand (1970), E.A. Johnson (1970) and Miller (1971:321) have expressed serious doubts about the application of central place theory to the Third World. Concerning the concept of a minimum viable market threshold, criticism has been levelled by numerous authors such as Bunge (1962), Davies (1968: 146), Daly and Brown (1964:6) and Scott (1970). Is it possible to identify a single threshold when one accepts that the urban economy comprises two subsystems, each of which is closely associated with a specific section of the population? The concept of threshold appears all the more problematical when, on the one hand, the middle classes appear capable of frequent consumption in either circuit, and, on the other hand, when the two economic circuits clearly interact.

Though the volume and complexity of lower circuit activities tends to diminish from centre to periphery, from metropolis to small town, its sphere of influence or 'urban field' tends to increase from the centre to the periphery. In the largest cities the lower circuit is confined to the relative outskirts of the agglomeration, whereas in the local town, territorial influence is exercised *through* the lower circuit (see Fig. 13). As for the upper circuit, its sphere of influence tends to be the greater, the higher ranking is the city within the urban system. Under monopolistic conditions, the urban market itself is often sufficient to justify the establishment of certain modern industries. However, some goods appeal to the entire national market: the gap between minimum viable market-size and potential market would, under these conditions, attain its maximum. This interval between minimum and maximum range tends to decline from the metropolis to the local city.

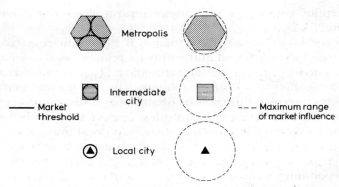

Figure 13 The lower circuit in the urban system

While the minimum viable market-size may coincide with urban population at the upper urban levels, at lower levels, a wider market surface must be covered. This partly explains why local towns can only with difficulty support modern activities: the minimum market threshold of these activities generally exceeds the absorptive capacity of the town and its maximum potential market.

For local towns, there is a purely 'hypothetical' threshold for upper circuit activities (Fig. 14); however, this scale is never attained. Under these conditions, the production or marketing of certain goods can only be managed by upper level cities. Consequently both minimal viable market-size and maximum range equally are hypothetical for low-ranking urban areas. Getis and Getis define the ideal range of market influence as being 'the maximum radius resulting from the increase of price with dista-

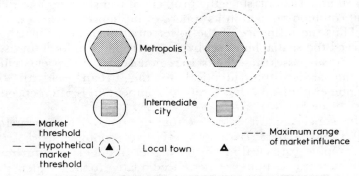

Figure 14 The upper circuit in the urban system

nce, until consumers will no longer purchase the product' (1966:221-2).

In the lower circuit, the situation is in certain respects the reverse of what is found in the upper circuit: in local towns, the difference between range and threshold is at a maximum. Due to the non-penetration of many modern activities, the lower circuit assumes the role of distributor of all commodities because of its more adaptable and flexible attitudes. The extension of the lower circuit's sphere of influence in the case of local towns is mainly due to the 'periodic market' phenomenon, as much in the cities as in the space around the lower-ranking agglomerations.

Depending on city size, the magnitude of lower circuit activities may vary during the year. The fluctuations are sharper in small towns: these are more dependent upon seasonal regional activities which generate much of the cash spent in the lower circuit. In big cities, so many activities are superimposed or inter-related that, over time, fluctuations are damped and the lower circuit's dimensions are maintained. The lower circuit in the metropolis is much larger than the lower circuit of smaller towns, yet it is unable to maintain relations with other agglomerations of the system, something only the upper circuit is capable of achieving.

In the larger cities, the lower circuit's operating costs are relatively higher than in other cities of the system. Money-relations have become more generalized, wage-earning more widespread, and wages themselves are higher. 'Subsistence' consumption involves a large number of goods and services: since, in the lower circuit, subsistence-employment is the rule and thus the cost of subsistence tends to rise. Transport costs must also be taken into account, since the problem of transporting lower circuit commodities within its sphere of influence also arises.

Thus the influence of the lower circuit can never match or exceed the spatial limits set by the metropolis: in local towns, it greatly surpasses these limits. In regional cities, the lower circuit's influence is often identical to the urban field of the agglomeration, and thus local-city competition is often encountered (see Fig. 15).

In conclusion, it is interesting to note that Friedmann (1961:100; 1963:357) defines 'effective economic space' as a geographical area within which a higher frequency of intra-zone economic transactions is experienced relative to the frequency of transactions with other areas, since this closely approximates the

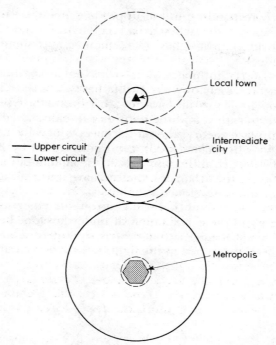

Figure 15 Spheres of influence and the urban hierarchy

definition of 'polarized space' advanced by Boudeville (1961) (though the latter does not make the assumption that economic behaviour within the area in question must be homogeneous). Friedmann's and Boudeville's concepts could be used with equal usefulness to characterize such complete metropolises as Buenos Aires or Cairo. But Friedmann's definition as it stands would exclude many dynamic urban-industrial regions (such as those surrounding large Third World cities such as Caracas or Abidjan), which act as the metropolitan centres of externally dependent, underdeveloped economies having frequent transactional relations with other economies.

Despite these shortcomings, it is interesting to apply Friedmann's concept of 'effective economic space' to the sphere of economic influence of the lower circuit of a small town, far removed from the national metropolis, since, in this case, the majority of economic transactions indeed occur *within* a given geographical space. In reality, every urban area has two market

circuits, corresponding to the upper and lower circuits of the
economy: even in the richest urban regions of the most advanced
Third World countries, these two economic subsystems function
side by side.⟩

The territorial influence of an urban agglomeration has two
fields of action: each town or city thus has two zones of influence,
each of which will vary in character according to the type of urban
area under scrutiny, and the nature of the individual circuits.

Central place theory, the basic concepts of which were formulated by Christaller (1933) and reintroduced by Berry and
Garrison (1958a, b and c), appears, in the light of our two-circuit
formulation of the urban economy, to have little relevance to the
analysis of underdeveloped economies.

The above analysis not only calls into question the use of central
place theory in the examination of underdeveloped economies
(Fig. 16), but also suggests that the concepts of *threshold* and *range*
need to be re-examined in the light of the lower circuit's existence.

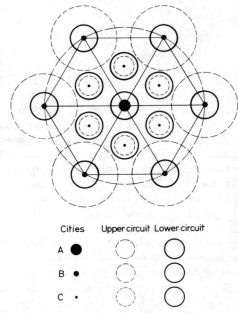

Figure 16 Christaller's hexagon marketing principle modified by the
existence of the two circuits of the urban economy in underdeveloped
countries

The spatial dialectic of the two circuits

'Solidarity and antagonism constitute the frame upon which intra-regional relations are woven' (Peillon 1970: Volume II, 88). In the two circuits of the urban economy, 'solidarity' is functional while antagonism is structural. The latter tends to be dominant and may even break relations of solidarity.

Competition between the two circuits for market hegemony and spatial control is shown by the upper circuit's tendency toward total unification and penetration of the market, and the lower circuit's tendency to claim some role in aggregate spatial organization, and to assert itself in competition with the upper circuit.

The true dialectic between the upper and lower circuits occurs at the local level because the lower circuit is only local. This dialectic operates at each urban echelon – metropolitan, intermediate and local – and has specific characteristics at each level.

The sphere of influence of the upper circuit is demarcated by various types of multidirectional, yet asymmetrical relations throughout the urban hierarchy. As regards the lower circuit, there are horizontal and symmetrical relations with the traditional activities of the urban area. Only in this respect could one perhaps revert to the classical concept of the central place.

The urban field of the lower circuit is continuous, while that of the upper circuit is not. If we take the national space economy as a whole, the upper circuit's market is unified whilst that of the lower circuit is highly fragmented. Therefore, it is difficult to accurately construct a demand cone (Lösch 1940) for the modern circuit's urban field: consumption possibilities are not extensively diffused, as in the developed countries, but are concentrated in certain points, as a spatial manifestation of the inequitable distribution of national income. For example, prices do not spatially vary in a uniform manner around the locus of production. The upper circuit's urban field is thus discontinuous, and despite its tendency to penetrate the entire national economy, it is currently incapable of achieving this in the underdeveloped countries: instead the lower circuit competes with the upper circuit for control of space.

In consequence, the existence of a powerful modern circuit in a city is not necessarily accompanied by its extension to the surrounding countryside. There is much evidence that the upper circuit is often incapable of directly extending its regional influence. For example, upper circuit activity may assume a monopolistic form and set high prices, or it may internalize essential external economies and impede local economic growth; it may pursue a wages policy with unfavourable repercussions on the labour market. In such cases, among others, despite its overall hegemony, the upper circuit has no real multiplier effects on rural areas and may even contribute to their impoverishment. The lower circuit then assumes the task of maintaining continuous relations with the immediate rural areas.

There is also a close relationship between a country's degree and type of industrialization and the form of diffusion of modern commodities. When national industry requires a large market, it puts pressure on the credit system, the expansion of which assures the effective demand necessary for industrial expansion.

In studying the dialectic of the two circuits we must take into account the role of modes of transport, which support both forms of urban economic organization. Transport facilities invariably *additional factors involved* benefit the upper circuit. The profitability of modern transportation, however, is linked to volume: if bulk transportation is not required, only the lower circuit will offer its services. It should be noted that ease of transport is not always equal to the quality and extent of the road network: the purchase-price and running costs of motor vehicles must also be considered. The composition of the final transport cost to the consumer plays an important role in determining the local viability of both circuits.

Proximity to large industrial metropolises will also determine whether a region has an integrated and well-used transport system; in such a case, the upper circuit penetrates the umland, whilst the rural poor, absorbed by the more developed labour-market, take refuge in the cities, swelling the ranks of those in lower circuit activities. Similarly, the demand profile of the poor is modified through contact with the city; since real incomes do not increase at the same rate as new consumption, recourse to the lower circuit becomes necessary, since only it is capable of furnishing credit adapted for those without steady employment.

The road-system barely reaches the peripheral urban areas, and this also encourages the lower circuit. Forms of upper circuit commercial monopoly can be maintained, but their high prices limit upper circuit consumption to the upper classes. The rest of the population are forced to use the lower circuit. Sometimes even upper circuit businesses adopt practices characteristic of the lower circuit. On the other hand, poor roads discourage the establishment of modern trade and reinforce the local power of wholesalers, whose businesses and profits are entirely founded upon the existence of the lower circuit.

Periodic markets and motor transport are two ways, one traditional, the other modern, in which national or foreign modern industrial products can be introduced into backward regions. If the upper circuit appears to be thus extending its influence beyond the city-limits, this is so only at the level of appearances: in reality, and irrespective of the types of goods sold, trade normally takes place according to the mode of operation of the lower circuit.

When economic activity is seasonal, the lower circuit generally has a greater chance of success. Seasonal activity is synonymous with irregular, temporary wage increases, and thus contributes to a raising of the threshold at which modern activities can be established; price fluctuations linked to seasonal activity produce similar results. In these circumstances, the lowest rather than the highest level of average incomes for the year in question will determine whether new commercial or manufacturing activities are established. The highest level induces higher levels of output, but never, in itself, stimulates the creation of new activities.

The dialectic between the two circuits indicates that the expansion of one takes place at the expense of the other: the penetration of modern activities or goods and the maintenance of non-modern activities is closely linked to spatial organization through transport, and the spatial distribution of activities and income. Competition between the two circuits and spatial organization have a reciprocal cause and effect relationship: the dialectic operates in spatial terms.

If present economic trends continue, there will be an accelerated circulation of means of production, commodities, capital and labour engaged in technologically modern activities, thereby accelerating the outflow of surplus value, since those enterprises capable of mobilizing these productive factors, would be also most able to control the economy.

It is clear that this situation will only benefit the upper circuit: the lower circuit will become progressively 'lower'. In absolute terms both the upper and lower circuits will develop, but the relative gap between them will become more pronounced.

The shared space and problems of national planning

Authentic enclaves are formed when the upper circuit of certain agglomerations consists mainly of extroverted firms, i.e. export or re-export industries, whose actions are governed only by their own internal interests, seriously inhibiting national or regional economic and political control. The weakening of local autonomy is maximized when the industries in question are least dependent on other regional or national firms. The effectiveness of national economic and spatial planning is further impaired if the enterprises are multinational, for decision-making then takes place outside the country.

Moreover, when industry develops in response to domestic demand, the multiplier effects tend to be much greater than when industry is export-based. In North America and Western Europe the urban network is organized on the basis of a horizontal spatial specialization on which are superimposed vertically specialized nodes of economic activity.

For these reasons, growth-pole theory and its variants do not provide a satisfactory explanation of the development of underdevelopment. It was believed that only the modern sector had the ability to generate growth and diffuse it to different social, economic, and geographical levels. The upper circuit generates growth but not development; furthermore, such a perspective neglects the important role of the lower circuit in the national economy as a whole and its impoverished regions.

In cities where domestically and export-oriented industrialization coexist, control over the urban economy is shared. Yet the influence of extroverted forms of industrialization on the surrounding region is limited and the 'domestic' forms of industrialization assume the regional role. In this situation, extroverted industrialization distorts the development of the aggregate urban economy and in particular of the industries themselves. When external economies are created *in situ*, extroverted industrialization increases in significance and imposes defensive sectoral shifts on the part of domestically oriented industry. The regional role of the city is therefore modified in response to the change in the balance of power between the two industrialization processes. Decision-making becomes increasingly an external matter, which poses difficult problems for planners, especially since increased industrial output often leads to the assumption that the city's sphere of influence should expand.

Given such industrial location patterns within the urban network, can we still accept that there is a reliable and consistent relationship (Zipf 1949) between the size and economic power of a city within a particular country or region? Similarly, how can we determine which activities are economically 'basic' or 'city forming', when, for example, export industries often require the co-operation of locally based, locally oriented activities, or when domestically oriented industry makes consistent use of foreign inputs?

The problem is not to examine, as Alexanderson (1969) has suggested, the existence of city-*forming* activities as opposed to city-serving activities, but to distinguish, within the urban network, nation-building and region-building activities from extroverted activities. The concept of urban hierarchy should also be reconsidered. Yet these theoretical problems are less important than the practical problems of evaluating the extent of the city's control over regional space: this makes clear the distinction between the dynamism of the urban economy and that of the region. A willingness to analyse the shared space in this way would greatly diminish the fundamental problems of regional planning.

In the national network, the role played by modern activities is dominant and dynamic, whilst those of the lower circuit tend to be subordinate. However, at the local level, even though the upper circuit tends to prevail over the lower circuit in the long run, this is not the case if one considers a given conjuncture, at which point activities in both circuits condition each other. Taking a somewhat longer view, the lower circuit is by no means completely passive: it constitutes a force of opposition to so-called modernization, thereby somewhat retarding unbridled upper circuit expansion.

However, the problem has further implications. Since the influence of the upper circuit is never uniform within the national territory, the lower circuit has to extend or replace upper circuit activities throughout the periphery (the term 'periphery' here applies to both the socio-economic and the geographical dimensions). While Berry believes that 'the spatial incidence of economic growth is a function of distance from the metropolis' (1971:115), we consider that the periphery is not only a collection of distant and impoverished rural and urban areas, but also can be contiguous with or even contained within Third World metropolises or other regions of dynamic growth. This periphery is precisely where the lower circuit's role in economic and spatial organization is most felt (Santos 1975). In spite of this, it is usually ignored by economic and social planners. This oversight has been responsible for the failure of a wide range of planning exercises and must be rectified if greater economic and spatial productivity is to be achieved.

13

Conclusion

The two circuits of the urban economy constitute a crucial aspect of the many problems presently faced by underdeveloped countries. Their existence bears witness to the failure of past and present development planning theory, at least in capitalist underdeveloped countries.

'Planning' usually means planning for a modernization predicated upon a rapid rate of economic growth; however, such increases in G.N.P. should be seen for what they are – mere statistics or 'an accountant's illusion' as Morice (1972) calls it. Poverty, in both absolute and relative terms continues to increase in rural and urban areas alike. The presence of an expanding lower circuit in the urban economy, co-existing with an equally dynamic upper circuit, is often considered a step towards the eradication of inequality and the equitable distribution of national income. Unfortunately, an analysis of the diverse situations encountered in Third World countries does not justify such optimism. Capital-surplus countries such as Singapore (Buchanan 1972:117) or countries with a high G.N.P. per capita (such as Venezuela) experience problems similar to other Third World countries, problems which have been aggravated by industrialization and modernization. The urban lower circuit plays an undeniable social and economic role, for it not only absorbs urban 'surplus labour' but most of the people who are expelled from the countryside. Because of this role, it is often concluded that the lower circuit should be protected and maintained for at least as long as the modern circuit continues to be unable to provide sufficient employment for the total labour force. Such a responsibility for the reduction of aggregate urban productivity and the lowering of average personal income of urban dwellers on the 'tertiarization' of the cities. But productivity must not be seen as an end in itself, nor should we fetishize average incomes: they very often conceal the most blatant inequalities. The lower circuit must not be preserved in its present form: though it provides employment and hence means of subsistence, its dominant trait is the perpetuation of poverty.

Through the multiple contacts it establishes with the mass of the population, the lower circuit is in a position to collect daily savings and earnings and transfer them to the capitalist sector. This is done through numerous mechanisms, such as that of the urban middle class of professionals, merchants and civil servants, much of whose limited accumulation (often the result of transactions with the poor) passes to the capitalist sector through their conspicuous consumption.

Current consumer goods production does not interest the more capitalist-oriented sectors, because other industrial activities offer greater profits. Intermediate cities can, as we have seen, create industrial activities which we have included in the marginal upper circuit. The lower circuit, which itself produces imitations of many modern goods as well as manufacturing traditional products, also distributes a large part of modern output. The capital thus accumulated is transferred to the upper circuit, often through financial and/or political channels.

In this way, the gap between the two capital markets tends to widen further. Since credit facilities are only offered to the modernized sectors, the limited supply of capital becomes progressively more expensive for the non-modernized sectors. The consequent and necessary recourse to the capital-market of the lower circuit implies higher interest-rates for those concerned. Thus, paradoxically, it is the poor who finance much of the modernization process, from which they reap so little benefit.

The lower circuit's cohesion and maintenance is assured by this *upward* flow of capital, for which there is no real counterpart in the opposite direction. The present operation of the urban economy requires that the output of the upper circuit is available to the lower circuit in return for the dependence and subordination of the latter. An analysis of the fundamental causes of the poverty generated by the urban economy would necessarily show the relationships between capital and credit scarcity and the other factors of lower circuit organization, irrespective of the level of industrialization, output and G.N.P. of the countries in question.

The way in which cities organize space in underdeveloped countries is yet another factor which supports and maintains the economic bi-polarization of the country. Improved transport, though it acts as a unifying factor between the large city and its periphery, does not greatly change the situation. Distance may be reduced, but the appropriation of surplus is not: improved communications place more people at the mercy of an alien consumption model imposed by the media, while prices, fixed by the 'interval' (though often externally oriented) motivations of the firm, continue to rise.

In any case, transport is only frequent and efficient between the principal cities of the urban network. It is only in these cities that industrialists can establish their own complementary services and bypass usurious middlemen. Elsewhere, the limited market-size confers a monopoly on a small number of merchants, who may charge virtually whatever prices they wish. The mass of the population, being relatively immobile, must pay these prices.

The spatial diffusion and penetration of the upper circuit also means the diffusion of impoverishment. This form of spatial organization therefore leads to the perpetuation of both the marginal upper and lower circuits. Yet such a spatial organization is the product of the capitalist system of production, the very system which has been responsible for the impoverishment of the periphery.

We are seeking a potential set of relations between the two circuits which would be capable of opening 'communications', and simultaneously permitting an increase in both the productivity and life-conditions of those now in the lower circuit. Such a solution would of necessity require both a *spatial* organization capable of redistributing national resources more equitably, and at the same time, an organization of *production* permitting an equitable spatial distribution of human and material resources. These are nothing more than different sides of the same solution, and thus inextricably inter-related. Thus the present system of relations must be replaced. Even in the poorest countries, the externally imposed growth model has, as it primary preoccupation, increased production, irrespective of any social objections or objectives, and is essentially oriented toward the international economic objectives of developed economies.

The domestic market is largely disregarded. Activities tend to be concentrated wherever locational advantages assure them the largest profits. Selective localization reduces the possibilities for increasing both production and consumption in other parts of the country. At the same time, poverty persists *inside* the dynamic growth centres themselves, since uneven and unequal growth merely accentuates the exodus from the rural areas to the largest cities.

It almost appears as if the poor had subconsciously decided to follow in the wake of their appropriated rural surplus, to press for a more equitable income-distribution. Is the city the place for this confrontation? The migration of the poor to the large cities results from the organization of the urban network itself. The distribution of economic activity among the various cities (associated with the effects of spatial and income disparities) makes the poor much more vulnerable in the small or middle-sized city than in the economic metropolis or primate city. The result is an unprecedented concentration of the poor in large cities, where their aspirations and expectations remain unsatisfied. Thus the city constitutes an arena of perhaps historical confrontation between rich and poor, since 'the introduction of the unemployed into a monetary exchange system can only reinforce the vicious circle of poverty' (Lambert and Martin 1971:195).

This 'vicious circle of poverty' results from the superimposition of two exploitive mechanisms, one economic and the other geographical. It is not only the result of the appropriation of popular savings by a small number of capitalist enterprises but also their accumulation as surplus by the minority (fostered by regional disparities based on the rigid requirements of the production-process). This mechanism, responsible for the maintenance of poverty in both the centre and periphery, also explains the existence of the lower circuit throughout the urban network: poverty and the lower circuit are synonymous.

Economic policy aimed at alleviating both the economic and spatial dimensions of poverty cannot be formulated in purely quantitative terms, but requires a social and political dimension.

An increase in income levels has been suggested as a solution, and land reform as one of the best methods of achieving it. Higher rural incomes would increase the amount of capital in a country and accelerate industrialization. Cities would therefore have new opportunities for commodity production. The urban masses would thus benefit and the entire population would have an improved standard of living.

This thesis has been discredited, for underdeveloped countries are currently industrializing without recourse to domestic capital. Neither agrarian reform nor industrialization by themselves can eradicate poverty in rural and urban areas. This is why the attempts to increase industrial employment through foreign capital and to establish re-exporting industries have not succeeded. These are at best tokenistic and partial answers designed to maintain hope rather than to find permanent and effective solutions.

It is wrong to imagine that either more, intermediate or appropriate technology could be a panacea; the problem is political, not technological. The primary emphasis should be on the breaking of society's subordination to an apparently given and autonomous production-process, and place the latter in the service of society. Under present conditions, a very small section of society receives the 'crumbs' of national surplus (for most profits are 'repatriated') while the masses become progressively impoverished.

For production to be placed in the service of the population, the concept of economic productivity must first be replaced by that of social productivity. Technology should henceforth play a subordinate role. Growth will only be meaningful if it benefits everyone; the quest for private and corporate accumulation would give way to a mass concern for equity and equality. Consumption would no longer be controlled by the requirements of the production system, but would be identified with collective welfare.

The implementation of such ideas presupposes a comprehensive and global approach in the economy. First the State, instead of protecting the modern sectors of the economy to the detriment of the non-modern sector, would be called upon to use modernization for the benefit of all society. From a practical viewpoint, the expansion of the 'dynamic' sectors of the economy must be subordinated to the expansion of the more progressive 'popular' sectors. This would permit an immediate expansion in the range of consumer products available to the mass of the population, the absorption of those currently termed 'the labour-surplus' (the affected industries would be more labour-intensive and less dependent on foreign countries) and an increase in *per capita* productivity in the lower circuit and in the rural areas.

Such a policy would have fundamental advantages. The gap between the upper and lower circuits would be narrowed: changes in the aims of production would facilitate 'communication' between the two circuits. The growth of the upper circuit would 'infect' the lower circuit, whose nature and role would change. In the strict sense of the word, the former would become less, and the latter more 'productive'.

The consequences would be from the viewpoint of spatial organization as well as that of production and distribution. First, foreign dependence would decrease and the promotion of local techniques would be encouraged, which would mean freedom from the need for large amounts of capital. The elimination, or in any case, the weakening of monopoly would permit the widespread creation of many industrial activities, the existence of which today is inconceivable, in regional cities. The latter would be more capable of absorbing and utilizing the rural surplus, and macrocephalous growth (both demographic and economic) would tend to diminish. Rural migration would henceforth be diverted towards a growing number of dynamic zones.

The rate of urbanization would not be reduced, but a different form of urbanization, with a larger number of big cities, would evolve. Cities other than the economic metropolis would be called upon for more complex and differentiated industrial production. The role of 'new' export industries (in other words, the Third World 'assembly plants') would tend to decline, for industry would become more domestically oriented.

The national budget of the State would increase, since the reserve funds of the monopolies would no longer be necessary. Consequently, the State would play a larger role. Funds designated for infrastructure, once required by ultra-modern industrial establishments, would be used in accordance with national criteria and for the creation of services intended for the population. The population would also see its purchasing power increase (in real terms), prices no longer being a function of monopolistic manipulation. This would again reinforce the influence of middle-sized and small cities.

The burden of oppressive macrocephalous cities would diminish; regional disparities would disappear rather than grow. The periphery would be less poor and the results of the stimulus to the rural areas would be shared between the latter and a larger number of cities. There would also be a wider diffusion of production and service activities due to better income distribution.

Thus, the intermediate cities would return to their original role as region-serving cities. True growth poles and growth centres would be created, designed to expand the production and consumption of essential goods and services, the prices of which would tend to fall.

Above all, since consumption would no longer be subordinated to production, the latter would tend to adapt itself not only to national, but also to regional conditions. Competition from the 'centre' would be consequently lessened, if not eliminated. There would be regionalized national modernization instead of modernization at a pace determined by national interests. This is the only way to integrate the lower circuit smoothly into the aggregate economy since the lower circuit is primarily fashioned by and responds to local conditions.

The difficulty in making this model operational is closely linked to the need to change the structure, objectives and organization of production. This is tantamount to the elimination of the present role of multinational enterprises and private monopolies. Such a task cannot be accomplished without a radical modification in the relationship between the State and the modern sectors of the economy; that is, without a change in the State's relations with the international system, which supposes a restructuring of the objectives of the State itself. Therefore the State, by using its regulative power, could distort the impact of external forces and significantly reduce the role presently played by multinational firms and monopolies in national spatial organization.

One should not, however, expect an immediate and radical change in the situation. Historical change, and the passage from one epoch to another is notoriously slow and fraught with setbacks and crises. The transformation of the State can no longer be made by an instantaneous break with conditions of the past which are still partially in operation. The lower circuit will consequently have a role to play in this process of change. Yet its *transitional* form must not be allowed to become ossified as an apparently 'permanent' solution.

The decline and demise of the present technological era will no doubt facilitate a more complete and rapid solution. It is also within the realm of possibility that the patience of the masses will run out and they will seek to persuade their leaders to abandon their 'wait and see' attitude and take decisive action. The trends presently imposed on production and consumption in the Third World are a source of cumulative distortion which causes an irreversible impoverishment of the mass of the population, a situation which, sooner or later, will force the contemporary State to act in the popular interest, or disappear.

Maybe a bit optimistic in this last part of conclusion.

Notes

Chapter 1 Towards a new paradigm

1 For example, see Lucien Pye (1962). For a bibliography, see F.F. Rabinovitz *et al.* (1967), and F.F. Rabinovitz (1968).

2 Boeke's book (1953) is a revised edition of two earlier books: *The Structure of Netherlands' Indies Economy*, New York, 1942, and *The Evolution of the Netherlands' Indies Economy*, New York, 1946.

Chapter 2 The two circuits: evolution and characteristics

1 For example, Myint's use of the term 'colonial financial system' (1970: 136), due to its imprecision, invalidates his subsequent conclusions.

2 The existence of this international demonstration effect is doubted by Bauer and Yamey (1957: 138-42). Moreover, Nurkse and Bauer suggest that domestic capital formation is a precondition of development; this is contradictory, since, under present conditions, 'development' is inextricably bound up with the demonstration effect, whether or not one takes domestic capital formation into account. These authors wrote, however, in a period when these relationships were not universally recognized by economic theorists.

Table 2.3 Increase in number of television sets in selected underdeveloped countries

Countries	Population (1000's)	1962	1963	1964	1965	1966	1967	Annual increase (%)	No. televisions per 1000 inhabitants (1967)
Ivory Coast	4,010 (1958)	–	1.5	1.6	6	–	–	100	1.5
Tunisia	4,560 (1966)	2	3.1	3.5	5	20	35	77.3	7.7
Egypt	30,907 (1966)	128	197	273	323	361	399	25.5	12.9
Argentina	23,255 (1960)	850	1200	1500	1600	1850	1900	17.4	81.7
Ecuador	5,508 (1962)	16	12	32	42	55	71	34.7	12.9
Costa Rica	1,594 (1963)	12	15	35	50	65	66	40.6	41.4
India	511,125 (1961)	0.4	0.5	0.7	0.8	4	6	71.9	0.01
Indonesia	110,079 (1961)	–	10	35	45	46	54	52.5	0.5
Hong Kong	3,834	16	25	36	50	58	93	42.2	24.2

Source: United Nations, Statistical Yearbooks, 1966 and 1968.

3 In underdeveloped economies, inequality in the distribution of income is often striking:

Table 2.4 Salvador 1966

Level of income (Cruzeiros)	Population (%)	Income (%)
0-10	5.7	0.6
10-20	14.4	3.2
20-40	26.0	11.7
40-80	25.4	22.0
80-160	22.1	38.0
160-240	3.3	9.7
240-400	3.1	14.8

Source: Banco do Nordeste (1967).

Table 2.5 Columbia 1961

Labour force (%)	Income (%)
top 1%	13
top 5%	29
top 10%	42
middle 25%	32
poorest 65%	26

Source: Adapted from Bird (1970:13).

Table 2.6 Pointe-Noire, Congo-Brazzaville

Monthly earnings (CFA francs)	% of wage-earners
under 10,000	52.7
20 – 20,000	31.9
more than 20,000	15.5

Source: Adapted from Vennetier (1968:363).

Table 2.7 Tananarive, Malagasy Republic

Monthly earnings (Malagasy francs)	% of working population
0 – 10,000	34.1
0 – 15.000	50.0+
25,000+	16.0
35,000+	7.6

Source: Adapted from Donque (1968:51).

4 In Goudet's survey of part of the Pointe-á-Pitre district of Guadalupe (1969), the proportion of residents owning the following durable consumer goods varied according to income:

Table 2.8

Income bracket (Francs)	Automobiles number	%	Refrigerators number	%	Televisions number	%
Less than 400F	3	5.2	10	8.1	1	2.6
400 to 600F	8	14.0	26	21.3	6	15.7
500 to 1000F	15	26.3	35	28.6	9	23.6
More than 1000F	31	54.3	51	41.8	22	27.8

The following data from Brazil clearly show that the higher income classes consume more, but that the gap between rich and poor is not the same for all commodites:

Table 2.9 Commodity consumption-ratios (rich : poor) in Aracaju, capital of the State of Sergipe, Brazil

Corn flour	1	Talc	3.5
Vinegar	2.5	Shaving cream	4
Vegetable oil	6	Sewing machine	2
Biscuits & crackers	8	Radio	3
Butter	9	Record player	21
Tooth-brush	1.5	Washing machine	32
Tooth paste	2	Floor-polisher	40
Toilet soap	3	Refrigerator	40

Source: Cidade de Aracaju, Consumo de Productos Industriaia, Departmento de Estudos Economicos, Banco do Nordeste do Brasil, Fortaleza (1967).

The following table indicates those commodities (i) in genral use, and (ii) those only used by a very small proportion of the population:

Table 2.10 Percentage of households having certain domestic items in Mossoro (The Rio Grande State of Northern Brazil)

Portable record player	3.6	Canned pork	4.1
Floor-polisher	7.3	Canned fruit	5.2
Record player	7.8	Condensed milk	12.4
Electric fan	10.4	Powdered milk	26.9
Kerosene stove	11.4	Chocolate	29.0
Charcoal stove	12.4	Canned fish	38.3
Refrigerator	17.6	Butter	56.0
Portable radio	19.0	Biscuits & crackers	66.8
Wood stove	33.7	Vinegar	73.6
Gas stove	40.9	Macaroni	74.6
Electric bulbs	59.0	Vegetable oil	79.3
Wireless	63.2	Nylon raincoat	3.1
Hammock	91.2	Fabric raincoat	6.2
Purified water	3.6	Plastic raincoat	21.8
Floor-wax	14.0	Tie	33.2
Detergents	30.0	Suit	36.8
Brooms	95.5	Dress shirt	36.8
Bar soap	97.9	Pyjamas	52.8
Vehicles	15.0	Blouse	66.3
Hats	31.0	Skirt	67.4
Clothes brush	38.9	Dress	71.5
Shoe brush	40.4	Sports shirt	83.9
Hair brush	42.5	Socks	88.9
Umbrella	58.5	Plastic shoes	14.5
Canned beans	2.6	Leather shoes	93.8

Source: Banco do Nordeste do Brasil, S.A. Consumo de Produtos Industrialis na Cidade de Mossoro, Rio Grande do Norte B.N.B., Fortaleza (1966).

5 In a previous work (Santos 1966:305-6), a dichotomy between a 'modern' and a 'traditional' system was proposed. This formulation has since been abandoned because the terminology had so many possible meanings that a valid distinction between 'modern' and 'traditional' could not easily be made.

Furthermore, it is not always possible to date accurately the activities of the upper circuit since they are not defined by their age, as are similar activities in developed countries, but rather by their organization and relationships. It seems difficult to call the lower circuit 'traditional', not only because it is a product of modernization, but also because it is in a process of continual transformation and adaptation (Hagen 1962), and because, in all cities, part of its supplies come, either directly or indirectly, from the so-called modern sectors of the economy.

216   *The Shared Space*

The phenomenon of the two circuits is easily verified in the field of manufacturing and in almost all branches of industrial activity in the underdeveloped countries. Polarization of economic activity manifests itself not only in the urban sphere but also at the *national* level. In many countries, small-scale and artisanal production accounts for a significant share of the total output of textile, metal and bakery products. The following table shows relative importance of what is officially called the 'modern urban' sector and the 'crafts' sector of manufacturing:

Table 2.11 Industrial production and urban crafts production (1966) – region of Bouaké, Ivory Coast (millions of CFA)

	Modern sector	Crafts sector	Total
Processing grains and flours	117.6	345.8	463.4
Drinks, ice cream	109.0	4.3	113.3
Other food industries, tobacco	1865.3	–	1865.3
Energy, water	160.0	288.0	448.0
Extractive activities	1.2	–	1.2
Construction materials	80.0	–	80.0
Chemicals, parachemical	–	19.4	19.4
Wood industry	100.9	123.5	224.4
Car repairs	217.8	180.6	398.4
Other electrical and mechanical industries	–	74.2	74.2
Textiles	1571.3	332.0	1903.4
Fat products	–	86.9	86.9
Leather shoes	–	46.0	46.0
Miscellaneous industrial products	–	92.5	92.5
Buildings and public works	1760.3	414.1	2174.4

The average number of employed persons is an indication of the technological level of the industry and consequently of its participation in either circuit of the urban economy. (For an illustration from Burma, see Angrand 1968.)

In north-eastern Brazil, the largest cities shelter an important number of small-scale industries. Manufacturing activities having fewer than 5 employees are well represented in cities of more than 50,000 inhabitants, which is related to the large number in low income classes (Robock 1963). In Lagos, in 1959, among 2419 industrial establishments, 69 per cent had fewer than 4 employees and only 7 per cent employed more than 20 (Mabogunje 1968:256). In Ibadan, the same phenomenon: in 1963, more than 200 small factories employed fewer than 10 persons and often less than 5. Of some 47 industries having more than 10 employees, only 9 had more than 100 persons, one among them having more than 500 employees (Mabogunje 1968:201).

In 1960, Istanbul's modern sector employed 130,975 persons and had a value added of almost 3 million NM; the unorganized manufacturing sector had a value added of under 1 million NM and employed 180,108 workers (Jurkart 1966). In 1958 almost 85 per cent of Costa Rican manufacturing enterprises employed less than five persons; only 69 per cent of the corresponding workers, however, were wage-employees (Lasserre 1967). In Venezuela, 'small' enterprises constitute 98.9 per cent of all establishments, and employ 63.2 per cent of the manufacturing labour-force (Avila 1969), whilst Jovito Valbuena (1966) finds the following distinction between industrial and craft enterprises in the Andean region of the same country:

Table 2.12

	Industry	Crafts
Value of materials used (bolivars)	763,985	91,646
Value of fuel and electricity (bolivars)	42,538	1,366
General expenditure (bolivars)	806,523	93,015
Fixed capital (bolivars)	8,131,500	1,023,000

Similar evidence can be advanced for the polarization of commercial activities (Erdens 1969).

Chapter 3 The colonial urban economy

1 Whilst some valid comparisons can be made in terms of the pervasive nature of underemployment (Chevalier 1950:77; Bedarida 1968: 276-7; Santos 1971:319; Sorlin 1969:92), data on the levels of remuneration, consumption and expenditure on essential commodities indicates that life in Industrial Revolution Europe was rather less exacting (Santos 1971:319; Beaujeu-Garnier 1965a). However, recent work (C. dos Santos 1971: Chapter 12) has demonstrated that the mechanisms which give rise to many of these apparent historical parallels are completely different in nature.

2 The word *ghetto* is used in the USA to designate a degraded urban district in which the poor usually reside; these latter are either Negro or of some other ethnic minority. In underdeveloped countries, the term *squattment* and *shantytown* designate the large poverty-stricken agglomerations which circle and even invade the city.

Chapter 4 The upper circuit

1 In this chapter, as elsewhere in the book, the word *monopoly* and the expression *monopolistic structure* are used to denote a monopoly as well as an oligopoly. This general meaning has been used in the past by Lenin, and is presently used by Galbraith (1967), Merhav (1969), Jalée (1969) as well as many others. In any case, no perfect monopoly exists (Ayres 1952:384). Some economists employ the terms 'monopolistic competition' and 'imperfect competition' interchangeably.

2 Martin (1966) describes the phenomenon of 'internalization' as follows:

> it is the result of a change in the international division of labour by which the exchange of raw materials for manufactured goods by underdeveloped countries is to some extent transformed into a division of local production for the domestic market between indigenous and foreign interests on the basis of either strategic importance or profitability

3 See Ikonicoff (1970: 685).

4 See Mishan (1967:3-8).

5 United Nations, 'World Economic Survey' 1969 and 1970 (1971: 151-4).

6 Between 1953 and 1968, total US production of synthetic textile materials increased from over 1 million metric tons to more than 11 million metric tons. (United Nations Statistical Yearbooks 1959, 1966, 1969).

7 According to the United Nations World Economic Survey 1969-70 (1971:233), US imports of rubber declined from $716 million in 1965 to $629 million in 1968. During the same period, however, imports of manufactured rubber products increased from $11 million to $17 million.

8 See Bauer and Yamey (1957:158).

9 In the Bouaké region of the Ivory Coast (Regional Survey of Bouaké 1966:218), modern commerce comprised 62 European, 58 Syrian or Lebanese and 14 African firms. Petty retail trade consisted of 5,742 African, but no European enterprises.

10 See Comite Interamericano de la Alianza para el Progreso 1966.

11 Between 1950 and 1967, $3000 million entered the Latin American economy whilst $12,800 million was withdrawn. Thus for every dollar it received, Latin America paid out four (Alia 1972:49).

12 The various divisions of multinational corporations can be categorized under three main headings: *subsidiaries* (when the corporation owns over 50 per cent of the shares), *branches* (when it owns 100 per cent) and *associates* (when less than 50 per cent of the shares

belong to the corporation).

13 In the Katanga of the 1950s, the textile industry used cotton and employed several thousand workers, whilst providing the peasant farmers of Kasai and Katanga with a large part of their incomes. The introduction of synthetic fibres and materials brought about a crisis in the cash crop sector upon which the region depended. (L'Industrie Katangaise, 1961:225).

14 Since the Taiwanese economy is totally oriented towards exports, of which 94 per cent go to the United States, the threat of a crisis precipitated by a reduction in American purchases is permanent.

15 In 1969, for example, France spent 14.5 billion francs (2.9 billion dollars) on R and D, 14 times the budget of the Ivory Coast; the United States in the same year allocated 26 billion dollars to R and D, which is equivalent to the G.N.P. of the entire African continent, excluding South Africa (Kamara 1971:745).

Chapter 5 The State and the upper circuit

1 Few case studies of monopolies in underdeveloped countries have appeared; work undertaken by Caio Prado Junior, Celso Furtado (1968), and Ruy Mauro Marini (1972b) on Brazil proved somewhat inconclusive, each writer adopting a particular point of view. For Greece, there is the study done by Ellis, Psilos, Westebbe and Nicolau (1964). The theme has also been studied by Samir Amin (1967) for the Ivory Coast, by Charles Bettelheim (1962) for India and by Maza Zavala (1964) for Venezuela. The greatest number of studies have been on Latin America, though they are generally recent and not always complete due to the difficulty of obtaining data.

2 From a study by the Conference Board (a non-profit business-sponsored research organization) we learn that,

> Of a gross world product of $3 trillion, approximately one-third is produced in the United States, one-third in the industrial nations of Europe, Canada, Japan, and Australia; and the remaining one-third in Russia, Eastern Europe, China and the developing nations elsewhere in the world.
>
> About 15 per cent, or $450 billion, is accounted for by multinational enterprises; $200 billion of this by U.S. based companies; $100 billion by production in other countries.
>
> The proportion contributed by multinational corporations is growing at a rate of 10 per cent per year. At this rate the multinational companies will generate one-half or more of the gross world product in less than 30 years. (cited in Rattner 1972a)

Innovations promoted by advertising assume an independent role in creating new investment opportunities. This refers to a type of autonomous investment brought about by any increase in 'modern' demand (Sylos Labini 1969:161).

4 In the same manner that investment tends to have a snowball effect,
lack of investment also tends to perpetuate itself. Without the impact
of investment the narrow market continues to remain so (Baran
1957: Chapter 6).

5 Excess capacity may be the result of tariff protection granted by
countries in the process of industrialization to entrepreneurs in their
country. As has happened in Ecuador, this may result in a rush
toward preferred branches such as textiles, where in 1961, 90 firms
were operating at less than 48 per cent of capacity (Bottomley
1965:84, 94); this situation is not unique however to Ecuador
(Frankman 1969:18n). Lack of protection, which opens up the country to an influx of foreign products as well as those of local industry,
can bring about the same phenomenon; for example, in the case of a
Laotian match factory operating below capacity due to competition
from imports (Labarthe 1969:64).

6 In 1964, in Algeria, the following sectoral levels of excess capacity
were recorded:

Metallurgic industries ⎞	
Mechanical industries ⎬	45%
Electrical industries ⎠	
Cotton	60%
Leather and shoes	30%
Paper and chemicals	20%

Source: (Isnard 1965:187).

7 The U.S. advertising budget of a company such as Kellogg's represents 9.7 per cent of sales (Cross 1970:198). Data is not available for
the corresponding budget allocation to underdeveloped countries,
however.

8 'In 1960, advertising expenditure in Brazil rose to approximately
$111 million, or 1.4 per cent of national income, divided among
television (37 per cent), radio (35 per cent), and other advertising. . . . Among the 300 advertising agencies in Brazil, eight foreign firms had a turnover amounting to 35 million cruzeiros out of a
total of 120 million' (T. dos Santos 1967:93). These 8 firms indirectly
controlled the other 292, through their power over local advertising.

9 'Spreading monopolization, as the almost immediate result of industrial growth, means that price competition, freedom of entry, constant return to scale – all the fundamental pre-requisites for the
classical process of continual growth in a private enterprise system –
do not exist from the outset' (Merhav 1969:6-7).

10 Varga believes there is a basic tendency toward the slowing down of
the growth of production in the capitalist world. Baran and Sweezy

believe that monopolistic capitalism undermined by its internal contradictions, creates an increasing surplus which under normal conditions, cannot be absorbed, and therefore will cease to be produced, resulting in underutilization of resources and consequent stagnation (Jalée 1969:164).

11 The Ivory Coast was well known for its liberal Investment Code of 1959 which gave fiscal exemptions and reductions to all enterprises given priority by the government: construction companies, industrial crops producers, and local manufacturing firms, 'import-substitution' entrepreneurs, mining industries and finally hydroelectric companies. All these categories were exempted from custom duties on imported equipment and intermediate goods. Domestic production and transactions also received either permanent or temporary tax exemption. Moreover, a long-term fiscal system guaranteed certain enterprises stabilization of taxes for a maximum of 25 years. Finally, operations were given relative freedom to cut back on investment, which means they might transfer their capital abroad.

12 The World Bank lent Malaysia $20 million for the development of water-resources, a major part of which was to be the Phason dam on the River Nann. Assistance for the provision of credit was also given to Malaysian Industrial Development Limited to promote joint-ventures with small local industry.

13 Marini (1972b) defines subimperialism as a combination of forces whereby (i) the super-exploitation of workers based on the concentration of both production and incomes, and (ii) a state of increasing external dependence induces (iii) a state of crisis during which the State evolves new forms of consumption (e.g. armaments, and infrastructural development) in the hope of achieving additional expansion of the capital goods market. Thus the State plays a central role in subimperialist development; a fusion of military and capitalist interests becomes one of the few paths which dependent capitalism can take in order to have some chance of reaching the monopoly- and finance-capitalist stages of capitalist development.

14 Not only central governments offer advantages: regional governments in Nigeria, for example, prior to 1966 granted special concessions and financial support to entrepreneurs wishing to locate in their area (Harris and Rowe 1971:148). Similarly, Dahomey, in its 1966 national budget of 318 million francs CFA, invested 10 million in an automobile plant, 30 million in a textile company and 70 million in a cement plant. The same year Niger allocated 202 million francs CFA out of a national budget of 923.5 million francs CFA for participation in a cement plant, a flour-mill, a brick-yard and a tannery (Tiercelin 1968:48).

In Pakistan, the private sector received support from the State ranging from direct financial aid to local market protection (Maddison 1970:168).

15 In underdeveloped countries, an average of 25 per cent of the budget is allocated to infrastructure investments compared to 6 per cent in developed countries (Prest 1962:165). In Nigeria, 66 per cent of public sector expenditure on fixed capital in 1963 was infrastructural. The State financed all water works, road and bus depot construction, 60 per cent of transports and communications, and 70 per cent of electricity. Moreover, the State assumed complete responsibility for health and education (Lewis 1967). Not surprisingly we find that American investment in Latin American service industries has diminished from 8.1 per cent of the total in 1961 to only 6 per cent in 1967 (Rockefeller 1969:82).

16 In Mexico, using 100 as a base for production of different industrial sectors for the year 1950, electricity generation had become almost entirely financed by the State by 1968 when it reached an index of over 514 while the corresponding level of industrial production was only 365 (Banco Nacionale de Mexico, S.A. 1965).

    While electricity in France was sold to industrial enterprises at prices varying from 2 to 5 francs, in the Cameroon, the Alucam company pays only 0.70 francs per KwH, which represents 7.6 per cent of the selling cost and 8.6 per cent of the cost prices of aluminium (Afana 1966:141).

    The percentage of electrical energy produced by the public sector for industries averages 39 per cent in Latin America, the rates in Chile, Brazil, Mexico and Argentina are 40 per cent, 36 per cent, 29 per cent and 24 per cent respectively. These figures should be compared with the proportion of the national population not consuming electrical energy: Chile 24 per cent, Brazil 26 per cent, Mexico 59 per cent, Argentina 14 per cent (Furtado 1970b:208).

17 In Argentina, 75 per cent of national public investments in 1970 went to 'overhead capital' and infrastructure compared with 80 per cent in 1966 (Robirosa 1971:48).

    In Tanzania, while the G.D.P. increased 67 per cent between 1960 and 1966, capital formation in the public sector of construction (buildings excluded) grew 181 per cent (Tanzania, An Economic Survey 1967-8, Table 49).

G.N.P. growth in Venezuela
(millions of Bolivars)

Year	Manufacturing industry	Construction	Water and energy
1950	1,274	827	69
1957	2,766	1,581	238
1964	4,526	1,473	644

Source:Avila (1969).

18 In Nigeria, expenditure on the civil service represented £11.3 millions in 1963, or approximately 18 per cent of public sector expenditure. In the same year, foreign investment in manufacturing totalled 68 per cent of the total investment in that branch (Lewis 1967).

19 Percentage of the state budget allocated to administration expenses:

Ivory Coast (1965)	73.0%
Senegal (1965)	75.7%
Upper Volta (1964)	93.3%
Mauritania (1967)	90.2%

20 After 1950, State saving in Columbia continued to decrease while corporate saving increased:

Year	Public saving (% of total)	Corporate saving (% of total)
1950	19.5	6.5
1952	28.4	6.3
1959	27.5	14.0
1960	22.8	14.1
1963	7.7	15.4

Source: Columbia, Cuentas Nacionales (1950-61 and 1960-6).

21 In the Ivory Coast, average public investment in the administrative and social sectors fell from 38 to 36 per cent between the periods 1950-60 and 1961-5, during which time the national budget significantly increased (Samir Amin 1967); investment in agriculture declined from 12 to 10 per cent and sectors directly serving the population lost State financial support (these funds being transferred to infrastructure construction needed for modernization).

22 'The government's tax and expenditure policies tend to accentuate inequality rather than diminish it' (Griffin 1971:23).

23

	Direct taxes %	Indirect taxes %
Great Britain (1968)	64	36
Latin America (1968)	35	53

Source:Thurow (1971:37).

24 'In general, only a small fraction of the surplus is channelled to the government and most tax revenues are raised through a highly

regressive system of indirect taxation. Progressive direct taxation is
unenforceable, even when it is enacted, because of the power of
wealth. Hence the tax burden falls largely on the poor' (Griffin
1971:23).

25 In Colombia, indirect taxes made up 9.6 per cent of total tax revenue
in 1951, and 17.8 per cent in 1966 (Bird 1970:10, Table 13). In Peru,
indirect taxes rose from 61.7 per cent of the total in 1950 to 75 per
cent in 1965 (Griffin 1971:17).

26 In the Communist Manifesto (part 1, paragraph 12), Marx states that
in monopoly capitalism, the executive power of the State is little more
than a management committee for the whole bourgeoisie's current
business.

27 'The success of . . . efforts to accelerate economic growth may
depend much more upon the manner of using the investable surplus
than upon its initial importance' (Dobb 1963).

Chapter 6 Third World poverty and the lower circuit

1 The E.C.L.A. study (1967) shows this to be true for Latin America,
and McGee (1967) and Amin (1967) illustrate this fact for Asia and
Africa respectively.

Chapter 7 Lower circuit employment

1 Out of 85,780 wage-earners enumerated in Martinique, only 28.4
per cent stayed with the same employer all year. A large number of
temporary wage-earners was found in trade and transport (47 per
cent), the hotel trade (66 per cent), and in building and public works
(72 per cent). Wages were lower for the temporarily employed. In the
building trade temporary workers received 1,283 F annually on the
average while permanent workers made 7,288 F per year. In the
hotel trade the difference was smaller but nevertheless considerable
– 1,483 F compared with 5,676 F (Cazes 1970:410-12).

2 Data from the Central Bank of Chile reported that in Greater Santiago in 1966, 18.3 per cent of the active population was non-
employed, that is 174,200 persons out of 862,000 (Bulletin of the
Banco Central de Chile 1966:No.461, 1021-4). In 1961, Morocco had
a non-employment rate of 28 per cent while Algeria, then suffering
an economic depression, had a non-employment and underemployment rate of 42 per cent.

3 On this subject see Slighton (1968:38), Herrick (1965:53, 103), Rao
and Desai (1965:341, 383), Lakdawala (1963:159), Mukerjee and
Singh (1961:116), Farock (1966:19) quoted by Joan Nelson
(1969:16) and others such as Laquian (1971).

4

Characteristics of Ivoirian craft activities
(in millions of 1965 CFA francs)

		Production	Gross income	Taxes	Wages
European crafts	1950	0.70	0.11	0.05	0.16
	1965	2.82	0.43	0.20	0.66
African crafts	1950	0.27	0.18		
	1965	1.06	0.70		

Source: Amin (1967:294).

5 'Boys' (domestic servants) represented 13 per cent of the total native population at Elizabethville, Belgian Congo in 1941; this percentage rose to 18 per cent in 1946 and 26 per cent in 1950, due to the city's economic growth which attracted many Europeans (Chapelier 1957:91).

6 At Ciudad Guyana, Venezuela, out of 4,956 self-employed, 2,709 worked more than 49 hours a week (1,617 more than 60 hours, 567 more than 70 hours (C.V.G. 1969). Out of a total labour force of 22,089, 2,879 worked more than 49 hours (C.V.G. 1968:26). The number of hours worked is greatest among employers, self-employed, and household employees.

7 In 1955 one resident out of 14 in Freetown, Sierra Leone was a hawker. At Kenema and Majamba, Sierra Leone, the ratio was even lower: 1 out of 12 and 1 out of 13 respectively (Cox-George 1957:25). Hawkers represented 3.6 per cent of income-earners in Calcutta (Kar 1962). In Lima they were estimated to number 250,000 in 1966 (Dollfus 1966).

	Number of hawkers	% of total population
Greater Bangkok	61,500	2.1
Kuala Lumpur	4,500	0.8
Greater Djakarta	100,000	2.3
Hong Kong	92,000	3.2

Source: McGee (1970b:14).

Chapter 8 Financial mechanisms of the lower circuit

1 'A carpenter I interviewed, also dealt in sugar, cement, bicycles, and iron sheets. When one of the big import firms landed a cargo of sugar, it would be bought up by wholesalers able to acquire large stocks on credit. These wholesalers would then get in touch with him,

and he might take 1000 pounds of sugar against a deposit of £200. He then sold in turn to smaller dealers, who were not in a position to deal on credit. He would distribute his stock among ten or so, each taking £50 to £100 worth. Some of these would retail to the public, others to petty traders. So the sugar passed through four or five hands.' (Marris 1962:76).

2   *Composition of the Money Supply in East Africa*, 1950-63*

June 30	Cash with public**	Demand deposits	Money supply	Proportion of cash to total
1950	19.4	51.1	70.5	27.5
1955	42.8	81.6	124.4	34.4
1960	46.7	70.0	116.7	40.0
1961	47.2	69.9	117.1	40.3
1962	48.2	75.0	123.3	39.2
1963	57.1	83.2	140.3	40.7

*   Kenya, Uganda and Tanzania.
** Cash with the public is currency in circulation minus cash in the banks.

It is to be expected that the currency component in East Africa is relatively high compared to highly developed countries such as the United States and the United Kingdom; on the other hand, it is a smaller part of the stock of money than in several other developing countries. Little significance, however, should be attached to the composition of the money supply as a measure of the degree of the economic development.

3 (A. Martin 1963:15-18; Katzin 1964:193; Garlick 1971:111-16). For example, in Porto Novo, capital of Dahomey, the houses in the diplomatic quarter are largely owned by market tradeswomen.

4

Sale of Manioc Bread at Brazzaville, Congo	*francs*
40 loaves of bread purchased at the village at 25F each	1000
Transport costs to the city	300
Trader's travel expenses (return)	500
Market tax	30
	1830
Sale at 60 francs each	2400
Profit	570

Source: Auger (1972:295).

5 The *Nath* is a savings association grouping together several trades-women of the same market in Dakar, Senegal, unknown in the rural areas. It has been developed in the cities due to the high demand for credit (Agnessy 1968:419).

6 A *Kye*, in general, consists of people who have some factor in common and who have a sense of mutual trust. Rules for the operation of a *Kye* are mutually established by the members and vary according to purpose. While the general purpose of *kye* formation is usually to accumulate a larger sum of money than could normally be possible for a single individual, the specific uses of the sum may vary consid-erably. A *kye* is frequently organized on a temporary basis to achieve some short-range goal and ordinarily consists of between 10 and 30 persons. (M.-G. Lee 1971:368-9). Twenty-three per cent of the mig-rants interviewed at Taegu, South Korea belonged to *Kyes*.

7

Accra: place of purchase by income level

	All households (%)	African (%)	Non-African (%)
Supermarkets	11	7	69
Stores	3	2.5	10
Street stalls	2	2.5	4
Street sellers and itinerant hawkers	14	14	4
Public markets	70	74	13
	100	100	100

Source: Lawson (1971: 381, Table 1).

In the 'Assainissement' quarter of Pointe-à-Pitre, Guadeloupe, it was observed that 'shops and department stores have complementary functions for one-third of consumers frequent at the same time both these types of commercial activities' (Goudet 1969:267).

8 On this subject see: Dewey (1962); Geertz (1963); Marris (1962:68-72) Belshaw (1965); Hawkins (1965:135); McKay (1968:74); Orlove (1969:43); Chapelier (1957:89-90, 109); Garlick (1971:71).

9 Issaac (1971:292) observed this in Pendembu, Sierra Leone, as did Garlick (1971:71) in Ghana: 'in trying to avoid bad risks in giving credit, the rough principle had evolved in Kumasi of selecting cus-tomers as credit-worthy on the basis that the nearer the customer's home, the better risk he was.'

10 The importance of credit in the lower circuit can be measured by the commercial value of the customer to the trader. Caracas small traders acquire middle-class clientele which buys food products such as

bread and milk delivered daily to their doorsteps, often with a news-paper, on credit. This system of commercialization is known as *la ruta* or the route, since each morning the owner or his employee make the same rounds on which he also tries to acquire new customers. Payment is made at the end of every month, a convenient arrangement for civil servants and employees, allowing the trader to collect simultaneously substantial sums of money. One of these traders who was about to retire sold his 'ruta' for almost 40,000 bolivars or $7,600.

11 These rates have been indicated by several writers, such as Dewey (1963:92) and Bhat (1970). In Southern India thousands of Pathans engage in this type of activity, those lending without a guarantee charge a monthly interest of 15 to 25 per cent.

12 Burlaz (1970) was able to obtain information from the largest commercial firm in Dahomey. This company divided its customers into two categories. The larger tradeswomen, retail-wholesalers (numbering around 15) could buy up to 80 million francs CFA, but the maximum credit granted was only 1.3 million francs CFA. The terms of payment were set at 30 days, with an increased interest rate after the twentieth day. In order to obtain credit, the tradeswomen had to pay cash for a year and prove her ability to sell merchandise. In addition to these traders, there were also 300 buyers of smaller quantites, who never received more than 150,000 francs CFA in credit.

13 The twelve outstandingly successful women traders in Onisha, Nigeria, were established customers of one or another of the large European trading firms, from whom they bought goods on credit to resell to a large number of smaller traders, a clientele each of them had built up over many years.

14 It was observed at Bouaké, Ivory Coast that the blacksmiths avoided paying their expenses in cash as much as possible (Étude Régionale de Bouaké, 1962-4 (1966:69).

15

Selling price of fish in the Copperbelt, Zaire
(francs per kilo)

	1 Producer	2 Wholesaler	3 Retailer	1/3 ratio
Fresh fish	4–5	9–10	15	3–4
Dried and salted fish	9–10	13–15	26–28	3
Smoked fish	13	26–28	40–60	3–4.5

Source: Miracle (1962:725).

16 The average return in the banana trade in the Congo (Brazzaville) is

8.7 per cent for wholesalers and 69.7 per cent for retailers over 15-day periods (Auger 1972). The earnings of the wholesaler are a function of the volume of his trade.

17 At Toulepleu, Ivory Coast the profit margins of the static hawkers, which averaged 15 per cent, make this form of hawking relatively more lucrative than that of the small stalls (Schwartz 1969:181). A *buhonero* or hawker in central Caracas selling toys disclosed that he earned on the average 8 bolivars for each sale, a profit of 32 per cent (El Nacional, September 13, 1970).

18 'We know that in most cases the consumer's demand for a commodity rises when its price falls, and falls when its price rises, although there are exceptional cases in which the reverse is true' (Scitovsky 1971:40).

Chapter 9 Adaptability in the lower circuit

1 A survey conducted in the African districts of Kinshasa (then Léopoldville) enumerated 7,070 self-employed 'entrepreneurs' employing a total of 4,619 wage-workers. The following year the number of 'entrepreneurs' had increased by 21 per cent, whilst that of wageworkers had risen by only 3.7 per cent (Denis 1954).

Chapter 10 Inter-circuit relations and growth

1 In a comparison of buying patterns in the Medina (old town) and new city districts, the following degrees of dependence of 'poor' and 'average' consumers on local small-scale production were found:

	Small-scale sales in the Medina (%)	Small-scale sales in the New City (%)
'Poor' consumers		
Clothing	73	6
Table linen	88	3
Household items	66	16
'Average' consumers		
Clothing	63	31
Table linen	75	19
Household items	44	46
'Rich' consumers		
Clothing	26	71
Table linen	41	55
Household items	20	75

Source: République Tunisienne (1972:20-21).

2 In the north-east Brazilian city of Fortaleza, traditional fishing, with its characteristic fluctuations in both supply and price, constituted the only source of fish. The modernization of this activity, hastened notably by the arrival of Japanese tuna trawlers, caused local fish prices to drop and the number of consumers to rise. It also brought about the modernization of trade in fish, which meant the elimination of credit-sales. Consequently, the lower circuit of fishing and fish trading was able to survive: despite lower prices in the modern sector, purchases now had to be made in cash. In the lower circuit, the availability of personal credit enabled the poor to continue purchasing, even though the fish-prices were relatively higher.

Chapter 11 Monopoly, State and macrospatial organization

1 See Paul Claval (1968), especially chapter VIII; this book contains a broad account of the influence of the State's activities upon the organization of the national space. Unfortunately this theoretical framework has not been followed by case studies of similar quality and scope. A more recent book (Navarro de Brito 1973) is one of the first theoretical studies of the spatial implications of the State in underdeveloped countries from a perspective of both the national and international system. De Brito studies what he calls 'the reciprocal effects of spatial input on the State and State output on space'.

2 In Istanbul, public expenditure is mostly controlled by the central government:

	Central government (%)	City (%)	Municipality (%)
Drinking water (1963-9)	73.63	19.27	7.10
Roads and sewers (1966-9)	52.00	31.00	17.00
Electricity (1963-9)	93.43	2.13	4.44

Source: Aru (1971:84-6).

In Mexico, total expenditure of the states and territories in 1964 made up only 1.3 per cent of the G.N.P., and municipal expenditure 0.4 per cent. Federal government expenditure reached 8.9 per cent of the G.N.P. Total income of all the states together was 12 per cent of that of the Federal Government. The municipalities and the Federal District collected 3 per cent and 5 per cent respectively of that collected by the federal government (Anguiano 1968).

3 The term periphery may be used in different ways and each scientific discipline gives it a special meaning. In geography, the periphery is not defined as the physical distance between a pole and its dependent zone, but rather in terms of accessibility. This accessibility depends primarily on the existence of transport and the possibility for individuals to use it to satisfy real or apparent needs.

4 Algerian air traffic gives a clear indication of the lack of relations between regional centres: 96 per cent of the flights out of Constantine go to Algiers, while 99 per cent of the flights from Oran went to Algiers. There was no direct flight between Oran, the second largest city, and Constantine, the third largest (Cote 1968:156). Out of 61,167 flights, 98.2 per cent were made from or to Algiers.

5 Travelling time between Ankara and Samoun, and Ankara and Adana in 1948 was 22 and 35 hours respectively. By 1962 this time had been reduced to 9 and 7 hours (Rivkin 1965:113). Barry Ridell (1970a:41) shows how in Sierra Leone, the time spent in 1920 to reach what is today the capital is now equivalent to that now required to travel halfway across the country.

In Bangladesh, the improved road network created in the early sixties (road density increased 7.5 times between 1963 and 1967) has contributed to the large increase in the number of vehicles in circulation, reducing transport costs by 40 per cent and increasing the prices paid to producers (from 8 to 34 per cent for products in primary markets and from 13 to 65 per cent in secondary markets). Also the improved highway network has aided the monetarization of the economy and considerably increased the importance of markets both for the number of traders and the dimension of operations (U.W. Thomas 1971:205-13).

6 On this subject see Mortimore (1972) and Madhusudan Singh (1964). Guatemala does not have an important highway network and those roads recently constructed have been large international highways such as the Pan American Highway, the Atlantic Highway (leading to Puerto Barrios), and the Pacific Highway (Whetam and Currie 1967).

7 A comparison between the situation found in Sweden (Karlqvist 1971) and that of the Eastern coast of Madagascar is interesting. In Sweden, 28 per cent of the population live within 7 miles of all services while only 20 per cent live in regions where journeys of up to 50 miles for certain services are necessary. The following table shows the situation for the East coast of Madagascar.

	Population served by a highway (%)	*Population less than a 2-hour walk from highway* (%)
Antalaha	20	38
Fenevive	19	41
Tamatave	20	48
Mananjary	25	47
Farapangana	29	61
Moramangara	23	42
Fort Dauphin	22	46

In the region of Kanpur in India, 37 per cent of the villages have no road, another third have unsurfaced highways generally inaccessible during the monsoons. The 4100 villages without roads have a population equal to that of Norway (E.A. Johnson 1970:194-5).

8 Bangladesh has 1.1 miles of road (which are often impassable) for each square mile of cultivated land. This index can be compared to that of the western nations where there is 3.5 to 4 miles of paved highway for each square mile of cultivated lane (Thomas 1971:205).

9 The price differential between the city and its surrounding region is often scandalous. In the region of Bouaké, Lechau observed a variation from 1 to 3.5. In the city, 1 kilogram of sugar would exchange for 4 kilograms of yams while in the jungle markets 14 kilograms of yams has a value equal to 1 kilogram of sugar.

   According to Wilmet (1964) 'the influence of the urban centre market makes itself felt particularly in a centripetal sense and the city thus weakens the surrounding countryside for its profit without it receiving any advantages. Yet, since tropical civilizations are essentially rural (*sic*) the development of cities as technical poles is slowed down.'

10 As Lean (1969:173) points out 'the community of laws, language, currency, etc., facilitates inter-regional exchanges within the same country, while differences due to these factors reduce the possibilities of trade between different countries.'

11 During the 1940s, in Algeria, for example, the distribution of certain goods such as textiles was rationed. Algerois, the region of Algiers, received a quota equivalent to 50 per cent of the available goods, yet its population represented only 20 per cent of the national total. The eastern region, where Constantine is located, has 37.7 per cent of the population, but received barely 20 per cent of the rations, despite the fact that Constantine was then the most important textile producer in North Africa. This is explained by the colonial situation and the location of the colonizers within the country, for they dominated the distriution system of imported products as well as locally produced goods.

12 Diverse unfavourable effects of 'polarization' probably also play a role. Competition from the north risks to upset the South's export and industrial activities, which while being comparatively unprofitable nevertheless create income. Insofar as the North's industrialization is based on the goods the South does not produce, the South again risks losing, since it must buy from the North manufactured products protected by recently raised tariff barriers in the place of similar products once imported more cheaply from abroad. (Hirschman 1964:214)

13 'The massive movement of rural population to the cities cannot be explained by studying the motive of individual migrants. Structural

changes in society must first be analysed' (Sjoberg 1966).

14 The often rapid development of the transport network facilitates the unification of the market for the benefit of the country's centre. The main highways link the major production centres to the principal consumption centres. In the intermediate cities' urban sphere of influence, the highway network is poor and transport is expensive, discouraging the establishment of modern activities in these cities and therefore encouraging their growth in the primate cities. On the other hand, if 'spatial friction' exists (Ratcliff 1959:302) the intermediate city will be favoured. The fate of the latter therefore depends to a considerable degree on transport organization.

The reduction of prices brought about by improved transport facilities offers those firms already established in the centre a supplementary advantage due to economies of scale (Roweiss 1970:29-30). The traditional or modern small firms, located in areas recently influenced by the large industries therefore tend to disappear. 'The reduction in transport rates . . . results in a trend toward agglomeration and large-scale production; this, in turn, leads to the downfall of small-scale industries serving local markets previously protected by spatial friction' (Roweiss 1970:31).

15 Essentially, the principle of accumulation is that when market forces are unrestrained a group of individuals, *a city or a region of a country*, which due to circumstances, are found in a historically dominant position, reinforce this position, while the position of the other groups remains stationary. Individuals, regions, or countries which fall under the domination of the first, remain outside the cumulative process (Marrama 1961:79).

A high degree of concentration is characteristic of the industrial structure in underdeveloped countries. This seems to be true for countries presenting wide differences in their degree of development, which also explains that the phenomenon is not transitory but permanent and structural, and whose roots are found in the technical constraints under which development is established in these countries. (Merhav, 1969:48-9)

Macrocephalous urbanization may also be the result of a poor choice on the part of the government. Preference given to certain types of industry 'leads to concentration or polarization of development in several cities, principally the metropolitan areas of the country' (Gauthier 1971:2).

16 'Dependent urbanization produces a superconcentration in the primate cities, a considerable gap between these agglomerations and the rest of the country and the rupture or nonexistence of an urban network functionally and spatially interdependent' (Linsky 1965).

17 The market mechanism leads to the geographical concentration of activity and population because of increased external economies of

agglomeration for firms due to the existence of overhead capital and a well-trained labour-force (Hansen 1971:193).

18 Kayser (1972b) shows how in Latin America the intermediate level should no longer be considered as important as it was given that the intermediate city increasingly lacks autonomy compared to regional activities. In Black Africa, both a relative and absolute decline has been observed in the role of secondary centres as regional poles (Marguerat 1972). L.V. Thomas (1972) believes it is not a weakening, but an *absence* of middle-sized cities in Senegal.

19 'The production of small, traditional factories in Merida, Venezuela is wholly consumed by the local market but this production faces relatively stiff competition from similar products brought in from elsewhere and sold through local retail outlets' (Valbuena 1966).

Chapter 12 The shared space

1 According to J.H. Johnson (1966), it was Dickinson who introduced the term *urban hierarchy*, though Smailes (1971:4) also claims credit for the expression.

2 Despite Higgins' view to the contrary (1967:141-2) it is difficult to accept that the growth of the non-urban modern sector and of the urban economy at the regional level are so closely correlated: often the surplus generated in the rural areas or mines goes directly to enrich a distant city.

3 'The principal lesson is that these basic industries have little multiplier effect on the other economic activities of the region. Petrochemicals and steel constitute highly integrated industries which neither contribute to nor utilize their immediate environment' (Alonso 1971:29).

4 According to Clarke (1972) this concept (the rank-size rule) was developed by Zipf (1949), though it was originally suggested by Auerbach (1959).

Bibliography

Abdel-Malek, Anouar (ed), *Sociologie de l'Impérialisme*, Ed. Anthropos, Paris.

Abiodun, Josephine Olun, (1967), 'Urban hierarchy in a developing country,' *Economic Geography*, vol. 43, no. 4, October.

—— (1968), 'Central place study in Abeokuta Province, South-western Nigeria, *Journal of Regional Science*, vol. 8, no. 1.

Adelman, M. A., (1966), 'La firme et son environnement', in F. Bloch-Lainé and F. Perroux (eds), *L'Enterprise et l'economie du XX$_e$ siècle*, P.U.F., Paris, pp. 33-52.

Agnessy, D., (1968), 'La femme dakaroise commercante du detail sur le marché', in *Dakar en devenir*, (Groupe d'études dakaroises) M. Sankale, L. V. Thomas, P. Fougeyrollas (eds), *Presence Africaine*, Paris.

Albertini, Pedro; Valdivieso, Amilcar; Alexander, Jeanine de; Burdeinick, Manuel and Alverez, Louis Magin, (1969), *Estudio regional de Calabozo*, Documento de trabajo, Projeto Venezuela 11 de las Naciones-Unidas, Maracay, April (mimeog).

Alia, Josette, (1972), 'Les paravents de Santiago', *Le Nouvel Observateur*, 24 April, Paris.

Almeida, Romulo, (1965), 'Integration Latino-Américaine', *Revue Tiers-Monde*, vol. VI, no. 23, July-September.

Alonso, William, (1968), 'Urban and regional imbalances', *Economic Development*, E.D.C.C., vol. 17, no. 1, pp. 1-14.

—— (1971), 'Les strategies de développement', *Le Nouvel Observateur*, no. 364, 1-7 November, Paris.

Amaral, Ilidiodo, (1968) *Luanda, estudo de geografia urbana*, Junta de investigacoes do Ultramar, Lisboa.

Amin, Samir, (1967), *Le Développement du capitalisme en Côte-d'Ivoire*, Ed. de Minuit, Paris.

—— (1971), *L'accumulation à l'échelle mondiale; critique de la théorie du sous-développement*, Ed. Anthropos,(2nd edn), Paris.

Amsdem, Alice Hoffenberg, (1971), *International firms and labour in Kenya: 1945-1970*, Frank Cass, London.

Anderson, Nelson, (1964), *Our Industrial Urban Civilization*, Asia Publishing House, New York.

Angrand, Claire, (1968), *Quelques aspects de l'industrialisation dans les grandes villes du Sud-Est asiatique*, Université de Bordeaux, November (typescript 288 pp.).

Anguiano, Roberto, (1968), *Las finanzas del sector publico*, Universidade Nacional Autonoma de México, Mexico.

Ardant, Gabriel, (1963), *Le Monde en friche*, P.U.F., Paris.

Arraes, Miguel, (1969) *Le Brésil, le peuple et le pouvoir*, Ed. Maspero, Paris.

Auerbach, (1959), 'Das Gesetz der Bevokerungskonzentration', Petermann's Mitteilungen.

Auger, Alain, (1972), 'Le Ravitaillement vivrier traditionnel de la population Africaine de Brazzaville', *La croissance urbaine en Afrique Noire et à Madagascar*, C.N.R.S., pp. 273-98.

Avila, Bernal Alvaro, (1969), *Elementos de reflexion para una politica de planificacion urbana y ordenamiento del territorio*, Ministerio de Obras Publicas, Caracas.

Avineri, Shlomo, (1970), *The Social and Political Thought of Karl Marx*, Cambridge University Press, London.

Ayres, C.E., (1952), *The Industrial Economy, its Technological Basis and Institutional Destiny*, Houghton Mifflin, Boston.

Bain, Joe S., (1956), *Barriers to New Competition*, Harvard University Press, Cambridge, Mass.

Balandier, G., (1955), *Sociologie des brazzavilles noires*, A. Colin, Paris.

Banco Central de Venezuela y Universidad de Los Andes, (1969), *Estudio sobre Presupuestos Familiares e Indices de Costo de Vida para las Ciudades de Merida, Valera, San Cristobal y Barinas*, Caracas, Merida.

Banco Nacional de Mexico, (1965), *Las 16 Cuidades principales de la Republica Mexicana*, Mexico.

Banco do Nordeste do Brasil, S.A. (1967), *Consumo de produtos industriais na Cidade de Aracaju*, B.N.B., Fortaleza.

—— (1966), *Consumo de produtos industriais na Cidade de Mossoro, Rio Grande do Norte*, B.N.B., Fortaleza.

Baran, P., (1957), *The Political Economy of Growth*, Monthly Review Press, New York.

—— (1969), *The Longer View*, Monthly Review Press, New York.

Baran, Paul, and Sweezy, Paul M., (1966), *Monopoly Capital*, Monthly Review Press, New York.

Barber, A., (1968), 'Emerging new power, the world corporation', *War Peace Report*, October.

Barringer, Herbert R., (1971), 'Migration and social structure', in Lee and Barringer (1971), pp. 287-334.

Barros de Castro, Antonio, (1971), *Sete ensaios sobre a economia Brasileira*, vol. II, Ed. Forense, Rio de Janeiro.

Bataillon, Claude, (1964), 'Mexico, capitale metisse', *Caravelle*, no. 3.

—— (1971), *Villes et campagnes dans la région de México*, Ed. Anthropos, Paris.

Bauer, P. T., (1954), 'Origins of the statutory export monopolies of British West Africa', *Business History Review*, September, pp. 197-213, and in Bauer and Yamey (1968), pp. 138-153.

—— (1957), *Economic Analysis and Policy in Underdeveloped Countries*, Cambridge University Press, London.

Bauer, Peter T. and Yamey, Basil S., (1957), *The Economics of Underdeveloped Countries*, University of Chicago Press.

—— (1968), *Markets, Market Control and Marketing Reform*, Weidenfeld and Nicolson, London.

Beaujeu-Garnier, Jacqueline, (1965a), *Trois milliards d'hommes*, Hachette, Paris.

—— (1965b), 'Population et économie en Nouvelle-Caledonie', *Bulletin de l'association des géographes français*, pp. 2-12.

—— (1967), 'La population de México', *Bulletin de l'association des géographes français*.

—— (1970), 'Large overpopulated cities in the underdeveloped world', in W. Zelinsky, L. Kosinski, R. M. Prothero (eds), *Geography and a Crowding World*, Oxford University Press, New York, pp. 269-78.

Becker, Joseph M., (1968), *Guaranteed Income for the Unemployed, the Story of Sub*. The Johns Hopkins Press, Baltimore, Maryland.

Bedarida, Francois, (1968), 'Londres au milieu de XIXe siècle', *Annales, économies, sociétés, civilisations*, March–April.

Beguin, H., (1970), 'Une carte du produit intérieur marocain', *Bulletin de la société belge d'études géographiques*, vol. XXXIX, no. 2.

—— (1971), 'La ville et l'industrie au Maroc', in Milton Santos (ed), *La ville et l'organisation de l'espace dans les pays sou-développés*, Revue Tiers-Monde, no. 45, P.U.F., Paris, pp. 145-166.

Belshaw, Cyril (1965). *Traditional Exchange and Modern Markets*, Prentice-Hall, Inc., Englewood Cliffs, N.J.

Berry, Brian, (1971), 'City size and economic development', in Leo Jakobson and Ved Prakash (eds), *Urbanization and National Development*, Sage publications, Beverley Hills.

Berry, Brian and Garrison, William, (1958), 'A note on central place theory and the range of a good', *Economic Geography*, vol. 34, pp. 304-311.

Bettelheim, Charles, (1950), *Le problème de l'emploi et du chomâge dans les théories économiques*, Ecole pratique des hautes études, Paris, (photocopy, 145 pp.).

—— (1962), *L'Inde indépendante*, Colin, Paris.

Bettignies, J. de, (1965), *Toumodi, étude monographique d'un centre semiurbain*, Université d'Abidjan, Institut de geographie.

Bhat, Shrikant, V., (1970), 'Le prêt d'argent', *Himmat*, 27 February.

Bienefeld, (1974), 'The Self Employed of Urban Tanzania', I.D.S. Discussion Paper No. 54, Brighton, U.K.

Bird, Richard M., (1970), *Taxation and Development, Lessons from Colombian Experience*, Harvard University Press, Cambridge, Mass.

Boeke, J. H., (1953), *Economics and Economic Policy of Dual Societies, as Exemplified by Indonesia*, H. D. Tjeenk Willink & Zoon N.V., Haarlem.

Bognar, Jozsef, (1968), *Economic Policy and Planning in Developing Countries*, Akademiai Kiado, Budapest.

Bohannan, Paul and Dalton, George, (1962), *Markets in Africa*, Northwestern University Press.

Borde, Jean, (1954), 'Santiago du Chili', *Cahiers d'Outre-Mer*, no. 25, January-March.

Bose, Nirmal Sumar, (1965), 'Calcutta, a premature metropolis', *Scientific American* 213, no. 3, September, pp. 91-102.

Bottomley, Anthony, (1965), 'Imperfect competition in the industrialization of Ecuador', *Inter-American Economic Affairs*, XIX, Summer.

Boudeville, Jacques, (1961), *Les espaces économiques*, P.U.F., Paris, (2nd edn. 1964).

—— (1966), *Problems of Regional Economic Planning*, Edinburgh University Press, Edinburgh.

Brasseur, P., and Brasseur, M., (1953), *Porto Novo et sa palmeraie*, I.F.A.N., Dakar.

Braudel, Fernand, (1958), 'Historia y ciencias sociales: la larga duraciôn', *Cuadernos americanos*, Ano XVII, no. 6.

Bray, Jennifer M., (1969), 'The Economics of traditional cloth production in Iseyn, Nigeria', *Economic Development and Cultural Change*, vol. 17, no. 4, July, pp. 540-51.

Brisseau-Loaiza, Jeannine, (1972), 'Le rôle du camion dans les relations ville-campagne dans la région du Cuzco (Perou)', *Les Cahiers d'Outre-Mer*, no. 97, January-March, pp. 27-56.

Brookfield, H. C., (1969), *Pacific Market Places. A Collection of Essays*, Australian National University Press, Canberra.

—— (1969), *The Market-place*, Australian National University Press, Canberra.

Browning, H., (1958), 'Recent trends in Latin American urbanization', *The Annals of the American Academy of Political and Social Science*, no. 316, pp. 111-20.

Buchanan, Ian, (1972), *Singapore in Southeast Asia*, Bell, London. *Bulletin economique et social du maroc*, (1966), October-December, and April-September.

Bunge, William, (1962), *Theoretical geography*, Universite de Lund, Gleerup Publishers, Lund.

Burlaz, E., (1970), Letter to the author.

Buron, Robert, (1964), 'La productivité en société capitaliste, en société marxiste et dans le Tiers-Monde', *Revue de la mesure de la productivité* no. 37.

Caire, Guy, (1971), 'Commentaire aux livres A. Huybrechts et J. Gouverneur', *Revue Tiers Monde*, vol. XII, no. 48, October-December, pp. 894-5.

Capelle, Emmanuel, (1947), La cité indigène de Léopoldville, C.E.S.A., C.E.P.S.I.

Caplovitz, David (1963), *The Poor Pay More, Consumer Practices of Low Income Families*, The Free Press of Glencoe, New York and Collier-MacMillan Ltd., London.

Cardona, Ramiro, (1968), 'Migration, urbanisation et marginalité', *Premier seminaire national sur ubranisation et marginalité*, Division des études de population, Bogota, Antares, and Revue Tiers-Monde.

Cardoso, Fernando Henrique, (1971), 'Commentario sobre los conceptos de sobrepoblacion relativa y marginalidad', *Revista Latino-Americana de ciencias sociales*, June-December, pp. 57-76.

Carnoy, Martin and Katz, Marlaine, (1971), 'Explaining differentials in earnings among large Brazilian cities', *Urban Studies*, vol. 8, no. 1, February, pp. 21-37.

Carrion, F.M., (1970), *Les domaines industriels et le développement régional*, *I.E.D.S. Université de Paris*.

Casimir, Jean (1965), Aperçu sur la structure sociale d'Haïti, *America Latina*, Ano 8, no. 3, July-September, pp. 40-61.

Castells, Manuel (1972), *La question urbaine*, Maspero, Paris.

Cazes, Georges, (1970), 'Problèmes de population et perspectives économiques en Martinique et Guadeloupe', *Cahiers d'Outre-Mer*, no. 92, October-December, pp. 379-424.

Champseix, C., Guibert, J.-J., Lazzari, C.-H. and Mignon, J.-M, (1972), *Contribution aux méthodes d'analyse régionale: le cas de la ville de Saida*, Institut d'études du développement économique et social, Université de Paris.

Chandler, G., (1970), 'The effect of the flow of private sector finance on employment in less developed countries', Background paper, Cambridge Conference on Development.

Chang, Yunshik, (1971), 'Population growth and labour force', in Lee and Barringer (eds) (1971), pp. 41-85.

Chapelier, Alice, (1957), *Elisabethville: essai de géographie urbaine*, Bruxelles.

Chauleur, Pierre, (1970), 'Les idées directrices de marchés tropicaux et méditerranéens', *Marchés tropicaux et méditerranéens*, supplement to no. 1306, 21 November.

Charleux, J.L., (1970), 'Étude sur Tindivanam, dans l'Inde de Sud', Institut de géographie, Université de Toulouse (typescript).

Chevalier, L., (1950), La formation de la population de Paris au XIXe siècle, P.U.F., Paris.

C.H.I.S.S. (Centre Haitien d'Investigation en Sciences Sociales), (1971), 'Le processus d'urbanisation a Port-au-Prince', *Revue haitienne de sciences sociales*, 5e Année, Special number, August.

Choldin, Harvey M., (1968), 'Urban cooperatives at Comilla, Pakistan: A case study of local-level development', *Economic Development and Cultural Change*, vol. 16, no. 2, 1st part, January, pp. 189-218.

Chollet, Jesus; Gadra, Sanchez; Bolivar, Mauro; Rodriguez, Jorge and Da Costa, Juan R., (1969), *Estudio Regional de Coro y Punto Fijo*, Documento de trabajo; Proyeto Venezuela 11, Caracas.

Christaller, W., (1966), *Central Places in Southern Germany*, Prentice-Hall, Englewood Cliffs, New Jersey.

Ciudad, Guyana, (1968), *Encuesta regional de Hogares por muestra, 1967*, C.V.G., Caracas.

Clark, Colin, (1957), *The Conditions of Economic Progress*, Macmillan, London.

Clarke, J. I., (1972), 'Urban primacy in tropical Africa', *La croissance urbaine en Afrique Noire et à Madagascar*, C.N.R.S., Paris.

Claval, Paul, (1968), *Régions, nations, grands espaces*, Ed. M.-Th. Genin, Paris.

Colombia, *Cuentas nacionales: 1950-1961 et 1960-1966*, Banco de la Republica, Departamento de estudio economicos.

Comite Interamericano de la Alianza para el Progreso, (1966), *Informe preparado para el gobierno de los Estados-Unidos*, Washington, February.

Conaps (1967), Oficina Nacional de Propriedad Social, Lima, Peru.

Cote, M., (1968), 'Note sur le trafic intérieur d'avions en Algerie', *Annales algériennes de geographie*, 3rd year, no. 5.

Courtheoux, Jean Paul, (1966), *La repartition des activités économiques*, Centre de recherches d'urbanisme, Paris.

Cross, Jennifer, (1970), *The Supermarket Trap*, Indiana University Press, Bloomington and London, 1970.

Cuber, John F. (1940), 'Marginal Church participants', *Sociology and Social Research*, vol. XXV, no. 1, pp. 57-62.

Daly, M., and Brown, J., (1964), *Urban Settlement in Central Western N.S.W.*, Geographical society of New South Wales, Research paper no. 8.

Dasgupta, Samir, (1964), 'Underemployment and dualism, a note,' *Economic Development and Cultural Change*, vol. XII, no. 2, January.

Davies, W. K. D., 'The need for replication in human geography: some central-place examples', *Tijdschrift voor economische en sociale geografie*, 59, pp. 145-55.

Davis, Kingsley and Hertz Golden, Hilda, (1954), 'Urbanization and the development of pre-indsutrial areas', *Economic Development and Cultural Change*, vol. III, no. 1, October, pp. 6-26.

Demonque M., (1966), 'La firme et son rôle dans les systèmes économiques français'. La grande entreprise française', in F. Bloch Lainé and F. Perroux (eds), *L'entreprise et l'économie du XXe siècle*, P.U.F., Paris, pp. 65-94.

Denis, J., (1954). Léopoldville, étude de géographie urbaine et sociale.

Desmond, Gerald M., (1971), 'The impact of national and regional development policies on urbanization', in Jakobsen and Prakash, *Urbanization and National Development*. Sage Publications, Beverly Hills.

Destanne de Bernis, G., (1971), 'Les industries industrialisantes et les options algériennes', *Revue Tiers-Monde*, vol. XII, no. 47, July-September, pp. 545-63.

Dewey, Alice G., (1962), *Peasant marketing in Java*, The Free Press of Glencoe, New York.

Directorio de Atividades Economicas, (1969), MOP-FUDECO, Barquisimeto, Venezuela.

Dollfus, O., (1966), *Remarques sur quelques aspects de l'urbanisation péruvienne*, Institut de géographie, Université de Strasbourg, April.

Dominican Republic (1970), Oficina Nacional de Estadistica Censo Poblacion.

Donque, Gerard, (1968), 'Tananarive', *Notes et études documentaires*, no. 3529-3530, Paris, 29 October.

Dos Santos, Carlos Nelson F., (1971), 'The possibilities of developing policies supporting autonomous housing action in underdeveloped countries: The Bras do Pina redevelopment project case', M.I.T., (mimeog.).

Dos Santos, Teotonio, (1968), 'El nuevo caracter de la dependencia', *Cuadernos del CESO*, no. 6, 1967; also in *Latin America: Reform or Revolution*, Fawcet Books, 1968.

Durroux, Y., (1970), *La surpopulation relative*, Université de Paris, (photocopy).

Eckaus, R. S., (1955), 'The factor proportions problem in underdeveloped areas,' *The American Economic Review*, vol. XLV, no. 4, September, pp. 539-65.

Eckert, Hedi, (1970), *Les populations du grand Tunis*, Projet Tunis-Carthage, (mimeog. 64 pp.).

Eisenstadt, S. N., (1966), *Modernization: Protest and Change*, Prentice-Hall Englewood Cliffs, N.J.

Ellis, H.S., Psilos, D. P.; Westebbe, R. N. and Nicolaov, C., (1964), *Industrial Capital in Greek Development*, Center of Economic Research, Athens, Greece.

Emmanuel, A., (1969), *L'echange inegal*, Maspéro, Paris.

Engberg, H. L., (1967), 'Commercial banking in East Africa', in Whetam and Currie (eds) (1967), pp. 48-69.

Erdens, Antonia Dea, (1969), *A Conurbação Barcelona-Puerto La Cruz e sua Regiao*, Caracas, (mimeog.).

Etude Regionale de Bouaké, 1962-1964, (1966), vol. II, *L'économie, République de la Côte-d'Ivoire*, Ministère du Plan.

Farock, G. M. (1966), *The People of Karachi: Economic Characteristics*, Monograph in Economic Development, no. 15, Institute of Development Economics, Karachi, Pakistan, July.

Fisher, Douglas, (1967), 'Modern small industry for developing countries – a paradox in planning economics', *Economic Development and Cultural Change*, vol. 15, no. 3, April.

Fox, Richard G., (1967), 'Family, caste, and commerce in a North Indian market town',*Economic Development and Cultural Change*, vol. 15, no. 3.

Frankenhoff, Charles, (1971), 'Economic Activities', in *Improvement of Slums and Uncontrolled Settlements*, United Nations, New York, pp. 127-49.

Frankman, Myron J., (1969), 'Employment in the Services in Developing Countries: a Reappraisal', McGill University, June (mimeog. 19 pp.).

Friedmann, John, (1963), 'Regional economic policy for developing

242   *The Shared Space*

areas', in *Papers and Proceedings*. The Regional Science Associations, vol. 11.
—— (1964), 'Cities in Social Transformation', in J. Friedmann and W. Alonso, *Regional Development and Planning*, M.I.T. Press, Cambridge, Mass.
—— (1966), *Regional Development Policy. A Case Study of Venezuela*, MIT Press, Cambridge, Mass.
—— (1971), 'Urbanisation et développement national: une étude comparative', Revue Tiers-Monde, no. 45, January-March.
Friedmann, J. and Lackington, Tomas, (1966), 'Hyperurbanisation and national development in Chile: some hypotheses', *Urban development programme* (CIDU), the Catholic University of Chile, Santiago, November, (mimeog. 38 pp.).
Fryer, D. W., (1963), The development of cottage and small-scale industries in Malaya and in South-East Asia, *The Journal of Tropical Geography*, vol. 17 (17).
Fuch, Jaime, (1959), *Le penetracion de los trusts Yanquis en Argentina*, Editorial Carago, Buenos Aires.
Funes, Julio Cezar, (ed), (1972), *La cuidad y la región para el desarollo*, Caracas.
Furtado, Celso, (1966), *Développement et sous-développement*, P.U.F., Paris.
—— (1968), *Um Projeto para o Brasil*, Editora Saga, Rio de Janeiro, Fourth edition.
—— (1970), *Obstacles to Development in Latin America*, Doubleday, Garden City, N.Y.

Gadgil, D. R., (1965), *Sholapur City: Socio-economic studies*, Gokhale Institute, Studies no. 46 (Poona), Asia Publishing House, New York.
Gakenheimer, Ralph, (1971), Analysis para la planificacion metropolitana en America Latina: La adaptacion de methodos, *Revista Eure*, vol. 1, no. 2, pp. 55-6.
Galbraith, J. K., (1967) *The New Industrial State* Hamish Hamilton, London.
Garcia, Juan Pedro, (1970), *Condiciones del proceso de industrialisacion de Barquisimeto*, Instituto de geografia, Universidad Los Andes, Merida, Venezuela.
Garlick, Peter C., (1971), *African Traders and Economic Development in Ghana*, Clarendon Press, Oxford.
Gauthier, Howard L., (1971), 'Economic growth and polarisation in Latin America: A search for geographic theory?' Conference of Latin Americanist Geographers, Syracuse, December, (mimeog. 17 pp.).
Geertz, Clifford, (1963). *Peddlers and Princes*, The University of Chicago Press.
Geiger, Theodore and Armstrong, Winifred, (1964), *The Development of African Private Enterprise*, National Planning Association, Planning Pamphlet no. 120, Washington, D.C.
Gendreau, F., (1972), 'Les centres urbains à Madagascar, Données recentes,' *La croissance urbaine en Afrique Noire et à Madagascar*,

C.N.R.S., Paris, pp. 591-609.

George, P., (1969), *Population et peuplement*, P.U.F., Paris.

Gerry, C., (1974), 'Petty producers and the urban economy: a case-study of Dakar', ILO World Employment Programme, Working Paper 8, Geneva.

Gormsen, Erdmann, (1972), 'Considerations on the formation of central places systems in developing countries', in W. Peter Adams and Frederick M. Helleiner (eds), *International Geography 1972*, University of Toronto Press, pp. 1293-5.

Goudet, Françoise, (1969), 'Croissance et rénovation urbaines en milieu tropical. Étude socio-économique du quartier d'assainissement à Pointe-à-Pitre.' Institut de Géographie, Université de Bordeaux, (mimeog.).

Greenhut, M. L., (1963), *Micro-economics and the Space Economy: the Effectiveness of an Oligopolistic Market Economy*, SCOTT Foresman, Chicago.

Griffin, Keith (ed), (1971), *Financing Development in Latin America*, Macmillan, London.

Gunder Frank, André, (1968), 'Le Brésil dans l'impasse,' *Partisans*, no. 26/27, Paris.

Gusfield, Josepp R., (1971), 'Tradition and modernity: misplaced polarities in the study of social change', in Jason L. Finkle and Richard W. Gable (eds), *Political Development and Social Change*, John Wiley and Sons, New York, 2nd edn, pp. 15-26.

Gutkind, P.C.W., (1968), African responses to urban wage employment, *International Labour Review*, no. 97.

Hagen, Everett E., (1962), *On the Theory of Social Change*, Dorsey Press, Homewood, Ill.

—— (1968), *The Economics of Development*, Irvin, Homewood, Ill.

Haig, R. Murray, (1926), 'Toward an understanding of the metropolis', *Quarterly Journal of Economics*; I, pp. 179-208, II, pp. 402-434.

Hallett, Robin, (1966), *People and Progress in West Africa. An Introduction to the Problems of Development*, Pergamon Press, Oxford and London.

Hanna, W. J. and Hanna, J. L., (1971), *Urban Dynamics in Black Africa: an Interdisciplinary Approach*, Aldine, Chicago.

Hansen, Niles M., (1971), *Intermediate-size Cities as Growth Centers*. Praeger Publishers, New York, Washington, London.

Harris, Britton, (1959), 'Urbanization policy in India', *Papers and Proceedings*, Regional Science Association, V, pp. 181-203.

Harris, John Rees, (1967), 'Industrial entrepreneurship in Nigeria', Thesis, North-Western University, Evanston, Ill.

Harris, John Rees and Rowe, Mary P., (1971), 'Entrepreneurial Attitudes and National Integration: The Nigerian case', in R. Melson and H. Wolpe (eds), *Nigeria, Modernization and the Politics of Communalism*, Michigan State University Press.

Harrison Church, R. J., (1972), The case for industrial and general development of the smaller towns of West Africa, *La Croissance urbaine en Afrique Noire et à Madagascar*, C.N.R.S., Paris, pp. 659-65.

Hauser, P., (ed), (1959), *Le Phénomène de l'urbanisation en Asie et en Extrème-Orient*, UNESCO, Paris.

Havens, Eugene and Flinn, William L., (1970), Diffusion of agricultural innovation as a factor of social change, in Havens and Flinn, *Internal Colonialism and Structural Change in Colombia*, Praeger, New York.

Hawkins, H. C. G., (1965), *Wholesale and Retail Trade in Tanganyika. A study in Distribution in East Africa*, Praeger, New York.

Hay, Alan M. and Smith, Robert, (1970), *Inter-regional Trade and Money Flows in Nigeria, 1964*, Oxford University Press, Ibadan.

Hayter, Teresa, (1971), *Aid as Imperialism*, Penguin Books, Harmondsworth.

Herkommer, Siegfried, (1966), Planeacion regional de transportes, *Revista de la Escuela de contabilidad economia y administracion*, Guadalajara, Mexico, vol. XVIII, no. 70.

Herrick, Bruce, (1965), *Urban Migration and Economic Development in Chile*, M.I.T. Press, Cambridge, Mass.

Hicks, J. R., (1969), *Essays in World Economics*, Clarendon Press, Oxford, p. 163.

Higgins, Benjamin, (1967), 'Urbanization, Industrialization and Economic Development', in Glenn H. Beyer (ed), *The Urban Explosion in Latin America*, Cornell University Press.

Hill, Polly (1962), 'Some Characteristics of Indigenous West African Economic Enterprise,' *The Economic Bulletin of Ghana*, vol. VI, no. 1, pp. 3-14.

—— (1966), 'A Plea for Indigenous Economics: The West African Example'. *Economic Development and Cultural Change*, vol. 15, no. 1.

Hirschman, Albert O., (1958), *The Strategy of Economic Development*, Yale University Press, New Haven.

Hoselitz, Bert, (1957), 'Urbanization and Economic Growth in Asia', *Economic Development and Cultural Change*, vol. VI, no. 1, pp. 42-54.

—— (1960), 'Generative and Parasitic Cities', in B. Hoselitz (ed), *Sociological Aspects of Economic Growth*, The Free Press of Glencoe.

Houssiaux, J., (1966), 'La grande entreprise multinationale', in F. Bloch Laine and F. Perroux, *L'Entreprise et l'économie du XXe siècle*, P.U.F., Paris, pp. 291-328.

Hoyt, Elizabeth, (1952), 'Economic Sense and the East African', *Africa*, vol. 22, pp. 165-70, quoted by M. Katzin, (1964) p. 184.

Hutchinson, Bertram, (1963), 'The Migrant Population of Urban Brazil', no. 6, no. 2, April-June.

Ianni, Otavio, (1971), *Estado e planejamento economico no Brasil, 1930-1970*, Editora Civilizacao Brasileira, Rio de Janeiro.

I.L.O. (International Labour Office) (1972), *Employment, Incomes and Equality: A Strategy for increasing productive employment in Kenya*. Geneva.

L'Industrie Katangaise, (1961) Publications de l'Université de l'Etat à Elisabethville.

Isaac, Barry L., (1971), 'Business failure in a developing town: Pendembu, Sierra Leone', *Human Organization*, vol. 30, Autumn, no. 3, pp. 288-94.

Isnard, H., (1965), *Le Maghreb*, P.U.F., Paris.

Jalée, Pierre, (1969), *L'Impérialisme en 1970*, Maspero, Paris.

Jefferson, Mark, (1939), 'The law of the primate city', *Geographical Review*, vol. 29, pp. 227-32.

Johnson, E. A., (1970), *The Organization of Space in Developing Countries*, Harvard University Press.

Jones, Emrys, (1966), *Towns and Cities*, Oxford University Press, London.

Jones, Graham, (1971), *The Role of Science and Technology in Developing Countries*, Oxford University Press, London.

Joshi, Lubell and Monly (1976), *Abidjan: Urbanization and Employment*, I.L.O. Geneva.

Jurkat, Ernest H., (1966), *Employment and value added in the regions and Villayets of Turkey, 1935-1960; 1977-1985*, Ministry of Reconstruction, Istanbul.

Kamara, Lai, (1971), 'Integration fonctionnelle et développement accéléré en Afrique', *Revue Tiers Monde*, no. 48.

Kaplan, Marcos, (1970), 'Estado, dependencia externa y desarollo en America Latina', Escuela de administracion publica, Caracas (mimeo).

Karlqvist, Anders, (1971), 'Regional planning and planning research in Sweden', Lecture held at M.I.T., SPURS Programme, October 27.

Katzin, Margaret F., (1959), 'Partners: an informal savings institution in Jamaica', *Social and Economic Studies*, vol. 8, no. 4, December.

—— (1964), 'The Role of the Smaller Entrepreneur', in M. Herskovitz and M. Harwitz (eds), *Economic Transition in Africa*, North-Western University Press.

Kay, George, (1970), *Rhodesia: A Human Geography*, Africana Publishing Corporation, New York.

Kayser, Bernard, (1972a), 'La survie imprévue du Tiers monde', *Revue Tiers Monde*, no. 47, pp. 515-24.

—— (1972b), 'Le nouveau système des relations Ville-Campagne: problèmes et hypothèses à propos de l'Amerique latine', Université de Toulouse Mirail, Departement de géographie, (mimeog. 10 pp.).

Kiskor, Braj and Singh, B. P., (1969), *Indian Economy through the Plans*, National Publishing House, Delhi.

Knapp, J., (1969), 'Vers une analyse keynesienne du sous-développement et des points de croissance', *Revue Tiers Monde*, no. 37.

Kotter, Herbert, (1964), Changes in urban-rural relationships in industrial society, in Nels Anderson (ed), *Urbanism and Urbanization*, E. J. Brill, Leyde, pp. 21-9.

Kuenne, Robert E. (ed), (1967) *Monopolistic Competition Theory: Studies in Impact*, John Wiley and Sons, New York.

Kuhn, Thomas S., (1962), *The Structure of Scientific Revolutions*, The University of Chicago Press, Chicago and London.

Kus'min, S. A. (1969), *The Developing Countries, Employment and Capital Investment*, International Arts and Sciences Press, White Plains, N.Y.

Kusnetz, Simon, (1966), *Modern Economic Growth: Rate, Structure and Spread*, Yale University Press, New Haven.

Laquian, A. (ed), (1971), *Rural-Urban Migrants and Metropolitan Development* Intermet, Toronto, 1971.

—— (1971), 'Slums and squatters in South and South-east Asia,' in Jakobson and Prakash, *Urbanization and national development, South and Southeast Asian urban affairs*, vol. I, Sage Publications, Beverly Hills, pp. 183-203.

Lasserre, G., (1958), *Libreville*, A. Colin, Paris.

—— (1967), 'Le Costa Rica', *Revista Geografica*, June, no. 66.

—— (1972), 'Les mécanismes de la croissance et les structures démographiques de Libreville (1953-1970); *La Croissance urbaine en Afrique Noire et à Madagascar*, C.N.R.S., pp. 719-38.

Lasuén, J. R., (1971), 'A Generalisation of the Growth Pole Notion', Paper prepared for the Commission on regional aspects of economic development, International Geographical Union, Vitoria, Brazil.

Lawson, R. M., (1967), 'The markets for food in Ghana', in Whetham and Currie (1967).

—— (1971), 'The supply response of retail trading services to urban population growth in Ghana', in C. Meillassoux (ed), *The Development of Indigenous Trade and Markets in West Africa*, Oxford University Press, pp. 377-98.

Lean, William, (1969), *Economics of Land-Use Planning: Urban and Regional*, The Estates Gazette Limited, London.

Lebeuf, Jean-Paul, (1951), *Bangui (Oubangui-Chari) Afrique Équatoriale Française*, Èditions de l'Union Française, Paris.

Le Chau, M., (1966), 'Problèmes économiques du commerce régional, région de Bouaké, République de Côte-d'Ivoire, *ORSTROM, Bulletin de liaison, sciences humaines*, no. 3, January.

Lee, Hy-Sang, (1971), 'An economic survey: efficiency, equity, and growth', in Lee and Barringer, (1971), pp. 187-219.

Labarthe, Christian, (1969), *Quelques aspects du développement des villes au Laos*, Université de Bordeaux, Institut de Géographie.

Labrasse, Jean, (1968), 'Planification et aménagement régional dans le Tiers Monde', *Revista Geographica*, no. 68, June, pp. 157-66.

Lacoste, Yves, (1968), *Géographie du sous-développement*, P.U.F., Paris.

Lakdawala, D. T. (1963), *Work, Wages and Well-being in an Indian Metropolis: Economic Surveys of Bombay City*, University of bombay, Bombay.

Lambert, Denis, (1965), 'L'urbanisation accélérée de l'Amérique latine et la formation d'un secteur tertiaire refuge', *Civilisations*, vol. XV.

—— (1968), 'Les mécanismes de l'inégalité sociale en Amérique latine', *Economie et humanisme*, August.

Lamicq, Helene, *Realité et limites du rôle de la ville de Maturin dans l'organisation de l'espace de l'Etat Monagas* (Venezuela).

Lee, Man-Gap and Barringer, Herbert R., (1971), *A City in Transition, Urbanization in Taegu, Korea*, Hollym Corporation Publishers, Seoul, Korea.

Leeds, Anthony and Leeds, Elizabeth, (1970), 'Brazil and the myth of urban rurality: urban experience, work, and values in "squatments" of Rio de Janeiro and Lima', in *City and Country in the Third World*, Sukenkman, Cambridge, 1970.

Lejars, Jocelyne, (1971), *Contribution à la connaissance de la situation industrielle de Vientiane (Laos)*, Université de Paris, Institut de géographie, (mimeog. 145 pp.).

Leloup, Yves, (1970), *Les villes du Minas Gerais*, Institut des Hautes études de l'Amérique latine, Université de Paris.

Lerner, Daniel, (1967), 'Comparative analysis of processes of modernisation', in Horace Miner, *The city in modern Africa*.

Lewis, Arthur, (1954), 'Economic development with unlimited supplies of labour', Manchester School of Economics and Social Studies, vol. XIII, May, pp. 139-51.

—— (1967), *Reflexions sur la croissance économique du Nigéria*, O.E.C.D., Paris.

Liebow, Elliot, (1967), *Tally's Corner*, Little, Brown and Co., Boston.

Linsky, Arnold S., (1965), 'Some generalizations concerning primate cities'. *Annals of the Association of American geographers*, vol. 55, no. 3, September, pp. 506-13.

Lopez, Gustavo; Arteaga, Victor Manuel; Gonzalez, Juan Gustavo and Zuleta, Herman (1968), *Le artesania en el departamento de Antioquia (Medellin)*. S.E.N.A. (Servicio Nacional do Aprendizaje), May.

Losch, August, (1954), *The Economics of Location*, Yale University Press, New Haven.

Loupy, Elisabeth, (1971), *Problèmes posés par le ravitaillement des marchés de Vientiane*, Université de Paris, IV, (mimeog. 86 pp.).

Lubell, H., (1974), *Urban Development and Employment: the Prospects for Calcutta*, I.L.O., Geneva.

Mabogunje, Akin L., (1964), 'The evolution and analysis of the retail structure of Lagos, Nigeria', *Economic Geography*, vol. 40, no. 4, October, pp. 304-23.

—— (1965), 'Urbanization in Nigeria, a constraint on economic development', *Economic Development and Cultural Change*, nov. XIII, no. 4, part 1, July, pp. 413-38.

—— (1968), *Urbanization in Nigeria*, Africana Publishing Corporation, New York.

Maddison, A., (1970), *Economic Progress and Policy In Developing Countries*, Allen and Unwin, London.

Maneschi, Andrea, (1971), 'The Brazilian public sector during the sixties', in *Brazil in the Sixties*, Riordan Roett (ed), Vanderbilt University Press (mimeog.).

Mangin, William, (1967), 'Latin American squatter settlements: a problem and a solution', *Latin American Research Review*, vol. 2, no. 3,

Summer, pp. 65-98.

Manne, A., (1967), *Investments for Capacity Expansion: Size, Location, and Timephasing*, M.I.T. Press, Cambridge,Mass.

Marguerat, Y., (1972), 'Réflexions provisoires sur la décadence de villes secondaires au Cameroun', in *La crossance urbaine en Afrique Noire et à Madagascar*, C.N.R.S., Paris.

Marini, Ruy Mauro, (1972a), *Sous-développement et révolution en Amérique latine*, Cahiers libres 217-18, Maspero, Paris.

—— (1972b), 'Brazilian subimperialism', Monthly Review, February.

Marrama, Vittorio, (1961), *Politica economica de los paises subdesarollados*, Aguilar, Madrid.

Marris, Peter, (1962), *Family and Social Change in an African City. A study of Rehousing in Lagos*, Northwestern University Press.

Marshall, Alfred, (1927), *Industry and Trade*, MacMillan, London.

Martin, Anne, (1963), *The Marketing of Minor Crops in Uganda. A factual study*, H.M.S.O. London.

Martin, J. M., (1966), *Industrialisation et développement énergétique du Brésil*, Université de Paris, Institut d'études de l'Amérique latine, Paris.

Mason, Edward S., (1967), 'Monopolistic competition and the growth process in less developed countries: Chamberlin and the Schumpeterian dimension', in Robert E. Kuenne (ed), (1967).

Maunder, W. F., (1960), *Employment in an Underdeveloped Area. A sample of Kingston, Jamaica*.

Maza Zavala, D. F., (1964), *Venezuela una economia dependiente*, Universidad central de Venezuela, Caracas.

—— (1969b), *El economista ante el subdesarollo*, Instituto de investigaciones economicas, Universidad central de Venezuela.

M'Buy, Leon Victor M., (1970), 'Habitat et urbanisme à Kinshasa', *Bulletin S.M.U.H.*, nos. 58 & 59.

McGee, T. G. (1967), 'Croissance et caractéristiques des grandes villes du Sud-Est asiatique: foyers du nouveau culte', *Revue Tiers-Monde*, t. VIII, no. 31, P.U.F., Paris, pp. 567-604.

—— (1969), 'Hawkers in Hong-Kong, an outline of research, project and fieldwork', Centre for Asian studies, University of Hong-Kong, December, (mimeog. 11 pp.).

—— (1970a), *Dualism in the Asian city: the Implications for City and Regional Planning*, Centre for Asian Studies Reprint Series no. 2, University of Hong-Kong.

—— (1970b), *Hawkers in Selected Asian Cities, a Preliminary Investigation*, Centre for Asian studies, University of Hong-Kong.

—— (1971a), *The Urbanization Process in the Third World*, Bell and Son, London.

—— (1971b), 'Têtes de pont et enclaves, le problème urbain et le processus d'urbanisation dans l'Asie du Sud-Est depuis 1945'. *Revue Tiers-Monde*, t. XII, no. 45, January-March, pp. 115-43.

—— (1972a), Letter to the author.

—— (1972b), 'Peasants in the cities: A paradox, a paradox, a most ingenious paradox', University of Hong-Kong, (mimeog. 18 pp.).

McKay, J., (1968), 'Commercial life in Freetown', in Fyje and Hones, pp. 65-76.

McKee, David L., and Leahy, William, (1970a), 'Urbanization, dualism and disparities in regional economic development', *Land Economics*, vol. 56, no. 1, February, pp. 82-5.

—— (1970b), 'Intra-urban dualism in developing economies', *Land Economics*, November.

McNulty, Michael L., (1969), 'Urban structure and development: the urban system of Ghana', *The Journal of Developing Areas*, III, January, pp. 159-76.

Medina, Echavarria, (1963), *Working Group on Social Aspects of Economic Development in Latin America*, Mexico City.

Meillassoux, Claude, (1968), *Urbanization of an African community, Voluntary Associations in Bamako*, University of Washington Press.

Meillassoux, Claude (ed), (1971), *The Development of Indigenous Trade and Markets in West Africa*, Oxford University Press.

Menauge, Jacques, (1969), *Les petits commerces de détail dans l'agglomération de Point-à-Pitre*, Institut de géographie, Université de Bordeaux, May (mimeog.).

Mende, Tibor, (1972), 'Le Tiers Monde, victime de la croissance', *Le Monde* 21-22 September.

Mendez, Elias, (1970), *Brèves consideractiones sobre los centros industriales, Caracas*, (typescript).

Merhav, Meir, (1969), *Technological Dependence, Monopoly and Growth*, Pergamon Press, Oxford and London.

Messner, Johannes, (1966), *L'entrepreneur propriétaire*, in F. Bloch-Lainé and F. Perroux (eds), *L'enterprise et l'économie du XXe siècle*, P.U.F., Paris, pp. 241-56.

Miles, Simon R., (ed), (1970), Metropolitan problems, Intermet, Metropolitan Studies Series, Methuen Publications, Toronto.

Miller Jr., V.P., (1971), 'Towards a typology of urban-rural relationships', *The Professional Geographer*, vol. XXIII, no. 4, October, pp. 319-23.

Mintz, Sidney W., (1956), 'The role of the middleman in the internal distribution system of a Caribbean peasant economy', *Human Organization*, vol. 15, no. 2, pp. 18-23.

—— (1964), 'Market systems and whole societies', *Economic Development and Cultural Change*, vol. 12, no. 4, July, pp. 444-8.

Miracle, Marvin P., (1962), 'African markets and trade in the Copperbelt', in *Markets in Africa*, P. Bohannan and G. Dalton (eds), Northwestern University Press, pp. 698-738.

Mishan, Esra J., (1967), *The Costs of Economic Growth*, Praeger, New York, and Pelican Books, 1969 and 1971.

Moore, Wilbert E., (1965), *The Impact of Industrialization*, Prentice-Hall Inc., Englewood Cliffs, New Jersey.

Morice, Gerard, (1972), *La croissance économique: une illusion comptable*, Pauvert, Paris.

Morrison, Ian, (1972), 'Intra-national migrations in Latin America', Term paper to GGR 341, University of Toronto, Department of Geography, December (typescript 37 pp.).

250   *The Shared Space*

Mortimore, Michael J., (1972), 'Some aspects of rural-urban relations in Kano, Nigeria', in *La croissance urbaine en Afrique et à Madagascar*, C.N.R.S., Paris.

Motti, Pascal, (1970), 'Mécanismes commerciaux et organisation de l'éspace dans un pays sou-developpé: les foires de la region de Salvador, Bahia (Brésil)', Université de Toulouse, Institut de géographie, (mimeog. 143 pp.).

Murerjee, R. and Singh, B., (1961), *Social Profiles of a Metropolis*, Asia Publishing House, Bombay.

Munoz Garcia, Humberto; de Oliveira, Orlandina, and Stern, Claudio, (1971), 'Migration et marginalité occupationnelle dans la ville de Mexico', *Espaces et sociétés*, no. 3, pp. 89-108.

Myint, H., (1965a), 'Economic theory and the underdeveloped countries'. Journal of Political Economy, vol. LXXIII, no. 5, October, pp. 477-91.

—— (1965b), *The Economics of the Developing Countries*, Hutchinson University Library, London.

—— (1970), 'Dualism and the internal integration of underdeveloped economies'. *Banca nationale del lavoro, Quarterly review*, no. 93, June, pp. 128-56.

Myrdal, Gunnar, (1969), 'L'État "mou" en pays sous-developpé', *Revue Tiers-Monde*, no. 37, January-March.

—— (1971), *Economic Theory and Underdeveloped Regions*, Harper & Row, New York (1st ed. Harper & Row, 1957, under the title, *Rich Lands and Poor*).

—— (1972), 'Political factors in economic assistance', *Scientific American*, vol. 226, no. 4, April.

Navarro De Brito, L. A., (1972), 'La région et le phénomène du pouvoir', *Revue Tiers-Monde*, no. 50, pp. 309-28.

—— (1973), *Politique et espace régional*, Ophrys, Paris.

Nelson, Joan, (1969), *Migrants, Urban Poverty and Instability in Developing Countries*, Harvard University Press.

Niemeyer Pinheiro, A. M. de, (1971), 'La problématique des conditions de travail des travailleurs urbains d'origine rurale dans les métropoles brésiliennes dans la phase actuelle de l'industrialisation', Université de Paris I, Institut de géographie, (typescript 49 pp.).

Norro, L., (1972), Urbanisation et développement économique dans les pays africains: théorie et méthodes de recherche, *La croissance urbaine en Afrique Noire et à Madagascar*, C.N.R.S. Paris.

Nun, Jose, (1969), 'Sobrepoblacion relativa, ejercito industrial de reserva e masa marginal', *Revista Latinoamericana de sociologia*, no. 2.

Nurkse, Ragnar, (1953), *Problems of Capital Formation in Underdeveloped Countries*, Oxford.

Onyemelukwe, J. O. C., (1970), 'Aspects of stable foods trade in Onitsha market', *The Nigerian Geographical Journal*, vol. 13, December, no. 2.

Orlove, Benjamin, (1969), 'Kinship and economics in the favela', Thesis (B.A.), Harvard University, 94 pp.

Paix, C., (1972), 'Approche théorique de l'urbanisation dans les pays du Tiers Monde,' Revue de Tiers Monde, no. 50.

Pallier, Ginette, (1972), (Les activites du secteur secondaire à Ouagadougou', *La croissance urbaine en Afrique Noire et à Madagascar*, C.N.R.S., Paris, pp. 905-10.

Park, Robert E., (1928), 'Human migration and the marginal man', *American Journal of Sociology*, May, vol. 33, no. 6, pp. 881-3.

Peattie, Lisa R., (1968), *The View from the Barrio*, The University of Michigan Press, Ann Arbor.

Peillon, Pierre, (1970), 'Économie urbaine', Université d'Alger, Institut d'urbanisme, Alger, (mimeog. 106 pp., and 97 pp.).

Pericchi, Juan Jacobo, (1971), 'Quelques idées sur la localisation industrielle au Venezuela', Revue Tiers-Monde, t. XII, no. 46, April-June, pp. 382-6.

Perlman, Janice Erlaine, (1971), *The Fate of Migrants in Rio's Favelas: The Myth of Marginality*, M.I.T., Cambridge.

Perroux, François, (1950), 'Economic space: theory and applications', *Quarterly Journal of Economics*, vol. 64.

—— (1955), 'Note sur la notion de pole de croissance', *économie appliquée*, vol. VII, nos. 1-2.

—— (1959), Une distinction utile à la politique des pays à croissance retardée: points de développement et foyers de progrès, *Développement croissance, progres*, Cahiers de l'I.S.E.A., no. 94, Paris, November.

—— (1960), *Grandes firmes et petites nations*, Rapport sur la politique de coopération avec les pays en voie de développement, Paris.

Peil, Margaret, (1972), *The Ghanaian Factory Worker: Industrial Man in Africa*, C.U.P., Cambridge.

Pinto, Anibal and Osvaldo Sunkel, (1966), 'Latin American economists in the United States', *Economic Development and Cultural Change*, vol. 15, no. 1, October.

Planungsgruppe Ritter, (1974), 'Report on two surveys', *ILO World Employment Programme, Working Paper No. 9*, Geneva.

Prebisch, Raul, (1972), 'Monetary ills in U.S. threaten Latins', *The New York Times*, 28 January.

Preiser, E., (1971), 'Property, power and the distribution of income', in Rothschild (1971), pp. 119-40.

Prest, A. R., (1962), *Public Finance in Underdeveloped Countries*, Praeger, New York.

Pye, Lucien W., (1962), 'The political implications of urbanization and the development process', in *United Nations Conference on the Application of Science and Technology for the Benefit of Less Developed Areas*, Geneva, 1963, United States Papers, U.S. Government Printing Office, Washington D.C.

Quijano, Anibal, (1970), *Redefinicion de la dependencia u marginalizacion en America Latina*, Facultad de ciencias economicas, Universidad de Chile, Santiago.

—— (1971), 'The marginal pole of the economy and the marginalised labour force'. E. & S. III no. 474.

—— (1972), Speech to the Conference on external dependence and development problems in Latin America and Caribbean, University of Toronto, March 6-9.

Rabinovitz, Francine F.; Trueblood, Felicity; and Savio, Charles, (1967), *Latin American Political Systems in an Urban Setting: A preliminary bibliography*, Gainsville, Florida.

Ramos, Joseph, R., (1970), *Labour and Development in Latin America*, Institute of Latin American Studies, Columbia University Press, New York.

Ranis, C., (1962), 'Production functions, market imperfections and economic development', *Economic Journal*, LXXII.

Rao and Desai, (1965), *Greater Delhi. A Study in Urbanisation*, Asia Publishing House.

Ratcliff, Richard U., (1959), 'The dynamics of efficiency in the locational distribution of urban activities', in Harold Mayer and Clyde Kohn (eds), *Urban Geography*, University of Chicago press, Chicago.

Rattner, Henrich, (1972), *The control of Technology Transfer to Developing Countries*, SPURS, M.I.T. Cambridge, Mass.

Ravenstein, E.G., (1885), 'Laws of Gravitation', *Journal of the Royal Statistical Society*, 48, June.

Recensement General d'Algerie (1966).

Redfield, Robert and Singer, Milton B., (1954), 'The cultural role of cities', *Economic Development and Cultural Change*, vol. III, no. 1, October, pp. 53-73.

Ree, T., (1968), 'Interrelationship between research at applied research organisations and academic institutions', *International Symposium on Development of Industrial Research in Korea*, Institute of science and technology.

Remy, Jean, (1966), *La ville, phénomene économique*, Ed. Vie Ouvriere, Bruxelles.

Remy, D., and Weeks, J. F., (1973), 'Economic characteristics of the informal manufacturing and processing sector: occupational structure and size of enterprise', mimeo, University of Sussex.

République Tunisienne, (1972), *Sauvegarde et mise en valeur de la Medina de Tunis*, Projet Tunis-Carthage, UNESCO, PNUD, TUN 71-532, Rapport préliminaire, October, (mimeog, 59 pp.).

Resources for the Future, (1966), *Design for a Worldwide Study of Regional Development*, Washington.

Richardson, Harry W., (1969), *Elements of Regional Economics*, Harmondsworth, Penguin.

Ridell, Barry J., (1970a), *The Spatial Dynamics of Modernization in Sierra Leone*. Northwestern University Press, Evanston.

—— (1970b), 'On structuring a migration model', *Geographical Analysis*, pp. 403-9.

Rivkin, Malcolm D., (1965), *Area Development for Nation Growth: The Turkish Precedent*, Praeger, New York.

Robirosa, Mario; Rofman, Alejandro; and Moreno, Oscar, (1971), 'Elementos para uma politica regional en la Argentina', Instituto Torcuato Di Tella, Centro de Estudios urbanos y regionales, (mimeog. 72 pp.).

Robock, Stefan, (1963), *Brazil's Developing Northeast: A Study of Regional Planning and Foreign Aid*, The Brookings Institution.

Rochefort, Michel, (1964), 'L'accroissement de la population dans quelques capitales du Brésil', *Caravelle*, no. 3, pp. 63-72.

Rockfeller, Nelson A., (1969), 'La calidad de la vida en las Americas. Informe presentado por una mission presidencial de los Estados Unidos al hemisferio occidental', New York, August, (mimeog. 136 pp.).

Rotberg, Robert I., (1962), 'Rural Rhodesian markets', P. Bohannan and G. Dalton (eds) *Markets in Africa* Northwestern University Press Evanston, pp. 581-600.

Rothschild, K.W., (ed), (1971), *Power in Economics*, Penguin, Harmondsworth.

Roumegous, Micheline, (1966), 'Port-Gentil: quelques aspects sociaux du développement industriel', *Les cahiers d'Outre-Mer*, 19th year, no. 73, January-March, pp. 321-53.

Roweiss, Shoukry T., (1970), 'Metropolitanization: fate or choice', M.I.T., (typescript, 53 pp.).

Rozental, Alek A., (1968), 'Branch banking in Thailand', *The Journal of Developing Areas*, III, October. 1968, pp. 37-50.

Ryad, Hassan, (1964), *L'Égypte nassérienne*, Éd. de Minuit, Paris.

Santos, Milton, (1965), *A cidade nos paises subdesenvolvidos*; ed. Civilizacao Brasileira, Rio de Janeiro.

—— (1971), *Les Villes du Tiers-Monde*, Ed. M. Th. Genin, Paris.

—— (1972), 'Los dos circuitos de la economia urbana de los paises sub-desarollados', in Julio Funes (ed), *La cuidad y la region para el desarollo*, Comision de administracion publica de Venezuela, pp. 67-99.

—— (1973), *Brazil: An Industrialized Underdeveloped Country*, University of Toronto, Dept of Geography, January.

—— (1974), 'Sous-développement et poles de croissance économique et sociale', Revue Tiers-Monde, 58, pp. 271-86.

—— 'The lower circuit: the so-called informal sector', mimeo, McGill University.

—— (ed) (1972), *Modernisations et espaces dérives*, Revue Tiers-Monde, no. 50, P.U.F., Paris.

Santos, Milton and Kayser, Bernard, (1971), 'Espaces et villes du Tiers-Monde', Revue Tiers-Monde, no. 45, January-March.

Sari, J., (1968), 'L'Évolution récente d'une ville pré-coloniale en Algérie occidentale: Nedroma', *Revue tunisienne de sciences sociales*, 5th year, no. 15, December.

Saylor, Ralph Gerald, (1967), *The Economic System of Sierra Leone*, Duke University, Durham, D.C.

Schneider, Erich, (1967), 'Milestones on the way to the theory of monopolistic competition', in Kuenne (ed) (1967).

Schumpeter, J. A., (1950), *Capitalism, Socialism and Democracy*, Allen and Unwin, London.

Schwartz, Alfred, (1969), 'Toulepleu; Étude socio-économique d'un centre semi-urbain de l'ouest ivoirien', *Cahier ORSTOM*, vol. VI, no. 2, pp. 51-70.

Scitovsky, Tibor, (1971), *Welfare and Competition*, Richard D. Irwin, Inc., Homewood, Illinois.

Scott, P., (1970), 'The hierarchy of central places in Tasmania', *The Australian Geographer*, vol. 9, pp. 134-47.

Seck, A., (1965), 'Les escales du fleuve Sénégal', *Revue de géographie de l'Afrique occidentale*, nos. 1-2.

Seck, A., (1970), *Dakar, métropole ouest africaine*, IFAN, Dakar.

Sen, Satyendranath N., (1960), *The City of Calcutta: A Socio-economic Survey, 1954-1955 to 1957-1958*, Bookland, Calcutta.

S.E.R.F.H.A.U., (1971), Boletim Informativo, vol. 5 no. 43, October ('Ministro Delfim Netto comenta o discusso do Presidente do Banco Mondiale').

Sethuraman, S. V., (1974), *Jakarta: Urban Development and Employment*, I.L.O., Geneva.

Short, Brock K., (1973), 'The velocity of money and per capita income in developing economies: Malaysia and Singapore', *The Journal of Development Studies*, vol. 9, no. 2, January.

Silvany, Augusto J., (1971), 'Aspects théoriques de l'urbanisation', in Revue Tiers-Monde, t. XII, no. 45, January-March, pp. 99-113.

Simon, Lucien, (1971), 'Le crépuscule de Tchang-Kai-Chek', *Le Nouvel Observateur*, Paris, no. 364, 1-7 November.

Singer, H. W., (1970), 'Dualism revisited: a new approach to the problems of the dual society in developing countries', *The Journal of Development Studies*, vol. 7, no. 1, October.

Singh, Madhusudan, (1964), 'The urban field of Meerut', *The Deccan Geographer*, vol. 2, no. 2, January, pp. 85-99.

Sjoberg, Gedeon, (1960), *The Pre-industrial City*, The Free Press, Glencoe.

Sjoberg, Gedeon, (1966), 'Rural-urban balance and models of economic development', in Smelser and Lipset, (1966) pp. 235-61.

Skinner, G. W., (1964), 'Marketing and social structure in rural China', Journal of Asian Studies, vol. 24, pp. 3-43; 1965, pp. 195-228 and 363-399.

Slighton, Robert, (1968), *Urban employment in Colombia: measurement, characteristics, and policy problems*, Rand RM 5393-AID.

Smailes, Arthur E., (1971), *Urban Systems, Transactions*. The Institute of British Geographers, Publication No. 53.

Smelser, Neil J. and Seymour Martin Lipset, (eds) (1966), *Social Structure and Mobility in Economic Development*, Aldine Publishing Company, Chicago.

Sorlin, Pierre, (1969), *La Société française, I, 1840-1914*, Arthaud.

Sovani, N.V., (1964), 'The analysis of "overurbanisation"', *Economic Development and Cultural Change*, vol. X, no. 2, January, pp. 113-22.

Staley, Eugene, (1962), 'Les programmes de développement des "microindustries"', *Methodes de développement industriel et leur application aux pays en voie de développement*, OCDE, Paris, Ch. 9, pp. 199-233.

Staley, Eugene and Morse, Richard, (1965), *Modern Small Industry for Developing Countries*, McGraw Hill, New York.

Stapleton, G. Brian, (1967), *The Wealth of Nigeria* Oxford University Press, Ibadan, London.

Stavenhagen, Rodolfo, (1968), 'Seven fallacies about America Latina', in James Petras and Maurice Zeitin (eds), *Latin America, reform or revolution? A Reader*, Fawcett World Library, Connecticut, pp. 13-31.

Sturmtal, A., (1955), 'Economic development, income distribution and capital formation in Mexico', *Journal of Political Economy*, June.

Sunkel, Osvaldo, (1970), 'Desarollo, subdesarollo, dependencia, marginacion y desigualdades espaciales; hacia un enfoque totalizante', *Revista Latino Americana de estudios urbano regionales*, EURE, vol. 1, no. 1.

Tagri, Shanti, (1971), 'Urbanization, political stability, and economic growth', in Jason L. Finkle and Richard W. Gable, (eds), *Political Development and Social Change*, John Wiley and Sons, New York, 2nd ed., ch. 7, pp. 212-226.

Thomas, L. V., (1972), 'Les problèmes spécifiques de l'emploi dans les villes d'Afrique Noire et de Madagascar', *La croissance urbaine en Afrique Noire et à Madagascar*, C.N.R.S., Paris, pp. 117-38.

Thurow, Lester C., (1971), 'Development Finance in Latin America: Basic principles', in Griffin, *Financing Development in Latin America*, Macmillan and Co. Ltd., London.

Tiercelin, Marie-Helene, (1968), *Un aspect du réseau métropolitain mondial: Les rapports entre métropoles d'Afrique occidentale et l'Europe*, Université de Bordeaux, Institut de géographie, (mimeog. 130 pp.).

Tissandier, J., (1970), 'Aspects des relations villes campagnes dans le dep. de la Haute-Sanaga (Cameroun). Colloque sur la croissance urbaine en Afrique Noire et à Madagascar', Bordeaux.

—— (1972), *La croissance urbaine en Afrique Noire et à Madagascar*, C.N.R.S., Paris.

Troin, J. F., (1968), 'Structures et rayonnement commerciaux des petites villes marocaines', *Revue tunisienne de sciences sociales*, 5th year, no. 15, December.

—— (1971), 'Essai méthodologique pour une étude des petites villes en milieu sous-développé. Les structures commerciales urbaines du Nord marocain', *Annales de géographie*, 80th year, no. 444, September-October, pp. 513-33.

Turin, Laurent, (1965), *Combat pour le développement*, Ed. Ouvrieres, Paris.

Turner, John, (1969), 'Uncontrolled urban settlements: problems and policy', in G. Breese (ed), *The City in Newly Developing Countries*, Prentice-Hall, Englewood Cliffs N.J., pp. 507-34.

Uchendu, Victor C., (1967), 'Some principles of haggling in peasant markets', *Economic Development and Cultural change*, vol. 16, no. 1, October, pp. 37-50.

United Nations statistical yearbooks, U.N., New York, 1959, 1966, 1968, 1969, 1970.

Uribe, Sylvia and Uribe, Beatriz (1965), *Bases para el desarollo de la pequena y mediana industria en Colombia*, Medellin.

Utton, M. A., (1970), *Industrial Concentration*, Penguin, Harmondsworth.

Valbuena, Jovito, (1966), *Aspectos de la geografia economica del area de Merida*. Universidade de Los Andes, Escuela de geografia, Merida.

Valladares, Licia, (1969), *El Tigre y su region*, Caracas (typescript.).

—— (1972), *The Brazilian Housing Policy and Rio de Janeiro's Favela Relocation Scheme*, Centre for Urban Studies, University College, London, April.

Veblen, Thorstein, (1904), *The Theory of Business Enterprise*, New York.

Vennetier, P., (1960), 'Un quartier suburbain de Brazzaville, Moukondji-Ngouaka', *Bulletin de l'Institut d'Etudes centrafricaines*, Brazzaville, Nos. 19-20.

Vennetier, P., (1968), *Pointe-noire et la façade maritime du Congo Brazzaville*, Mémoires ORSTOM, no. 26, Paris.

Weisslitz, Jacqueline, (1971), Migration rurale et intégration urbaine au Pérou, *Espaces et sociétes*, no. 3, pp. 45-69.

Wheatley, Paul, (1969), *City as Symbol, An Inaugural Lecture Delivered at University College, London*, H. K. Lewis and Co. Ltd., London.

Whetam, Edith H. and Currie, Jean I., (1967), *Readings in the Applied Economics of Africa*, Cambridge University Press, London.

Wilmet, J., (1964), 'Adaptation du concept et des méthodes de régionalisation économique aux pays en voie de développement, l'exemple de l'Afrique centrale', *Geographia polonica*, 4.

Wingo, London, (1969), 'Latin American urbanization, plan or process?' in Bernard F. Frieden and William Nash (eds), *Shaping an Urban Future*, M.I.T. press. Cambridge, Mass., pp. 115-146 (Resources for the future, no. 75, January 1969).

Zipf, George, (1949), *Human Behaviour and the Principle of the Least Effort*, Addison-Wesley, Cambridge, Mass.

Author index

258   *The Shared Space*

Subject index